Development, Power, and the Environment

Unmasking the neoliberal paradox, this book provides a robust conceptual and theoretical synthesis of development, power and the environment. With seven case studies on global challenges such as under-development, food regime, climate change, dam building, identity politics, and security vulnerability, the book offers a new framework of a "double-risk" society for the Global South.

With apparent ecological and social limits to neoliberal globalization and development, the current levels of consumption are unsustainable, inequitable, and inaccessible to the majority of humans. Power has a great role to play in this global trajectory. Though power is one of most pervasive phenomena of human society, it is probably one of the least understood concepts. The growth of transnational corporations, the dominance of world-wide financial and political institutions, and the extensive influence of media that are nearly monopolized by corporate interests are key factors shaping our global society today. In the growing concentration of power in few hands, what is apparent is a non-apparent nature of power. Understanding the interplay of power in the discourse of development is a crucial matter at a time when our planet is in peril—both environmentally and socially. This book addresses this current crucial need.

Md Saidul Islam is Assistant Professor in Sociology at Nanyang Technological University, Singapore.

Routledge Studies in Development and Society

For a full list of titles in this series, please visit www.routledge.com.

Development, Power, and the Environment

Neoliberal Paradox in the Age of Vulnerability

Md Saidul Islam

Routledge
Taylor & Francis Group
NEW YORK LONDON

First published 2013
by Routledge
711 Third Avenue, New York, NY 10017

Simultaneously published in the UK
by Routledge
2 Park Square, Milton Park, Abingdon, Oxon OX14 4RN

*Routledge is an imprint of the Taylor & Francis Group,
an informa business*

Library of Congress Cataloging-in-Publication Data
Islam, Md Saidul.
    Development, power, and the environment : neoliberal paradox in the
age of vulnerability / by Md Saidul Islam. — 1st Edition.
        pages cm. — (Routledge studies in development and society ; 34)
    Includes bibliographical references and index.
    1. Economic development.   2. Power (Social sciences)   3. Global
environmental change.   I. Title.
    HD82.I85 2013
    338.9—dc23
    2012051047

ISBN13: 978-0-415-54002-5 (hbk)
ISBN13: 978-0-203-76881-5 (ebk)

Typeset in Sabon
by IBT Global.

SUSTAINABLE   **Certified Sourcing**
FORESTRY   **www.sfiprogram.org**
INITIATIVE   SFI-01234
SFI label applies to the text stock

Printed and bound in the United States of America
by IBT Global.

To my respected father, Md Adul Hossain, who always wishes me to be a paragon of social change, and my beloved mother, Mrs. Zayeda Khatun, whose unsurpassed love and affection makes me feel the importance of the Mother Nature for our existence.

Contents

PART III
Sustainable Earth amid Vulnerabilities

14 Towards a Sustainable Earth?   219

     Notes   233
     References   237
     Index   257

Tables

Glossary/Abbreviations

TNCs	Transnational corporations
IFIs	International financial institutions
UNEP	United Nations Environment Programme
IPCC	Intergovernmental Panel on Climate Change
CBD	Convention on Biological Diversity
UNCGG	United Nations Commission on Global Governance
UNCED	UN Conference on Environment and Development
ICC	International Chamber of Commerce
WBCSD	The World Business Council for Sustainable Development
CEFIC	The European Chemical Industry Council
GEF	Global Environmental Facility
UNFCCC	United Nations Framework Convention on Climate Change
UNCBD	United Nations Convention on Biological Diversity
GATT	General Agreement on Tariffs and Trade
WTO	World Trade Organization
LDCs	Least developed countries
MDCs	Most developed countries
CBNRM	Community Based Natural Resource Management
HEP	Human Exemptionalist Paradigm

Preface

The planet under neoliberal global governance is now on the path of destruction. There are apparent ecological and social limits to neoliberal globalization and development. Current levels of consumption are *unsustainable, inequitable,* and *inaccessible* to the majority of humans. Despite massive productive forces and sometimes 'epidemics of over production', about fifty thousand people are dying every day because of hunger and hunger-related disease. Power has a great role to play in this global trajectory. Global problems like this necessitate a critical unmasking of the complex nexus between development, power and the environment.

Though power is one of most pervasive phenomena of human society, it is probably one of the least understood concepts. The growth of transnational corporations, the dominance of world-wide financial and political institutions, and the extensive influence of media that are nearly monopolized by corporate interests are key factors shaping our global society today. In the growing concentration of power in few hands, what is apparent is a non-apparent nature of power. Understanding the interplay of power in the discourse of development is a crucial matter at a time when our planet is in peril—both environmentally and socially. *Development, Power and the Environment* addresses this current crucial need.

In the run-up to the June 2005 G8 leaders meeting in Gleneagles Scotland, Rock singer Sting took the stage and admonished the powerful world leaders to address global climate change and to pursue meaningful development initiatives that can help the helpless. "Every step you take, every vow you break, we'll be watching you . . . " he sang to a roaring crowd. From the first earth summit in Stockholm in 1972 through to Gleneagles in 2005, from the Kyoto Protocol in 1997 to Copenhagen Summit in 2009, the issue of how power and development can damage and/or save the global environment has been the source of protest, congressional and parliamentary debate, and reform efforts at development agencies around the world.

Much ink has been spilt on the question of development and the environmental issues, but we still lack a complete and coherent account of the interplay of power and development in addressing environmental issues and challenges. What are different trajectories of power in social organizations? How is power understood in different schools of development paradigms? How are power and development conjoined together in creating and addressing environmental problems? How is power sometimes camouflaged and obscured in the discourse of development, and what are the ways and approaches to unmask that? What appropriate relationship between power, development, and environment can we think of to envision for a sustainable earth? Scholars have yet to systematically address these crucial questions of our time.

As we turn the millennium, concern is growing again among a new generation of students, but they confront a literature on the environment and development which is largely descriptive, dated and does not contain the complex dealings and pervasiveness of power. While teaching courses on environment and development, I have found that existing books have a few compilations with uneven and disjointed chapters. I have used several books in courses and assembled clippings in course-packs, but the students find themselves wishing to know more about environmental issues vis-à-vis power and development and needing a more coherent structure with which to understand them. The book aims to meet the growing needs of this new generation of students, as well as academics, conscious citizens, and policy-makers.

Md Saidul Islam
23 November 2012
Singapore

Acknowledgments

The idea of a book dealing with the complex nexus of power, development and the environment came to my mind about a decade ago. Since then many individuals and institutions have contributed to broadening my understanding. I'm particularly indebted to individuals such as Peter Vandergeest, Stuart Schoenfeld, Hira Singh, Syed Serajul Islam, Himani Bannerji, Ratiba Hadj Moussa, Peter Brosius, George Ritzer, Kwok Kian Woon, Arthur P.J. Mol, J. Timmons Roberts, and Arun Agrawal. Among the institutions and organizations, I acknowledge the contributions of Nanyang Technological University (NTU), Singapore (for providing excellent support in producing this book); York Centre for Asian Research, Canada; The College of William and Mary, Virginia; International Development Research Centre, Canada; and Social Science and Humanities Research Council, Canada.

A special 'thank you' to my research assistants and readers such as Quek Ri An, Iris Carla De Jesus, Tania Chowdhury, and Lai Zhi Xian Daniel. Ri An's contribution was particularly significant in data collection and during my writing phase. As a token of appreciation, I have therefore put his name in the first chapter. I'm grateful to my colleagues at NTU for their collegial support and inspiration. Last, but not the least, I will always remember the understanding and unceasing encouragement of my beloved wife, Salma Sultana, my daughter Ulfat Tahseen, and son Rawsab Said. They are all a source of my peace and tranquillity.

Part I

Concepts and Theories

1   Challenges of Our Time
Environmental and Social Vulnerabilities

with Quek Ri An

INTRODUCTION

"Anything that can go wrong will go wrong."—Murphy's Law

In March 2011, the world was reminded once more of the frailty of man-made systems, the uncertainties of technology, and the magnitude of destruction they can bring onto the environment supporting human societies and other ecosystems. Technological advancements and social systems are meant to benefit humanity and help societies cope with the vagaries of nature. On the other hand, the nuclear disaster at Fukushima—following the impact of the Tohoku earthquake and tsunami—resulted in the destruction of ecosystems, human lives, and property. The magnitude of destruction, coupled with the likelihood of further, yet-unknown effects on future generations, serves to remind us of the need for reflection and reexamination of the environmental and social vulnerabilities confronting humanity in the twenty-first century. It gives us a glimpse of the danger posed to both human and non-human communities (including the physical environments that support these communities) when the systems we build—to safeguard ourselves against the risks brought about by new technological applications and the hazards of natural disasters—fail, as nature's wrath is unleashed upon us.

This chapter explores the relationship between development, power, and the environment, considering environmental and social vulnerabilities and their distribution between and within countries, nations, communities, and societies undergoing different stages of development. While every community and country in the world today is susceptible to some degree of environmental and social vulnerability, differences in culture, economy, and political circumstances may explain why some countries are much more vulnerable than others. A community's level of vulnerability also correlates with its ability and resources to manage and control the risks it faces, both real and potential. Development, power, and the environment interact in complex ways to explain how and why the impact of environmental problems is more serious in less developed countries (LDCs) and why they lack the power within existing international political and economic structures to improve their situation and reduce their vulnerabilities. This chapter argues that the current trajectory of development, directed as it is by the dominance of powerful transnational corporations (TNCs) and international financial institutions (IFIs), continues to generate significant environmental, economic, and social vulnerabilities for developing countries and marginalized communities in the face of global environmental problems, threats, and risks into the twenty-first century.

We first begin the chapter by examining key environmental and social vulnerabilities confronting humanity in the twenty-first century. We proceed by analyzing how transnational corporations, dominant international financial and political institutions, and the extensive power of mass media exacerbate or mitigate the vulnerabilities experienced, specifically for developing and Third World[1] countries. The chapter then goes on to examine the unique situation of LDCs, which experience an unequal distribution of risks (ecological and social) as compared to developed countries, where communities possess the ability, technology, skills, capital, and other resources to deal with the risks more efficiently or to redirect the risks elsewhere.

UNDERSTANDING VULNERABILITIES

> Vulnerability refers to the susceptibility or potential for harm to social, infrastructural, economic, and ecological systems. It is the result of a set of conditions and processes that influence the way that these systems are harmed by natural and technological hazards or extreme events. Vulnerability is closely associated with resilience, which involves the capacity of these systems to bounce back from disasters or their capacity to both respond to and cope with extreme hazard events. Expressed in a different way, vulnerability is the result of our exposure to hazards and our capacity to cope and recover in a sustainable manner. (Pine 2009:136)

We discuss here two dimensions of vulnerability: environmental and social. Social vulnerability suggests a differential capacity of groups and individuals to deal with the adverse effects of hazards, based on their positions within the physical and social world. Social vulnerability often refers to the capacity of human societies and their social systems to cope with and recover from environmental changes and disasters. It also refers to the extent to which human societies, each with differing levels of resources and abilities available in their social systems, will be impacted by the environmental hazards and disasters. Ecological dimensions of vulnerability refer to the capacity of natural systems to bounce back from disaster. It is the ability, or lack thereof, of our natural systems to deal with stress that may change over time and space (Pine 2009).

Table 1.1 The Twenty-One Emerging Issues

No.	Issue Title	Ranking*
	Cross-cutting issues	
1.	Aligning Governance to the Challenges of Global Sustainability	1
2.	Transforming Human Capabilities for the 21st Century: Meeting Global Environmental Challenges and Moving towards a Green Economy	2
3.	Broken Bridges: Reconnecting Science and Policy	4
4.	Social Tipping Points? Catalyzing Rapid and Transformative Changes in Human Behaviour towards the Environment	5
5.	New Concepts for Coping with Creeping Changes and Imminent Thresholds	18
6.	Coping with Migration Caused by New Aspects of Environmental Change	20
	Food, biodiversity, and land issues	
7.	New Challenges for Ensuring Food Safety and Food Security for 9 Billion People	3
8.	Beyond Conservation: Integrating Biodiversity across the Environmental and Economic Agendas	7
9.	Boosting Urban Sustainability and Resilience	11
10.	The New Rush for Land: Responding to New National and International Pressures	12
	Freshwater and marine issues	
11.	New Insights on Water-Land Interactions: Shift in the Management Paradigm?	6
12.	Shortcutting the Degradation of Inland Waters in Developing Countries	15
13.	Potential Collapse of Oceanic Systems Requires Integrated Ocean Governance	13
14.	Coastal Ecosystems: Addressing Increasing Pressures with Adaptive Governance	19
	Climate-change issues	
15.	New Challenges for Climate Change Mitigation and Adaptation: Managing the Unintended Consequences	7
16.	Acting on the Signal of Climate Change in the Changing Frequency of Extreme Events	16
17.	Managing the Impacts of Glacier Retreat	21
	Energy, technology, and waste issues	
18.	Accelerating the Implementation of Environmentally-Friendly Renewable Energy Systems	7
19.	Greater Risk Than Necessary? The Need for a New Approach for Minimizing Risks of Novel Technologies and Chemicals	10
20.	Changing the Face of Waste: Solving the Impending Scarcity of Strategic Minerals and Avoiding Electronic Waste	14
21.	The Environmental Consequences of Decommissioning Nuclear Reactors	17

Source: UNEP (2012:4).

*Ranking based on scoring by the UNEP Foresight Panel and after considering the polling results of more than 400 scientists worldwide.

Social vulnerability is highest in developing countries, as they have less capacity to cope with environmental changes and threats. They are more vulnerable to the devastating impact of disasters on their economies, infrastructure, and public health. Such factors as wealth, technology, education, information, skills, and infrastructure influence the vulnerability of these developing countries to environmental threats. Poverty is arguably the most important cause of vulnerability; the poor tend to possess lower capacities for coping, thus suffering "a disproportionate burden of the impact of disasters, conflict, droughts, desertification and pollution" (UNEP 2002:303). Social indicators, such as age, also affect vulnerability; children and the elderly are more vulnerable to environmental threats. Marginalized social groups, such as the racially or ethnically marginalized, are more vulnerable too, as they lack the physical resources and social support to respond to such threats. Environmental vulnerability, in turn, has to do with the resilience of the environment to both human and natural threats. Developing states experience higher environmental vulnerability due to an interplay of factors, such as remoteness, geographical vulnerability to natural disasters, ecological fragility, high degrees of economic openness, small internal markets, and limited natural resources (UNEP 2002:313). United Nations Environment Programme (UNEP 2012) has identified twenty-one pressing issues for the 21st century (Table 1.1), clearly showing the magnitude of environmental and social vulnerabilities the planet is facing.

The impacts of environmental change on ecosystems, the environment, and human societies are closely intertwined. The social and human impacts of environmental change will rebound on the well-being of human communities. Environmental changes and threats lead to concurrent environmental and social vulnerabilities, and the effective management of both types of vulnerability is important to protect both human and non-human communities from harm.

GLOBAL ENVIRONMENTAL PROBLEMS

Twenty years after the Rio summit in 1992, world leaders met in Rio once again to discuss the environmental challenges facing humanity. It was a time for them to reflect on how successful and effective the international community has been over the previous two decades in managing the major identified environmental problems. Are we still facing the same environmental problems? Has the situation improved, or are we worse off? Environmental and social vulnerabilities will continue to exist twenty years from now and beyond. The question is what kind of steps can and should be taken to manage these vulnerabilities? Have they been taken? Do countries across the globe experience the same type and degree of vulnerabilities? Or is the distribution of these vulnerabilities uneven? How is the distribution of these vulnerabilities decided and by whom?

The environment—referring to the physical surroundings (both living and non-living physical elements, including energy and matter) that support all life forms on planet Earth—is highly vulnerable. By this, we mean that it is susceptible to 'attacks', to 'hurt', to 'damage', and to 'destruction'. Environmental problems, caused by human activities, natural causes, or both, threaten the biophysical environment that supports both human and non-human communities. R. Scott Frey has identified two general types of environmental problems: the first is "resource depletion," and the second is "pollution" (2001:4). UNEP's 2011 yearbook identifies the depletion of the ozone layer, climate change, natural resource depletion, and biodiversity loss, among others, as the key environmental challenges the world is still facing twenty years after the 1992 Rio summit (UNEP 2011). These challenges reflect the vulnerability of our environment to the hazards caused by human activities and natural environmental changes. The extent and magnitude of environmental and social vulnerabilities are shaped by the ability of communities to deal with these environmental problems.

In the following section, we look at some of the global environmental problems causing environmental and social vulnerabilities for both developed and developing countries. Emphasis is placed on developing countries that are more vulnerable to these environmental problems. We may speak of a vulnerability gap where there is an increasing gap within, between, and across regions, countries, and communities in terms of the risks they face from environmental change and disasters.

Climate Change and Global Warming

Climate change is perhaps the most prominent global environmental issue for the international community in recent decades. This community—which includes governments, non-governmental organizations (NGOs), industries, the United Nations and its various branches, and ordinary citizens across borders—are increasingly involved in negotiating multilateral environmental agreements to resolve the issue of climate change. Examples of such agreements being reached include the 1989 Montreal Protocol and the 1997 Kyoto Protocol. The prominence of climate change as an issue is a result of increased media coverage and the interest generated by scholarly and popular articles, research papers, and books. Much of the discourse on climate change is now accepted by the majority of people in the developed world. This discourse includes attributing the causes of climate change to human activities, discussing the adverse impacts climate change has on human societies and ecosystems, and arguing the need for immediate and coordinated responses from the international community to tackle the issue. This section examines the underlying forces driving climate change, the effects of climate change on development issues, and the vulnerabilities of poorer communities and developing countries confronting climate change.

Climate change refers to "the changes in climate directly or indirectly related to the impact of human activities" (Harris 2011:107). Climate change is more popularly known by the non-scientific and sometimes politically incorrect term 'global warming'; the latter has more negative connotations, whereas 'climate change' has more scientific and value-neutral implications. Global warming arises in part from the considerably increased emission of greenhouse gases due to human activities since the twentieth century. Climate change as a real and serious global environmental problem is affirmed by authoritative reports from the Intergovernmental Panel on Climate Change: "[The] warming of the climate system is unequivocal, as is now evident from observations of increases in global average sea level" (IPCC 2007:30).

Global consumption patterns are the underlying driving force behind climate change, ensuring that production to meet such demand continues endlessly, thereby increasing the emissions of greenhouse gases into our stratosphere. Greenhouse gases include carbon dioxide, methane, chlorofluorocarbons, ozone, and nitrous oxide. These gases are emitted through human activities, such as the burning of fossil fuels, agriculture (in particular, cattle ranching and rice cultivating, where the animals used for such activities emit methane), deforestation, and other industrial processes (DeSombre 2002). Climate change causes adverse impacts on human societies and ecosystems by increasing the possibilities of droughts, higher sea levels (as a result of melting ice caps), and heat waves, among many other consequences.

Vulnerabilities of human societies are reflected by the alarming impact of climate change on the health of millions; experts observe "increases in malnutrition; increased deaths, diseases and injury due to extreme weather events; increased burden of diarrheal diseases; increased frequency of cardio-respiratory diseases due to higher concentrations of ground-level ozone in urban areas related to climate change; and the altered spatial distribution of some infectious diseases" (IPCC 2007:48). Vulnerabilities of the physical environment and ecosystems to climate change are an increasing concern, too. Expert assessments note, "[T]he resilience of many ecosystems is likely to be exceeded this century by an unprecedented combination of climate change, associated disturbances (e.g., flooding, drought, wildfire, insects, ocean acidification) and other global change drivers (e.g., land-use change, pollution, fragmentation of natural systems, overexploitation of resources)" (IPCC 2007:48).

The impact of climate change will be felt most in countries and communities where environmental and social vulnerabilities to natural environmental changes and natural disasters are higher. Such groups as the elderly, the young, and the poor will suffer more from the risks of climate change; such groups exist in countries regardless of their developed or developing status. The impact of climate change will vary from region to region, depending on their geographical vulnerabilities; the coastal and delta regions of Asia may face increased flooding, Australia may face loss of biodiversity, and North America may face water shortages and heat waves (Harris 2011:109). "The impacts of climate change on natural ecosystems and on human society and economies are potentially severe, particularly in parts of the world where geographic vulnerability and poverty make adaptation difficult or impossible" (Brainard et al. 2009, cited in Harris 2011:108).

Efforts to respond to and resolve the climate change issue have been hampered by global politics between the Global North and South, perceived injustices felt by developing regions, and the unwillingness of developed countries and industries to accept proposed emissions reductions. The failure of the Kyoto Protocol, which "required actual reductions in emissions of greenhouse gases of varying amounts for developed countries, with an average of a 5 percent reduction from 1990 emissions by the period 2008 to 2012" (DeSombre 2002:101), reflects the disagreements between developing and developed countries over who should bear the responsibility for reducing emissions. Developing countries argue that since the developed countries were the ones that have historically contributed to the huge amounts of carbon emissions, the latter should be the ones that have more obligations to reduce emissions. The developing countries, furthermore, are resistant to attempts to limit and control their emissions, as doing so will affect their own development ambitions. The issue is complicated by the pollution estimates showing that developing countries are fast overtaking developed nations as the main contributors of carbon emissions as a result of their industrialization programs. Developed countries, most notably the U.S., are resistant to adopting emissions reductions, as corporations and industries are worried about the impact that doing so will have on their profits. Business and industry groups, specifically those from the petroleum, electric utilities, and automobile sectors, lobby for legislators and governments to avoid climate-related laws and the ratification of international agreements, such as the Kyoto Protocol, that will likely lead to "green taxes" or "carbon taxes'" (Harris 2011:114). In short, efforts to resolve environmental issues, such as climate change, are complicated by the politics of development and economic growth (details in Chapter 9).

While international negotiations continue to attempt to get more developed and developing countries to agree to cuts, emissions of greenhouse gases continue to increase at alarming rates. Even if the developed countries were to agree to substantial emissions cuts, the developing countries' emissions will continue to increase. At the moment, it appears that the conflicts in relation to reducing carbon emissions between the developed and developing countries or the Global North-South divide will not be resolved in the near future. The impact of climate change will continue to be felt across the globe, especially in those areas with higher environmental and social vulnerabilities to environmental changes.

Loss of Biodiversity

'Biodiversity' refers to the variability among living organisms from all sources, including terrestrial, marine, and other aquatic ecosystems and the ecological complexes that they are part of. It includes diversity within species (genetic diversity), between species, and of ecosystems (UNEP 2002:120). Despite international and national initiatives to protect it, bio-diversity continues to decline (UNEP 2002:126).

The loss of biodiversity is often linked to the loss of habitats, a result of increasing urban development requiring destruction of natural habitats to convert the land for economic or other human uses and in the process wiping out ecosystems and the diversity of living organisms supported by these habitats. According to the UNEP reports, global biodiversity is being lost at a rate many times higher than that of natural extinction due to land conversion, climate change, pollution, unsustainable harvesting of natural resources, and the introduction of species. Reports also estimate that from 1972 to 2002, about 24 percent of mammals and 12 percent of bird species were regarded as globally threatened (UNEP 2002:xxi). The three levels of biodiversity—i.e., ecosystem diversity, species diversity, and genetic diversity—are closely interrelated in that the loss of one level leads to the loss of other levels. Destruction of ecosystems leads to the loss of a variety of species residing in and supported by the ecosystems and habitats. This destruction in turn leads to the loss of the valuable (at least to the biologists) "range of genetic information coded in the DNA of a single population species" (Hannigan 2006:123).

The loss of biodiversity has negative impacts on human and non-human communities. Scholars have argued that non-human species and living organisms have intrinsic values and a right not to be destroyed through human activities. It is argued that biodiversity provides aesthetic value for human appreciation. Human communities also lose valuable resources in the production of drugs and pharmaceuticals made possible by genetic diversity. Traditional medicines also directly depend on the level of biodiversity. Thus the loss of biodiversity affects human health and well-being. The loss of biodiversity, alongside global warming, is one of the major global environmental issues gaining widespread attention. Efforts to conserve biodiversity have led to international agreements, such as the Convention on Biological Diversity (CBD).

Deforestation

Forests are important to human and non-human communities. They are the natural habitat for various ecosystems. The rate of deforestation has been alarming in the past few decades. Forests are being cleared at rates higher than their natural replacement rates or even attempts at replanting (i.e., reforestation). It is estimated, for instance, that *each day* humans destroy 180 square miles of tropical rain forest while creating over 60 square miles of desert (Frey 2001c:v). The impetus for deforestation comes from population growth and increased affluence, leading to increased market demands for trade and consumption of forest products. Poverty and the lack of strict regulations are among the main impediments to developing countries' efforts at curbing unsustainable deforestation. Forests are also cleared for other land uses, including agricultural expansion, but most often the trees are cleared for commercial purposes—to be processed into paper, fuel-wood, industrial wood, and other forest products. While deforestation may occur naturally, as a result of spontaneous forest fires, extreme climatic events, insect pests and diseases, and human-related activities have increased the pace and magnitude of deforestation, clearing trees at unsustainable rates—i.e., faster than they can naturally be replaced.

The impact of deforestation is most severe on local populations, often in developing and Third World countries. Industrial logging causes local populations to lose valuable sources of food, fuel, medicines, and areas for livestock rearing. Soil erosion is also a serious effect of deforestation that affects the agricultural practices and livelihood of local populations. The development of global trade enables multinational corporations to exploit the natural resources of developing countries, making profits for themselves while transferring the risks of ecological and environmental destruction onto local populations. Many Third World countries are caught in a dilemma between, on the one hand, allowing foreign companies' exploitation of their forests to promote foreign investment for national development and economic growth and, on the other, having to protect their forests for reasons of sustainability and for their own citizens' interests, specifically those who live off the forests, both economically and culturally. National development and economic growth are often prioritized over environmental protection, as national governments also have to consider other important and immediate problems, such as poverty and hunger.

Water Pollution

Although 70 percent of Earth's surface is covered by water, chronic shortages of safe drinking water affect many populations, specifically in developing Third World countries and poor communities (even within developed countries) with inadequate infrastructure to provide safe drinking water. Water pollution comes from the dumping of industrial waste from factories located conveniently close to rivers, which unfortunately represent the only fresh water source for millions of people. Lack of access to safe water supplies and sanitation results in hundreds of millions of cases of water-related diseases and more than five million deaths every year (UNEP 2002:xxii). Water pollution from human and industrial wastes also affects marine ecosystems. Millions of dollars have to be spent on clean-up operations.

Three major factors that are increasing water demand over the past century are population growth, industrial development, and the expansion of irrigated agriculture (UNEP 2002:152). For many of the world's poorer communities, untreated water remains one of the main threats to their health and well-being. Sources of water pollution include the discharge and dumping of untreated sewage waste; petroleum leaks and oil spills; chemical, agricultural, and industrial waste; and so forth.

To be sure, many developing countries' populations still suffer environmental and social vulnerabilities stemming from polluted water supplies unsafe for drinking and other daily uses. As the UNEP report concludes: "While developed countries have made significant strides in addressing water quality issues, the situation has actually worsened in developing countries, with many of them experiencing rising water demand and pollution" (2002:157). Aside from water pollution, access to and control over the sources of water are also key sources of tension in various regions of the world.

WHEN NATURE STRIKES

Are natural disasters a result of 'natural' causes, or are human activities in some way responsible, too? Michael M. Bell argues that most flooding today is caused by "two centuries of human-induced landscape change: deforestation, the destruction of wetlands, the channelling of rivers, the spread of roads and other impermeable surfaces, and the like" (2009:221). Deforestation and poor forest-management practices, which partially contribute to global warming, indirectly also lead to the wildfires and heat waves we experience today.

Perhaps the dubious 'naturalness' of a natural disaster, such as Hurricane Katrina in 2005 (and the flooding that came thereafter), reflects the increasing role of human activities in exacerbating the impact of natural disasters while also indirectly causing them. Human communities are increasingly losing trust in the security of the world and, more importantly, the faith we can put in technological advancement and human institutions. While Hurricane Katrina is neither the first nor the biggest hurricane to have hit New Orleans, it did cause the most damage. Scholars have attributed partial responsibility for the magnitude of destruction by Katrina to the shipping canal connecting New Orleans to the Gulf of Mexico (known as MRGO) built in 1963 (see Bell 2009:221).

Sociologist Kai Erikson calls the development of human-induced disasters—i.e., "between those disasters that can be understood as the work of nature and those that need to be understood as the work of humankind" (1994:19)—"a new species of trouble." He argues that while natural disasters suggest events that are beyond the control of human beings, human-induced disasters suggest a perceived *loss* of control over the processes that were thought to be preventable or at least manageable. Such a perceived loss leads to dread and fear of the unknown and unmanageable. Poor communities and countries often find themselves in a more precarious position against the threats posed by human-induced disasters, as they lack the resources and capabilities to respond to, manage, and cope with such threats.

THE DOMINANCE AND INFLUENCE OF
TRANSNATIONAL CORPORATIONS

Traditionally, it has been accepted that 'nation-states' are the key players in the decision-making processes of international politics, including global environmental politics and policy issues. In recent times, however, scholars of globalization studies and international relations have been highlighting the decline of 'nation-states' and their roles as actors in international politics. Instead, the rise and dominance of 'transnational' actors, including transnational corporations, NGOs, and transnational environmental movements, are being acknowledged in international governance over such matters as global environmental issues: "Increasing transnational activism is attributed to the perceived powerlessness of the state in a globalizing world, particularly when it comes to so-called global issues, such as environmental degradation" (Ford 2011:29). As the 1995 United Nations Commission on Global Governance (UNCGG) report suggests, NGOs and global business are becoming an "even more clearly identifiable sector with a role in global governance" (255).

Since the 1960s, transnational environmental movements and NGOs around the world have increased popular awareness and politicization of environmental issues. As a result, there is increasing scrutiny on many fronts over the relationship between the environment and the organization of social, political, economic, and cultural institutions within societies. Lucy Ford aptly sums up the turning point for transnational actors' role in global environmental politics:

> The 1992 UN Conference on Environment and Development (UNCED) is usually quoted as the watershed for transnational actor involvement in global environmental politics, where close to 1,500 NGOs organized a parallel conference and many more movements and NGOs rallied from across the globe. Ten years later, over 6,000 officially registered NGOs gathered in Johannesburg for the 2002 International Summit on Sustainable Development, alongside countless 'unofficial' groups and movements. Movements and organizations across the world also campaigned on climate change in the run up to the UN Climate Change Conference in Copenhagen in December 2009. (2011:33)

Over the last three decades, TNCs—referring to corporations that conduct their operations across more than two countries—have gained prominence as key players in global environmental politics. They may be headquartered in one host state but establish regional and continental offices, subsidiaries, production facilities, and markets in other locations. Their operations usually involve the movement of people, resources, and capital across national boundaries. Examples of TNCs include oil corporations, such as British Petroleum (BP) and Shell, and food conglomerates, such as Nestlé. In terms of financial power, Walmart is currently the largest transnational corporation: "If Wal-Mart [Walmart] were a country, its revenues would make it on par with the GDP of the 25th largest economy in the world by, surpassing 157 smaller countries" (Trivett 2011:1). Among hundreds, twenty-five major American corporations' 2010 revenues surpass the 2010 gross domestic product (GDP) of entire countries, often with a few billion to spare. Even some major countries, such as Norway, Thailand, and New

Table 1.2 Twenty-Five U.S. Mega Corporations: Where They Would Rank if They Were Countries (2011)

No.	Corporations	Corporation's Revenue (US$ Billions)	Bigger Than (Country)	State's GDP (US$ Billions)	Ranks as State
1.	Walmart	421.89	Norway	414.46	25th
2.	Exxon Mobil	354.67	Thailand	318.85	30th
3.	Chevron	196.34	Czech Republic	192.15	46th
4.	Conoco Phillips	184.97	Pakistan	174.84	48th
5.	Fannie Mae	153.83	Peru	152.83	51st
6.	General Electric	151.63	New Zealand	140.43	52nd
7.	Berkshire Hathaway	136.19	Hungary	128.96	57th
8.	General Motors	135.59	Bangladesh	104.92	58th
9.	Bank of America	134.19	Vietnam	103.57	59th
10.	Ford	128.95	Morocco	103.48	60th
11.	Wells Fargo	93.249	Angola	86.26	62nd
12.	Proctor and Gamble	79.63	Libya	74.23	64th
13.	Costco	77.94	Sudan	68.44	65th
14.	Microsoft	62.48	Croatia	60.59	66th
15.	Apple	65.23	Ecuador	58.91	68th
16.	Pepsi	57.83	Oman	55.62	69th
17.	Cisco	40.04	Lebanon	39.25	81st
18.	Morgan Stanley	39.32	Uzbekistan	38.99	82nd
19.	Amazon.com	34.2	Kenya	32.16	86th
20.	McDonald's	24.07	Latvia	24.05	92nd
21.	Consolidated Edison	13.33	Congo	13.13	112th
22.	Nike	19.16	Paraguay	18.48	102nd
23.	eBay	9.16	Madagascar	8.35	129th
24.	Visa	8.07	Zimbabwe	7.47	133rd
25.	Yahoo	6.32	Mongolia	6.13	138th

Source: Adapted from Trivett (2011).

Zealand, can be bested by certain U.S. firms (Table 1.2). TNCs organize themselves and protect their interests through business advocacy groups, such as the International Chamber of Commerce (ICC), the World Business Council for Sustainable Development (WBCSD), or the European Chemical Industry Council (CEFIC).

The relationship between industry actors and environmental degradation has been strongly debated. TNCs are driven by profit motives, and their growth imperative results in increased demands on the extraction of resources, often contributing directly or indirectly to environmental degradation. Pollution-heavy industries, specifically those from the manufacturing sectors, still hold influence over policy matters in their host countries (DeSombre 2002). There are an estimated 79,000 TNC parent firms globally and 790,000 foreign-affiliate firms, making up for 11 percent of the world's GDP and one-third of world exports in the year 2008 (UNCTAD 2008). TNCs are key investors in environmentally damaging industries, such as resource extraction, chemical production, and electronics (Clapp 2011:47).

Matthias Finger and James Kilcoyne (1997:142) argue further that TNCs are subverting "the efforts by the United Nations to prevent the further degradation of the natural environment" through their influence over governments and under the guise of sustainable development. TNCs and business advocacy groups routinely protect their interests by obstructing the establishment of regulatory regimes that may harm their business operations. Carbon taxes and stricter environmental legislation are examples of such regulations harmful to business. Alternatively, TNCs threaten to, and sometimes do, relocate to host countries that have lower environmental standards and fewer regulations, mostly developing regions known as 'pollution havens'. These developing countries have lower environmental standards and laxer regulatory and enforcement mechanisms, often purposefully so, in order to attract foreign investment for their development programs or to fulfill their international loan obligations.

There is an increasing concern over the power TNCs wield, "particularly vis-à-vis impoverished developing countries" (DeSombre 2002:89). The power of TNCs and business advocacy groups is manifest through the assets and resources they possess and control, often much more than some nation-states. In addition, TNCs are important agents of development and engines of economic growth by virtue of the foreign investment and job creation their operations can bring to host nations. While the business community is generally warming up to the idea of 'sustainable development', and actively voicing the argument that new technological innovations and applications can reduce the environmental impact of their business operations, they have found ways to "discursively integrate environmental problems without substantially changing [their] social and material productive practices" (Ford 2011:36). Such efforts are reflected in *The Business Charter for Sustainable Development: Principles for Environmental Management*, adopted in 1990 and first published in 1991, which articulates a separation of economic processes from environmental degradation. In the words of Jennifer Clapp (2011:48): "transnational corporations, by engaging in the formation of the discourse of sustainability, can shape it in ways that maintain their goals of economic globalization, openness to global investment, and the favouring of soft, voluntary approaches over hard, regulatory approaches to environmental policy."

Ford argues that there appears to be a privatization of *environmental governance* where transnational actors, particularly TNCs and business advocacy groups, are growing in their influence on policy making. Environmental governance is increasingly privatized through institutions, such as the International Organization for Standardization (ISO), that promote voluntary codes of conduct in environmental management. The adoption of ISO global standards in environmental management reflects an unequal power relationship between developed and developing nations. The membership of ISO consists of a mixture of governments, mixed public-private actors, and private-industry associations (Ford 2011). Much of the membership is dominated by representatives from the developed nations and private interests, thus ensuring that developing nations have little say over the establishment of global standards to which they are equally subject. As Peter Newell (2000:159) has argued, "Business actors clearly have more 'tacit power' over state actors on account of their close connection to economic growth creation."

The dominance of TNCs in global environmental politics, through their influence on the decision-making processes of global environmental policy formulation, is magnified through their close relationship with other transnational financial institutions, such as the World Bank and the International Monetary Fund (IMF). These world financial institutions ensure that together with TNCs, developing and Third World countries are caught in a web of dependency through financial instruments established under the veil of environmental management. Such financial instruments include both traditionally structured loans and the establishment of new environmental finance facilities—which provide loans to aid developing countries in their pursuit of sustainable development and incorporation of environmental protection into their development projects. For TNCs, business growth and expansion continue, often at the expense of environmental degradation in developing regions, increasing those regions' environmental and social vulnerabilities.

After the Second World War, former European colonies, such as those in Africa and the other colonies of the now weakened British Empire, were decolonized and (re)gained their independence. While formal colonialism was in retreat, there emerged a new form of colonialism through the establishment of a new international financial system. In 1945, African leaders meeting in Manchester, England, declared that they would no longer tolerate European colonization of their much-abused continent. As the Second World War ended, independence struggles broke out across the colonized world; and the European overlords, in their postwar weakness, could not suppress indigenous resistance indefinitely. Instead they joined with U.S. plans to use political and economic advantage to set up a new financial system for indirect, non-military influence over a stabilized international trade and investment market. At Bretton Woods, New Hampshire, in 1945, the soon-to-be-victorious Allied powers created a set of international financial institutions (IFIs)—the World Bank, the IMF, and General Agreement on Tariffs and Trade (GATT)—through which they could shape the postwar economy without directly governing any 'client' countries. Instead of guns and bombs, the tools were to be the global manipulation of capital, credit, and legal and allied expertise (M. S. Islam 2009; McMichael 2008; Young 2002).

Voting power was based on member states' contributions to the institutions, and, unsurprisingly, the U.S. government was the major donor. In 1994, the World Trade Organization took over from the GATT; however, this did not change the dominant influence of the IMF and the World Bank over the development trajectories of developing countries that needed loans. The World Bank has enormous influence and power over the developing nations, largely due to the postwar role it undertook. Having been overshadowed by the U.S. Marshall Plan in the task of rebuilding war-shattered Europe, the World Bank decided to focus its efforts on the newly independent and developing states of what has come to be known as the Global South. Through planning and financing projects for infrastructure development and economic reform in such sectors as transportation, mining, education, and agriculture, the World Bank's work largely benefited transnational firms and national elites, justifying their programs with the goal of aiding economic growth in these host countries. Reports show that "by the end of the 1990s, nearly half of the $25 billion-odd paid out annually as World Bank loans had been disbursed directly to Northern corporations contracted to carry out projects in the South, and $2.5 billion in consultancy contracts privately distributed" (Young 2002:23).

Much of the 'Third World debt' is created and managed by IFIs. The World Bank and the IMF together have a huge influence in shaping the national development of the Global South. Terms and conditions for the loans often include demands on national governments to pursue economic growth through attracting foreign investment, loosening their social and environmental regulations, and allowing foreign investors and TNCs access to their raw materials. These conditions are geared toward ensuring that Third World debtor countries can at least repay the interest for their loans—at the expense of exposing their people to social and environmental risks. Social risk results from the loans' terms and conditions for reduced public expenditure, leading to lower spending on public programs, such as education, welfare, and health care systems. Such measures impede the ability of populations to get themselves out of the poverty cycle and increase their standard and quality of life. Third World nations suffer more environmental vulnerabilities when the projects funded by IFIs and managed by TNCs have no qualms about extracting as many natural resources as possible while dumping industrial and chemical wastes back onto the rivers and land that local populations depend on for their livelihoods.

Elites (i.e., politicians, managers of corporate and para-state companies, entrepreneurial elites, and experts), specifically those coming from the better-off semi-periphery developing states, are co-opted into the capitalist world system, where they accept and adopt 'Western liberal-modeled' legal and bureaucratic systems. The political rule of international capital and TNCs is secured through the co-option of these elites. Most Southern governments are not blameless for the situation they find themselves in. Corruption remains one of the main reasons for many Third World countries' remaining in debt. For instance, in Indonesia, General Suharto has been accused of leaving his country deep in debt while he appropriated and transferred many of the loans into businesses controlled by his family and cronies.

The 1970s and 1980s saw the rise of environmentalism, particularly in the North. Environmental concern was fast becoming acknowledged as a geopolitical force making its way into Western agendas for local and international governance. Radical environmentalists started protesting against the adverse environmental impact brought about by development and economic growth. IFIs were, and continue to be, challenged and criticized for neglecting the environmental damage caused by many of their funded projects, which furthermore have benefited mostly TNCs and an international class of capitalist elites. IFIs had to react and respond to the challenge from environmentalism and regain their legitimacy to fund development projects while remaining in control over the needs of the developing nations and protecting the interests of their major donors. In 1987, the World Bank gained a specialist environment department (Young 2002:39), reflecting the compatibility it was attempting to establish between development and the environment.

Through hiring and engaging specialists and experts to legitimize its development initiatives and justify the environmental impact of its projects, the World Bank ensured that environmentalist discourses did not threaten the interests of its major donors. In 1991, the Global Environmental Facility (GEF) was created in the World Bank and was tasked with financing the protection of the 'global environment' and, in effect, 'sustainable development'. It funded international conservation projects justified under the United Nation Framework Convention on Climate Change (UNFCCC) and the United Nations Convention on Biological Diversity (UNCBD). The GEF was the World Bank's tool for legitimizing itself amid environmentalists' protests against the adverse socio-environmental impact of its development initiatives on Third World countries and their populations. Multilateral environment agreements, such as the Montreal Protocol and the Convention on Biological Diversity, were supported and funded through the GEF, effectively ensuring the continued dominance of IFIs in shaping environmental and social vulnerabilities, especially in the developing world, despite the environmentalists' challenge. The dominance of the U.S. and rich countries of the North, such as the UK, France, and Germany, was reflected in the consultation and preparation process of the GEF. From the birth of the idea to the administration of the GEF, Southern governments had little or no say in the decision-making process. The South had little choice but to accept the GEF, largely on the terms and vision set out by the major donors of the facility—the richer Northern governments. Zoe Young's (2002) research findings on the GEF demonstrate the subsequent dependence of Third World countries on IFIs, such as the World Bank and the IMF, for loans to finance their 'national development projects'. A new kind of "green hegemony" led by the World Bank (Goldman 2005:7) started.

The Western European donor governments' plan for a fund to finance environmental conventions for 'global' benefit was therefore presented in some fora as a means to shape economic development to the needs of the global environment, while elsewhere it was conversely seen to shape environments and environmentalism to support global economic priorities. Thus were professionals in environmental protection and economic development to be brought together: each wanting the other to adapt to their own norms and conceptions of 'global' benefits, and neither fully able to enforce their priorities given real-world complexities (Young 2002).

There is an increase in international efforts to set up funds to help developing countries implement policies to protect the environment and reduce their carbon emissions while they pursue industrial and other development projects. During the UNCCC held at Durban in 2011, an agreement on the broad design of a global Green Climate Fund was reached. This fund will "funnel some of the $100 billion a year that rich countries have promised to make available to poor ones by 2020, to help them cut emissions and adapt to climate change" (*The Economist* 2011a). It remains to be seen how effective this fund will be in achieving its aims and helping poor countries do more for environmental protection.

In sum, through such instruments as the GEF, IFIs are able to retain their power, control, and dominance over development initiatives in the Southern developing regions while protecting the financial interests of their major donor governments. In the face of the challenges posed by environmentalism to their work on development and loan facilities, the GEF helps the World Bank regain its perceived legitimacy as a global financial institution working for the benefit of all.

TNCs AND THE ROLE OF GLOBAL MEDIA

TNCs are also increasingly successful in lobbying for their interests on the international stage. Through international organizations, such as the World Trade Organization (WTO), they have been able to promote the need for freedom of movement of capital, technology, and so forth. Often, binding regional and global free-trade agreements are established that allow TNCs to undermine efforts from governments and other NGOs that may favor increasing regulation of TNCs within borders. TNCs—largely profit driven—are increasingly operating with little public accountability (E. Campbell 2009). How is this possible? The explanation can be found in the role of global media industry—increasingly owned by a handful of TNCs—and how they shape and influence what the global public knows and does not know about environmental issues. While such emerging channels as the Internet and social media are increasingly changing the 'rules of the game', our analysis here is concerned with traditional mainstream mass media, which are still the major source of information for the public, specifically those poorer countries and communities where access to the Internet is not as readily available.

The public depends on the global media industry for environmental news, which shapes their perception of environmental issues and which in turn influences how, and which, issues receive greater public scrutiny. This increases the possibilities for collective action, such as lobbying and protests, for more environmental regulation or protection from the state. In John Hannigan's (2006:79) own words, "[M]ost of us depend on the media to help make sense of the bewildering daily deluge of information about environmental risks, technologies and initiatives."

Mass media are often taken for granted in being 'objective' in their reporting of 'facts' and 'events'. However, this 'objectivity' is debatable. Reporters, editors, producers, and other media professionals have to decide what and how they report. This selective agenda-setting process, specifically in relation to environmental news and issues, is increasingly influenced by TNCs that own the global media firms. Elizabeth H. Campbell (2009:69) observes that "environmental issues are often debated in such ways as to ensure that corporations are never pointed out as a cause or source of environmental degradation." Instead, TNCs use their control over the global media industry to promote "the ideology that the free market economy is actually free and that what is good for corporations is good for the people" (2009:77); such an ideology is in line with TNCs' interests in minimizing regulation and free-market principles. The content and the slant of environmental news in the mass media is hence a reflection of the interests of power holders in societies, and in contemporary modern societies, TNCs have a huge influence in ensuring that the global mass media protect and prioritize their interests. In addition, TNCs establish resourceful and effective PR departments, thus ensuring that criticism and reports of events putting them in a bad light will be dealt with swiftly; this often involves discrediting the individual reporters and the reports themselves. Media professionals submit themselves to the power of the TNCs, knowing well the cost of offending the powerful.

TNCs exercise their influence in public debates over environmental issues through their control of the global media industry, ensuring that consumption as the driver of economic expansion in contemporary societies is not questioned overtly. Public debates over the relationship between consumption and environmental degradation are minimized and avoided altogether if possible. Advertising is a lucrative industry and a vital source of revenue for media companies in their hyper-competitive markets. Advertisements that promote consumerism in creating more desires and wants for goods, services, and lifestyles are found extensively across all media platforms. The encouragement of consumption through the advertisement industry ensures that economic growth is sustained, often at the expense of continued environmental degradation.

Despite an optimistic upswing in media interest over environmental issues since the environmentalist social movements in the late 1960s and 1970s, the 'objectivity' of environmental news reporting is still questionable, as important questions on the relationship between environment and development remain largely ignored by the mass media. As Colin Lacey and David Longman (1993) have noted, reporting of environmental issues has increasingly taken on a 'show business–like' and commercialized approach. The predominant editorial and political bias of many media firms maintains the common tendency to ignore or 'artificially separate' the relationship between environment and development. The issue of dumping hazardous waste and toxins from the developed countries into the developing ones is an example of the lack of public awareness in environmental problems, as such issues are deliberately presented as 'non-issues' by powerful corporations and states. Environmental news reporting increasingly favors the idea of 'sustainable development', with its coverage promoting the compatibility of businesses with green transformation to resolve environmental problems while still allowing for economic growth to continue. Developing and Third World countries continue to be under the control and influence of TNCs and IFIs. Environmental and social vulnerabilities of the communities in these regions increase in the face of human-induced environmental and technological risks.

In sum, the global media industry is increasingly influenced and controlled by a handful of powerful TNCs. These TNCs use the mass media to advance their corporate and profit driven agendas while ensuring that environmental issues are debated and discussed within discursive boundaries that do not question the importance of business and free-market liberalism.

"POWERLESS": DILEMMAS OF THIRD WORLD DEVELOPMENT AND THE ENVIRONMENT

Environmental problems are also development problems, as "environmental degradation can hit development strategies" (Martell 1994:43). For James O'Connor (2001; cf. 1998), the relationship between development and the ecological crisis is clear: development (i.e., the accumulation of capital through economic expansion) in both developing and developed regions is the driving force behind environmental and ecological degradation (pollution and resource depletion). But he argues, "The worst human and ecological disasters as a rule occur in the Third World and the 'internal colonies' of the First World. The human victims of ecological degradation are typically the rural poor—the land-poor and landless masses for whom ecological questions are a matter of life and death—and the unemployed and underemployed in the cities, as well as the oppressed minorities and poor in the First World" (O'Connor 2001:152).

When agribusinesses from the developed countries bring their operations to LDCs where the climate may be favorable for the mass production of certain cash crops, the agricultural practices employed are usually damaging to the land, causing soil degradation that, in turn, damages its ability for future crop production. The companies simply leave the damaged land holdings when their yield decreases. The local farmers of the LDCs are left with these problems of environmental degradation that affect their livelihood and ability to produce crops for sustenance and income. Pollution is exported from the First World to the Third World; "dangerous chemicals banned in the First World find their way into industrial and agricultural production in the Third World" (O'Connor 2001:157).

Third World countries are more susceptible and hence more vulnerable to environmental hazards. Their dependency on developed countries and IFIs often results in unfair loan conditions requiring their agreement to the exploitation of their natural resources at extraction rates that in turn affect their ability to pursue sustainable development. For example, in promoting fisheries 'development', the World Bank may offer a government credit to buy large boats and refrigeration and processing factories to serve global markets, but its take next to no responsibility for the resulting decline of fish stocks and local markets and immiseration of artisanal fishing communities, let alone the damage to marine ecosystems and spawning grounds by industrial-scale fisheries (Young 2002).

As alluded to earlier, Young's research findings on the GEF—an establishment in the World Bank to finance international conservation projects justified under the UNFCCC and the UNCBD (Young 2002:2)—demonstrate the dependence of Third World countries on such IFIs as the World Bank and the IMF for loans to finance their 'national development projects'. These institutions—and specifically the GEF—are funded mainly by rich donors from the 'West': governments from the UK, France, Germany, Italy, and the Netherlands. Often, loans and aid are approved for the developing countries in exchange for Southern governments' giving up a degree of sovereignty over the use of their countries' natural resources.

Third World countries have been unhappy that developed countries seek to place unfair restrictions and limitations on their use of natural resources, practices that they regard as vital for economic and national growth to the level of material comforts that the developed countries enjoy now. Environmentalism has thus been criticized as being insensitive to the "particular needs of Third World countries where growth needs are acute" (Martell

1994:39). In addition, certain social and political choices, such as the alleviation of poverty, may be valued highly and more urgently than environmental
and natural resource protection. The environmental concern may be a 'luxury'
or 'privilege' of those already materially well-off—and one should bear in
mind that such distinctions of 'haves' and 'have-nots' exist both between and
within countries. "LDCs have enough on their plates trying to foster development and growth and eradicate poverty, starvation and inequality without
worrying about environmental consequences. They have too many pressing material concerns on their hands for them to worry about non-material
issues" (Martell 1994:40). Environmental activists retort that environmental
protection issues are still vital for these LDCs. First, they argue that environmental problems affect everyone, both North and South, developed and less
developed countries. Instead of playing the blame game now, LDCs should
understand the severity of the issue at hand and contribute to resolving it
rather than exacerbating the issue by insisting on industrial development.
Second, the environmental consequences of developed countries' industrial
development should lead the LDCs to look for alternative models of development that can avert the same kind of mistakes previously made, which both
North and South are now suffering for.

LDCs continue to depend on investment, aid, loans, and technological
transfer from developed countries for their survival and development. As
such, they are in a vulnerable position to adopt environmentally damaging practices, either through pressure from those whom they depend upon
or by their own account. To attract investors for development projects to
take off, many LDCs have loosened environmental protection regulations,
often negligible, making it more attractive for multinational corporations
to outsource their operations to these areas. Often, hazardous waste and
toxics are freely dumped into the grounds of LDCs, which makes them
more vulnerable.

Scholars have pointed out that the web of dependency spun by Third
World aid and debt creates environmental problems. The financial interests
of First World creditors and the development needs of debtors combine
to ensure that loans are usually dedicated to big projects geared to rapid
industrial development, with little thought for their environmental impact.
Furthermore, debt has to be paid off in foreign exchange, so Third World
countries are keen in bringing this in by developing export industries, such
as cash cropping and mining. These, of course, are industries that have
a large environmental impact, because they involve the use of soil and
resource extraction (Martell 1994).

In their book *Refashioning Nature: Food, Ecology and Culture*, David
Goodman and Michael Redclift (1991) analyze the impact of our modern
food system on the environment. For them, the developing and Third World
countries experience higher environmental vulnerability as a result of the
demands and pressures of a modern food system involving agricultural intensification through new developments in technology and the implementation

of agricultural development policies. Developing countries have to rely on external loans and credit from IFIs to finance their agricultural projects. Goodman and Redclift argue that developing countries are effectively caught in a "scissors movement" (1991:214). In such a movement, the developing countries have to bear the double costs of conserving natural resources on one hand while also having to bear the costs of "revamping their economic policies under the exigencies of structural adjustment, and other packages emanating from international financial institutions" (1991:214). While understanding fully the environmental costs of modern agriculture practices, developing countries find it more difficult to prioritize environmental protection over the 'gains' from economic growth, which include the higher yield and productivity that modern agricultural practices can generate. Such economic growth is often valued more highly for its potential in alleviating poverty, hunger, and starvation due to food shortages.

The unfair treatment that Third World and developing countries feel they are subjected to from the bullying tactics of the developed world is reflected in the unwillingness of developed countries to conform to the same standards and restrictions of international agreements that they expect the developing countries to adhere to. The failure of the Kyoto Protocol has been widely publicized in mainstream media across the globe. The Protocol, not ratified by the U.S. government, passed its expiry deadline in 2012. Even Canada, whose citizens generally take pride in being 'green', announced its withdrawal from the protocol after the Climate Conference in Durban in 2011 as it attempts to escape the penalty for failing to meet the targets of emission reduction it promised (*The Economist* 2011b). The alarming lack of political will among the developed nations to make sacrifices for environmental protection through changes in their economic policies has emboldened developing nations, such as China and India, to resist pressure for them to reduce emissions as well. In short, a waiting and blaming game between the developing and developed countries over who should and how to resolve issues regarding emissions reductions continues endlessly; international negotiations often amount to nothing, and even the agreements are toothless. While the bickering continues, the impact of economic growth on environmental degradation nonetheless continues, and the unequal distribution of environmental and social vulnerabilities that developing countries face persists.

Much of the blame for the global environmental problems we face today can be attributed to the excesses of developed countries, which had contributed much to carbon emissions and environmental damage during their industrialization and economic expansion throughout history. However, scholars are also acknowledging the environmental degradation that many developing countries are causing as a result of their development projects. As Avijit Gupta (1998) argues in his work *Ecology and Development in the Third World*, many Third World countries are trying to improve the living conditions of their citizens. Economic expansion that involves the logging of timber, extraction of natural resources, intensification of agri-cultural practices, and establishment of industrialization programs similar to those of the West appears to be the preferred development strategy for these Third World countries. This strategy and its component steps bring increasingly adverse impacts on the environment. It is not that Third World countries completely lack the power to decide on matters that will impact their environment and development ambitions. For many Third World governments, the desire for industrialization and the acceptance of envi-ronmental degradation and resource exploitation are political and social choices, a price they are willing to accept to tackle immediate problems of poverty and hunger.

In sum, the relationship between development and the environment is clear: development (in modern times often synonymous with economic growth and expansion) brings with it environmental degradation. What is more complicated is the question of who is at fault. Accompanying that question, who should take responsibility for resolving the environmental problems associated with development? The search for a consensus on the answers to these difficult questions continues as the debate between devel-oped and developing nations continues on the international stage and aca-demic world. It is hard to think of the possibility of any nation in the world being willing to sacrifice much economic growth and development for the purpose of environmental protection. Developing countries are more sus-ceptible to the risks of environmental degradation and natural disasters, given their environmental and social vulnerabilities. Third World countries face a perennial dilemma: trying to improve the living conditions of their citizens entails economic expansion even though they recognize that their development steps will cause environmental degradation that will come back to haunt them, affecting their ability and resources for further devel-opment. For many Third World countries, the only viable path of develop-ment is the same road of industrialization taken by the developed world.

STRUCTURE OF THE BOOK

With this background, the remaining chapters of Part I (Chapters 2–5) provide a robust conceptual and theoretical examination and synthesis of power, development, and the environment. Chapters 2 and 3 elucidate con-cepts and theories of power and how power is understood and expressed in different paradigms of development, including modernization paradigm, dependency school, postmodern critique of development, and community-based natural-resource management. While exploring contemporary theo-ries of nature-society relationships, such as the treadmill of production, risk society, theory of metabolic rift, and ecological modernization, Chapter 4 proposes a new synthesis of a 'double-risk' society. Chapter 5 examines neoliberalism and uncovers some of its inherent paradoxes.

In Part II, this book discerns at least four conspicuous yet interrelated 'projects of power' dealing with development and the environment: the colonial project, the development project, the neoliberal globalization project, and the neoliberal security project. These 'projects of power' have been examined and expressed through a number of case studies on key global issues and challenges, such as underdevelopment (Chapter 6), food regimes (Chapters 7 and 8), climate change (Chapter 9), dam building (Chapter 10), identity politics (Chapter 11), and neoliberal security regime (Chapter 12). In the final part (Part III), the book offers a new framework of a 'double-risk' society for the Global South (Chapter 13) and possible pathways for a sustainable Earth (Chapter 14).

2 Understanding Power in Social Organization

INTRODUCTION

> "Every social act is an exercise of power, every social relationship is a power equation, and every social group or system is an organization of power." (Hawley 1963:422)

Power is perhaps the fundamental process of social relations and hence one of the most central concepts in sociology. However, it was perhaps one of the least studied and least understood concepts for a long time. In the 1860s, power relations between social classes were fundamental to the sociological writings of Karl Marx (1818–1883). In the early 1900s, power relations were again a critical factor in Max Weber's (1864–1920) writings. Subsequently, most sociologists, especially in North America, overlooked power for several decades. Marvin E. Olsen and Martin N. Marger (1993) show that American sociology was dominated for a long period of time by two foci that did not involve power: (a) social psychological concerns with the behavior of individual in society, and (b) Parsonian theory, with its emphasis on value consensus and normative expectations.

The rediscovery of power in sociological studies began in the 1950s with the publication of two pivotal books: Floyd Hunter's *Community Power Structure* in 1953, which demonstrates the exercise of power in communities, and C. Wright Mills's *The Power Elite* in 1956, which controversially debates the role of the elite in modern societies. The 1960s saw many American sociologists returning to Marx's writings, producing new interpretations of his theoretical ideas. The social upheavals of the civil rights and antiwar movements during that time consequently led many American sociologists to radically shift scholarly interest toward the field of power relations, stirring a new awareness of the role of power in social organizations (Lukes 1986; Olsen and Marger 1993). A new understanding of power, albeit in a new form, was brought to light in academia by the writings of Michel Foucault in the 1970s and post-Foucauldian authors in the 1990s.

Today, the exercise and structuring of social power is a major concern not only within political sociology but also in other areas of sociology—most recently in the areas of environmental and development sociology. This chapter provides a comprehensive yet concise survey and analysis of the nature of social power and its role in social organization and provides a discussion through different perspectives on social power.

NATURE AND CHARACTERISTICS OF SOCIAL POWER

Power is not a monolithic concept and hence has no universally accepted single definition. There are, however, some conspicuous problems in defining social power.[1] Nevertheless, we can deduce the essential idea stressed by most writers attempting to define social power, which is that *power is the ability to affect social activities.*[2] It is, as Olsen and Marger (1993:1) claim, a "dynamic process, not a static possession, that pervades all areas of social life." Sociologists are usually concerned with broad and relatively stable patterns of power, mainly for analytical convenience, rather than with every isolated and minute instance of power exertion. The idea of affecting social activities logically implies overcoming whatever resistance, opposition, or limitation that may be encountered. Nevertheless, reference to resistance adumbrates that the exercise of power is usually a reciprocal process among all participants and is rarely determined by a single actor, no matter how unequal the situation may appear (Olsen 1993). Hence, two ideas are central to the notion of social power: (a) social power is a generalized rather than a narrowly limited capacity, and (b) the exercise of power necessitates overcoming resistance.

The notion of 'influence' and 'control' are used by some writers as synonyms to 'power', while many distinguish 'power' from these concepts, usually on the ground that "the effects of power on the recipient are to some extent involuntary, while 'influence' and 'control' are seen as producing a motivational change within affected individuals so that they more or less willingly comply" (Olsen 1986:3). In this view, 'influence' refers to overt participation, whereas 'control' rests largely on unconscious norm internalization. The distinction may seem arbitrary, since "what begins as wholly involuntary compliance may over time shift to willing cooperation, while what seems to be voluntary compliance may be simply a decision to abide by an inescapable directive" (Olsen 1986:3). Therefore, a more meaningful use of these terms is to keep social power as an inclusive or generic concept, while using 'influence' and 'control' to describe the determinacy of possible outcomes as seen from the perspective of the power wielder: "the exercise of social power can vary from relatively indeterminate social influence to relatively determinate social control, depending on the type and amount of power being exerted and the relative power of the other actors involved" (Olsen and Marger 1993:1–2).

The actors who exercise power can be organizations (the size of which varies from small groups to total societies) as well as individuals. In the former, the activity is sometimes called 'organizational' or 'interorganizational' power, while in the latter, it is referred to as 'personal' or 'interpersonal' power (Olsen 1986; Olsen and Marger 1993). Unlike social psychology, which studies interpersonal power relations, sociology views power as entirely 'social' and 'organizational'. Someone might have 'personal power', but that is not an isolated phenomenon. Instead, it is connected with, and contingent upon, that person's location in society or the social organization. "Although it is of course true that relationships among organizations are carried out by individuals enacting organizational roles, it is nevertheless the organization as a whole—not individual spokesmen for the organization—which is wielding power" (Olsen 1986:3).

Within the dynamics of the power-exertion process, if a power relationship becomes an established feature of any pattern of social ordering, it can be regarded as a structural characteristic of that organization. Weber (1978) and, more recently, Anthony Giddens (1984) have both referred to such structured patterns of social power as 'domination' and have emphasized their perpetuation, stability, and relative predictability in social life. From the analysis and the debate around the notion of social power by different sociologists, we can discern some conspicuous characteristics of social power, as summarized by Olsen and Marger (1993:2–3):

(a) As social power is an *interactive process*, it always resides within social interaction and relationships, never in individual actors. A single actor may possess resources that provide a potential basis for exerting social power, but power does not exist until it is expressed in the actions of two or more actors as a dynamic relationship. Moreover, both the power attempt made by an exerter and the resistance offered by a recipient are crucial in determining the actual power exercised in any situation.

(b) The ability of an actor to exercise social power can be either *potential* or *active* at any given time. An actor exercises potential power when he or she possesses resources, is capable of employing them, and indicates that possibility to others. Power becomes active when those resources are actually converted into actions toward others.

(c) Power exertion is a *purposeful activity* that is intended toward others in certain ways, but it may also have unintended effects. Most sociologists restrict the concept of power to actions that are intended to affect the recipient, because otherwise virtually every action by every actor could be labeled as power exertion. The issue of intentionality is clouded in many situations, however, by three features of many power actions. First, for strategic reasons, actors often attempt to hide or disguise the purpose of their power wielding, attempting to influence others without others' being aware of it. Second, power can be exerted indirectly through intermediaries, a process that can mask the primary intentions. Third, in addition to its intended outcomes, an exercise of power can have numerous unintended (and sometimes unrecognized) consequences for others.

(d) The exercise of social power can affect actors' actions and ideas in either of two directions: it can enable or cause them to do things they would not otherwise do, or it can hinder or prevent them from doing things they would otherwise do. In other words, power can be used in either a *promotive* or a *preventive* manner. If we wish to emphasize the preventive use of power, we may speak of exercising power *over* others to control them. If we wish to emphasize its promotive use, we may speak of exercising power *with* others to attain common goals. The first expression often conveys the value that power exertion is undesirable, because it restricts individuals' freedom of action, whereas the second expression conveys the value that power is desirable for collective endeavors.

(e) The interactions and exchanges that occur between participants when power is exerted can vary from evenly *balanced* to grossly *unbalanced*. In relative balanced situations, each actor exerts approximately the same amount of influence or control on the other actor(s) so that everyone receives approximately equal benefits. In a highly unbalanced situation, one or a few actors exert much greater influence or control than everyone else and consequently receive most of the benefits. Relatively balanced power is usually more stable and is viewed as more desirable than highly unbalanced power conditions, although, for various reasons, the latter often occur.

FORMS OF SOCIAL POWER

There are various ways in exerting social power. Six fairly distinct types or forms of social power are frequently discussed by sociologists—force, dominance, authority, attraction, ideology, and discipline—although any specific situation may include more than one form, and sometimes in an overlapping manner.

(a) Force: According to Olsen, force is a form of social power that involves "the intentional exertion of social pressures on others to achieve desired outcomes" (1993:29). Olsen and Marger (1993) add that when exerting force, an actor brings pressures to bear on the intended recipient by giving or withholding specific resources or threatening to do so. The actor must therefore commit particular resources to that interaction and expend them to whatever extent is necessary to obtain the intended outcome. Amita Etzoni (1964, 1993) identifies three different forces to exert social power: (a) with utilitarian force (also called 'inducement' or 'compensation'), the recipient is given desired benefits in return for compliance; (b) with coercive

force (also called 'constrain' or 'deprivation'), punishments are meted out or benefits are suspended to obtain compliance; and (c) with pervasive force (also called 'information' or 'communication') messages are conveyed that alter the recipient's beliefs, values, attitudes, emotions, or motivations in an attempt to produce compliance.

(b) Dominance: Dominance is a "form of social power that results from the performance of established roles or functions" (Olsen 1993:31). While exerting dominance, an actor effectively carries out a set of established activities or social roles on a regular basis. To the extent that others depend on the performance of those activities, they are vulnerable to being enforced or controlled by that actor. This form of power, as Olsen and Marger (1993) explain, does not require the commitment of any additional resources to the interaction but relies entirely on the successful performance of the dominant actor's usual activities or roles. The ability to exert dominance depends heavily on one's position in a social network or organization, so that the closer an actor's position to the top or center of the social structure, the greater the possibility of dominance.

(c) Authority: "When exerting authority, an actor draws on a grant of legitimacy made by the recipient as a basis for using authoritative directives" (Olsen and Marger 1993:4). As the legitimacy has been voluntarily granted by those subject to the directives, they are expected to comply with them. Olsen (1993) explains that legitimacy is sometimes granted to an actor through direct procedures, such as formal votes or informal agreements, but more commonly it is indirectly expressed as one joins an organization, remains a member of it, and supports the action of its leaders who claim legitimacy.

Weber (1947:324–325, 1993:39–47) identifies four bases on which legitimate authority often rests within societies: (a) *rational knowledge* or expertise relevant to specific situations; (b) *legal rights* based on formal arrangements; (c) *traditional beliefs* and values sanctified by time; and (d) *charismatic appeal* of revered leaders to their followers.[3] In addition to this, Olsen (1993) mentions another form of authority, which rests on *passive acceptance*. It comes from established customs and conventions. The recipients do not overtly grant legitimacy to the authority wielder but simply follow his or her directives out of habit, an act that constitutes an implicit grant of legitimacy. Authority is by far the most stable form of power exertion, although sometimes it may take abnormal forms, such as diplomatic bribery and intimidation by the superpower to acquire formal compliance from the powerless nations.

(d) Attraction: Olsen defines attraction as a "form of social power that lies in the ability of an actor to affect others because of who he or she is" (1993:33). When exercising attraction, an actor draws on the diffuse appeal that he or she has for others in order to influence them. That appeal, unlike a grant of legitimacy, may have no connection with social power. A skillful actor may be able, nevertheless, to transform that appeal into power

exertion with which others voluntarily comply. Olsen (1993) identifies three common sources of appeal/attraction, which are cognitive *identification* with, positive *feelings* toward, and attribution of *charisma* to an individual or an organization. Attractive power is often unstable and transitory, but at times it becomes extremely compelling.

(e) Ideology: Marx is credited with uncovering and theorizing the concept of ideology, albeit a different version than what we conventionally understand ideology to mean. Ideology, to Marx, is a reified cover used by the bourgeoisie—the dominant class in the society that controls the means of production and hence difference sources or resources of power—that obscures the power relation between the bourgeoisie and the proletariat and masks the exploitation of the latter class. Ideology is put forward as what is believed to be a form of doing a certain kind of thought or belief, "an active epistemological gesture" (Himani 2001:27), whose method of production is uncovered by the 'three tricks' that have been paraphrased by Dorothy E. Smith (1990) from Marx:

> Trick 1: Separate what people say they think from the actual circumstances in which it is said, from the actual empirical conditions of their lives, and from the actual individuals who said it.
>
> Trick 2: Having detached the ideas, arrange them to demonstrate an order among them that accounts for what is observed. (Marx and Engels describe this as making 'mystical connections'.)
>
> Trick 3: Then change the ideas into a 'person'; that is, set them up as distinct entities (for example, a value pattern, norm, belief system and so forth) to which agency (or possible causal efficacy) may be attributed. Finally, redistribute them to 'reality' by attributing them to actors who can now be treated as representing the ideas. (A deeper analysis of the Marxist notion of power is discussed in the coming section.)

(f) Discipline, Discourse, and Knowledge: There is a dialectical relation between knowledge and power: knowledge is power, and power produces knowledge. The notion of governmentality, as propounded by Foucault, is particularly important here. In the coming section, it is discussed in detail.

THEORETICAL PERSPECTIVES ON SOCIAL POWER

Up to the 1970s, three principal theoretical perspectives on social power pervaded sociological thought: Marxian (or class) theory, elite theory, and pluralist theory. The writings of Foucault during the 1970s added a novel understanding of power to sociological thought. None of these is a formal theory; nevertheless, these broad perspectives tend to shape the overall manner in which sociologists view the role of power in social organizations. Each of these theories is briefly outlined below.

The Marxian Perspective

Political philosophers from Plato onward have written extensively on the exercise of power, and most of them have linked their discussions of power to the state, seeing government and related organizations, such as the military, as the main foci of power in society. Marx must be singled out, as he breaks sharply with this tradition. He argues instead that power originates primarily in economic production; that it permeates and influences all aspects of society; that the principal units within power dynamics are social classes, the main wielder of social power in society; and that the government is largely a servant of the dominant social class (Bottomore and Rubel 1956; Olsen 1970). Marx thus expands the concept of power from an especially political phenomenon to a ubiquitous social process and offers a theory of societal development based on the exercise of power.[4]

There are three major components of Marxian theoretical perspective, as identified by Ralf Dahrendorf (1962, 1989) and Joseph Schumpeter (1962): (a) a sociological model based on the primacy of economically generated social power, (b) a historical model describing the process of dialectical social change, and (c) a connecting thesis—that is, social classes in conflict. The sociological model that underlies all Marxian theory is often called the 'materialistic' conception of history (Heilbroner 1980) or the 'base-superstructure' model (Wacquant 1985). When we relate them to social power, however, both carry inappropriate connotations. Olsen and Marger (1993) use a more precise term: 'economic-base power model' of society. This model contains two principal arguments.

First, *all societies rest on an economic foundation or base.* Mankind's need for food, shelter, housing, and energy are central in understanding the socio-cultural system. "The first historical act is," Marx writes, "the production of material life itself" (1964:60). Unless men and women successfully fulfill this act, there will be no other. All social life is dependent upon fulfilling this quest for a sufficiency of eating and drinking, for habitation and for clothing. The quest to meet basic needs is humanity's primary goal. As people must produce goods and services in order to survive and attain any goals, the economic production processes—which Marx calls 'modes of production'—that prevail in a society constitute the foundation on which other aspects of social life rest. Societies may contain several modes of production; nevertheless, one of them, at any given time, tends to dominate the economy and hence is the society's 'dominant mode of production'. Thus, feudal society is dominated by a 'feudal mode of production' (agriculture) in which the class of landlords extracts a surplus from a rural population bound to the land. In modern capitalist society, the mode of production is manufacturing. The economic base and its dominant mode of economic production shape and influence other features of society—known as 'superstructures'—that include all other social institutions, such as government, education, culture, ideas, beliefs, and values. It does not mean that the rest of the society is determined by the economic base. It is important to recognize that other parts of the society may contain some functional autonomy and may, to some extent, influence the economic base (Bottomore and Rubel 1956; Olsen and Marger 1993; Schumpeter 1962).

Second, a mode of production contains two components—forces of production and means of production. *Forces of production* refer to all those factors that determine how that particular form of economic production is preferred, including its necessary resources, relevant technology, production techniques, labor force, organizational structures, division of labor, and so on. All these forces are important within the economy; nevertheless, their effects are limited to their own realms of activity. *Relations of production* consist of the social, economic, political, and legal arrangements that define who owns and/or controls that mode of the economic production process. In addition to linking a mode of production with the rest of society, *the relations of production constitute the primary source of social power.* Because of the functional primacy of the economic base in any society, whoever owns or controls its dominant mode of economic production has access to its major resources and hence becomes the principal wielder of social power in that society. In other words, whoever controls the dominant mode of economic production in a society determines how the existing technology will be utilized and how the resulting resources will be distributed. Consequently, these persons exercise power throughout the whole of society (Bottomore and Rubel 1956; Olsen and Marger 1993; Schumpeter 1962).

This theoretical perspective provides the key for Marx in his understanding of the power dynamics of all societies, but it does not explain long-term trends in human history. For this, he turns to the idea of dialectic social change that Olsen and Marger (1993:76) calls "dialectic social evolution." From philosopher G.W.F. Hegel, Marx takes the dialectic model and applies it to historical social change. This model consists of three stages: (a) an initial thesis, or existing set of social conditions; (b) an alternative antithesis, or radically different set of conditions that develops from the initial conditions but is not necessarily the complete opposite of the first stage; and (c) an integrating synthesis, or wholly new set of conditions that emerges from both the thesis and antithesis conditions, contains portions of both of them, and resolves the fundamental contradictions inherent in each of them. That synthesis then becomes the thesis for a succeeding dialectic, so that, theoretically, the process can continue indefinitely (Marx, Engels, and Lenin 1975). The dialectic process is for Marx not an inherent tendency within human society but rather an analytical tool with which to explain the broad sweep of human history—at least in Western Europe. In other words, dialectic change is never inevitable, but when major social changes do occur, they tend to follow the dialectic process (Zeitlin 1967).

Marx would have left two fundamental questions unanswered if he had ended his analysis at this point. First, what are the segments of society that compete for control of the means of production, and how do they relate to one another? Second, why would socialism not become the thesis for further dialectic change? He answers both questions by bridging the theoretical gap between his sociological perspective and his philosophy of history with the thesis of conflicting social classes. This thesis consists of a definition of classes, an analysis of the nature of capitalism, and an argument for class conflict and revolution. The opening line of *The Communist Manifesto* states, "The history of all hitherto existing society is the history of class struggles" (Marx 1998:34). Marx believes that the real struggles within any society are between the different classes, with each class struggling for mastery. Even the dominant class must continually struggle to conquer for itself the political mastery of its country. The prevailing class must subjugate the working class, while the middle class tries to maintain its precarious position above the lower class. All the while, the lower class is trying to climb up to a higher level. He analyzes the capitalist economic system in great depth to discover why it produces the extreme exploitation of workers he observes in all industrialized societies. He concludes that the dialectic social change will end only if social classes are completely abolished (Olsen 1970).

The Elitist Perspective

As a response to Marx's economic-based power model, a new outlook of power emerged—the elitist perspective. Many of the ideas of this power model, however, can be found in the writing of Plato, Machiavelli, and many other philosophers. As a theoretical perspective on social power, elitism is formulated by Vilfredo Pareto (1935), Gaetano Mosca (1939), and Robert Michels (1968). The common thesis among these scholars is that the concentration of social power in a 'small set of controlling elite' is inevitable in all societies, a thesis that negates Marx's vision of evolutionary change toward a classless society with power equality. At the same time, they hold that some social change can occur through gradual circulation of elites without overt class conflict or societal revolution. The basic principles of elitism, as summarized from Michels's (1968) famous 'Iron Law of Oligarchy', are as follows:

- Within all societies and other larger organizations that function beyond the subsistence level, there have been—and presumably always will be—one or a few sets of powerful controlling elites. Regardless of the nature of the government or the economy, there is always oligarchy, or rule of the few over many. The masses cannot and will not govern themselves.
- Although the elites are always a tiny minority of the population, they control a large proportion of the available resources, are usually well organized, and are quite cohesive. Consequently, the elites are highly effective in wielding power throughout society.
- Elites commonly employ all available means to protect and preserve their power and to enhance it whenever possible. They share power

with others only if it is in their self-interest, and they never voluntarily
surrender power.

- To rule their society, elites employ a wide variety of techniques. These
  include controlling the government, dominating the economy, using
  police and military force, manipulating the educational system and
  the mass media, sanctioning or eliminating those who oppose them,
  and creating ideologies (beliefs, values, myths, etc.) that legitimize
  their power and rule.
- Elites may permit or even encourage limited social change, but only to
  the extent that they see it as contributing toward the goals they seek
  and not threatening their power. Major social transformations are
  strongly resisted by the elites.
- As societies are getting increasingly large and complex, the power
  of the elites tends to be less visible, because it is embedded within
  numerous organizational social structures. As a consequence, however, their rule becomes more pervasive and effective.

In short, the elites exercise most of the power in a society; the masses do
not. Therefore, to understand any society, we must examine its powerful
elites, the bases of their power, the manner in which they exercise it, and
the purposes for which they exert power. Seemingly, many tenets of elitism may seem similar to Marx's theory of the 'bourgeoisie' class, which,
despite its minority position, controls the whole means of production in a
given society. However, two clear differences can be drawn between these
two theoretical perspectives. First, Marx views that the rule of the few, the
power of the bourgeoisie, is not an essentialized feature of society. Exploitation of the powerless—he calls them the 'proletariat'—is inherent in this
rule, and the prospect exists for social change through revolution. To the
proponents of elitism, oligarchy is a necessary condition for, and a common
feature of, all societies; hence, they do not see any prospect for revolution-
ary social change. Second, none of the proponents of elitism makes explicit
reference to the central Marxian concern with economic production and
economically based power. Elitists generally focus primarily on the polity
and give little or no attention to the economy as a source of social power.

The Pluralist Perspective

Despite differences between Marxian and elitist models of social power,
both hold a common view that the few elites in a society or organization
are the ones who exercise dominant power. The theory of social pluralism rejects that idea and holds that in modern industrialized democratic
societies, power is at least moderately dispersed—and could be extensively
decentralized if the pluralist model were fully implemented. "Pluralism is
thus partially an empirical-descriptive model of what is and partially a the-
oretical-ideal model of what might be" (Olsen and Marger 1993:83).

The idea of a division of power in a political system, as a means of preventing tyranny, has been discussed by political philosophers since antiquity. Aristotle points out the benefits to be gained from differentiating various governmental activities, and Montesquieu in the eighteenth century stresses the desirability of separating legislative, executive, and judicial functions between different bodies. In addition, the federal model of government divides political power along geographical lines, with the national state sharing sovereignty with one or more levels of local government (Olsen 1971).

The pluralist model goes far beyond the political system, however, to encompass the entire society. James Madison's *The Federalist, Number 10*, sketches the main features of this model, but it is Alexis de Tocqueville's *Democracy in America, Volume 2* ([1835] 1961), written in the 1930s, that fully develops pluralism as a societal model of power structuring. Tocqueville sees mass equality, created by the breakdown or the absence of traditional hierarchies of feudal authority, as providing fertile ground for the emergence of a 'tyranny of the majority' in place of a tyranny of the kings or other elites. His conception of socio-political pluralism is intended to prevent both forms of tyranny in modern societies (Olsen 1971; Olsen and Marger 1993). As the pluralism model has evolved, it has taken three somewhat different forms: elite pluralism, mediation pluralism, and mobilization pluralism.

Elite pluralism, presented by Robert Dahl (1956), acknowledges that there are numerous groups of competing elites in modern communities and societies. It asserts, however, that in most settings, "no single set of elites is powerful enough to dominate critical decision making or exert control over the entire community or society" (Olsen and Marger 1993:84). Power remains moderately dispersed, although various sets of elites may compete with one another for dominance.

Mediation pluralism, which is propounded by Toqueville and later by William Kornhauser (1959) and Robert Presthus (1964), also acknowledges the existence of numerous sets of elites but allows for the fact that, in many settings, one set of elites may largely dominate the others. Empirically, it is close to the Marxian and elitist model of social power; however, it differs sharply from them in its insistence that "power can be structured to allow non-elites to exert some influence on both competing and dominant elites" (Olsen and Marger 1993:84). In practice, the extent of this non-elite involvement varies widely, but in theory it could become quite influential. To disperse power and involve non-elites in power processes, the pluralist model calls for "a proliferation of autonomous groups, associations, and other organizations" (84) located throughout a society. These are sometimes called 'special-interest' associations, or 'intermediate' organizations. The intermediate organizations must possess several characteristics if pluralism is to operate effectively:

- The overall network they compose, but not necessarily each organization itself, must extend from grassroots up to the national government.

- Each organization must also have sufficient resources to exert some amount of influence upward, and those that operate at the national level must wield sufficient power such that governmental and other elites pay attention to them and involve them in decision-making processes.
- Each organization must be relatively specialized in its concerns and limited in its power exertion, so that none of them becomes so large and powerful that it can dominate the others. In other words, there must be a rough balance of power among all the said organizations.
- The organizations must have cross-cutting or overlapping memberships that link them and prevent individuals from becoming too strongly attached to any single organization.
- The organizations must be functionally distinct and yet interdependent so that they need to cooperate as well as compete with one another.
- Finally, there must be widespread acceptance of a set of rules specifying how the organizations will operate in their efforts to wield power and influence the government (Olsen and Marger 1993:84–85).

Mobilization pluralism, as outlined by Gabriel A. Almond and Sidney Verba (1963) and Olsen (1982), is an extension of the mediation pluralism. It addresses the question of how individual citizens can be mobilized to participate in the political system through voting and other political activities. The thesis of mobilization pluralism is that "citizens can be mobilized for active political participation through involvement in all kind of non-political organizations and activities" (Olsen and Marger 1993:86). These include not only voluntary special-interest associations but also neighborhood and community affairs and decision-making processes within one's workplace. Two features of this mobilization process are especially noteworthy:

- Mobilization can occur even when the level of social involvement is not extensive; non-active membership in one or two local associations will often lead to greater political activity.
- The mobilization process operates at all social-class levels and hence can overcome the political apathy and feelings of powerlessness that are widespread among people with low socio-economic status (86).

The Foucauldian Perspective

Many of Foucault's works demonstrate the constructed nature of some of our most established assumptions. Our notions of power, selfhood, sexuality, and reason, among others, are shown in his work to be historically contingent cultural products. His studies challenge the influence of German political philosopher Marx and Austrian psychoanalyst Sigmund Freud. Foucault offers new concepts that challenge people's assumptions about prisons, the police, insurance, care of the mentally ill, gay rights, and welfare (Bracken, Giller, and Summerfield 1997). The main influences, I find, on Foucault's thought are German philosophers Frederick Nietzsche and Martin Heidegger.

Foucault's thought explores the shifting patterns of power within a society and the ways in which power relates to the self. He investigates the changing rules governing the kind of claims that could be taken seriously as true or false at different times in history. He also studies how everyday practices enable people to define their identities and systematize knowledge; events may be understood as being produced by nature, by human effort, or by God. Foucault argues that each way of understanding things has its advantages and its dangers. In all the books of his last period, Foucault seeks to show that Western society has developed a new kind of power that he calls bio-power—that is, a new system of control that traditional concepts of authority are unable to understand and criticize. Rather than being repressive, this new power enhances life. Foucault's historical studies that reveal the power relations inherent in social practices may seem sometimes morally disturbing to many people. However, his intellectual sophistication, his discovery of power in every facet of society, and his creation of a new stream between broad conflict and functional paradigms of sociology are indeed astounding.

His notion of 'governmentality' is important to our understanding of the prevalence, continual extension, and complexity of power in societies. The term 'governmentality' ('*gouvernementalite*') is a neologism Foucault presented and explored at the end of the 1970s (see Foucault 1979, 1984, 1991) that implies the establishment of complex social techniques and institutions to intensify and expand the mechanism of control and power over the population in the name of what has become known as the 'reason of state'. Governmentality, for Foucault, refers famously to the "conduct of conduct" (2000:211), which is a more or less calculated and rational set of ways of shaping conduct and securing rule through a multiplicity of authorities and agencies in and outside the state and at a variety of special levels, which he calls "art of government" (1979:5), albeit negatively.

There are two aspects to governmentality in Foucault's writings: first, it is a concept based on the European historical context; and second, it implies a novel definition of power that has profound implications for our understanding of contemporary political power and in particular public policy. For Foucault, governmentality is the unique combination of three components: institutional centralization, intensification of the effects of power, and power/knowledge (Foucault 1979). These components combined denote "governmental rationality" (Gordon 1991). In speaking of governmentality, Foucault refers not only to the domain of civil/political government as it is conventionally understood but to a broader domain of discourses and practices that create and administer subjects through the presence of a variety of knowledge-making apparatuses. The central focus of a Foucauldian study of policy is on the broader impact of state policy, particularly the effects of power across the entire social spectrum (macro-level) down to individuals' daily lives (micro-level). Governmentality for Foucault refers not to sociologies of rule; quoting Nikolas Rose (1999:21), it refers to the

> studies of stratums of knowing and acting. Of the emergence of partic-
> ular regimes of truth concerning the conduct, ways of speaking truth,
> persons authorized to speak truth . . . of the invention and assemblage
> of particular apparatuses for exercising power . . . they are concerned
> with the conditions of possibility and intelligibility for ways of seeking
> to act upon conduct of others.

For Foucault, governmentality is a fundamental feature of the modern state. Most significantly, Foucault sees state authorities and policies as mobilizing governmentality, which works toward incorporating the economy and the population into the political practices of the state in order to be able to govern effectively in a rational and conscious manner (Foucault 1991; Luke 1999). Governmentality, then, applies techniques of instrumental rationality to the art of everyday management exercised over the economy, the society, and the environment.

Recently there have been attempts to extend the concept of governmentality into the realm of development (for example, see Watt 2003) and environment (see Agrawal 2003; Brosius 1999; Darier 1999; Escobar 1995; Luke 1999). Éric Darier, for instance, deploys Foucault's analytic tools to deconstruct contemporary environmental discourses, specifically the relations and technologies of power/knowledge that underpin them and the effects they have on individual conduct in private, daily life (cf. 1996a, 1996b, 1999). He applies the Foucauldian frame to the deployment of citizenship in Canadian environmental discourse in theorizing what he calls "environmental governmentality":[5]

> Environmental governmentality requires the use of social engineering
> techniques to get the attention of the population to focus on specific
> environmental issues and to instill, in a non-openly coercive manner,
> new environmental conducts. . . . [T]he challenge for the state is to find
> ways to make the population adopt new forms of environment conduct.
> If coercion is not the principal policy instrument, the only real alterna-
> tive is to make the population adopt a set of new environmental values,
> which would be the foundation of new widespread environmental ways
> of behaving. These new environmental values will be promoted by the
> establishment of an 'environmental citizenship'. (Darier 1996b:595)

The vision of 'power-as-repression-and-production' presented in Foucault's *Discipline and Punish* has been both embraced and rejected by many scholars. Foucault himself rejected this vision of power at the end of his life.

Steven Lukes (2005) calls it both extreme and misleading. However, Foucault's knowledge/power regime propounded in his theory of governmentality is still a powerful framework for many postmodern scholars.

CONCLUSION

Based on our sociological understanding of different models of social power, a taxonomy of power in social organizations may be outlined as follows:

Table 2.1   Taxonomy of Power in Social Organization

Model	Source(s) of Power	Power Dynamics	Methods of Power Exertion
Marxist	• Power emanates from economic production • Relations of production: the class that controls the key means of production	• Minority class (bourgeoisie) exerts power over the majority (proletariat) • Constant conflict toward social change • Prospect for power equity in society	Ideology (by bourgeoisie) and force or violent revolution (by proletariat)
Elitist	• Focus primarily on the polity, give little attention to the economy as a source of power • Small set of controlling elite, oligarchy	• Oligarchy is necessary/ inevitable for social organization • Hence, no need for social change toward power equity • Masses do not govern themselves but rather need to be governed	All means: force, dominance, authority, ideology, and knowledge
Pluralist	• Many actors (power is not centralized to a few, but decentralized so as to be exerted by many) • Space for everyone to be in power; the non-elite, many interest groups involved in power exertion	• Elite pluralism: more than one elite competes for power • Mediation pluralism: among many elites, one set of elites tends to dominate • Mobilization pluralism: to mobilize individuals to participate in decision-making process	Decentralization, mobilization, cross-cutting membership, etc
Foucauldian	• Knowledge • Discipline • Institution	• Bio-power: a new system of control that traditional concepts of authority are unable to understand and to criticize • Rather than being repressive, this new power enhances life	Problematization, institutionalization, and normalization of power

Power is one of the most pivotal as well as contentious concepts in sociology. Despite having a contested and ambiguous nature, power remains a useful analytical tool in sociology as well as other disciplines of social sciences. For instance, discourses of development comprise, among many other schools, four conspicuous paradigms: Marxist/dependency, liberal/modernization, community-based resource management (CBRM), and postmodern critiques of development, each drawn from an understanding of power from different perspectives discussed in this chapter. The dependency paradigm of development (see Hoogvelt 2001; Khor 2001) is based on the Marxist understanding of power. The modernization paradigm embraces the elitist vision of power (for example, Hunt 1989; Rostow 1960) while CBRM is drawn from the pluralist model of power (Brosius, Tsing, and Zerner 1998; Li 2002; Lynch and Talbot 1995). Postmodern critiques of development (development as a knowledge/power apparatus) propounded by James Ferguson (1990), Arturo Escobar (1995), Timothy W. Luke (1999), J. Peter Brosius (1999), M. S. Islam (2005), McMichael (2000) and some others, then, is largely based on the Foucauldian understanding of power (more details in Chapter 3, this volume). A comprehensive analysis of and debate about all perspectives of power would provide us with a better understanding of this important yet complex and contentious concept in social organization.

ACKNOWLEDGMENTS

The earlier version of this chapter was published in *Bangladesh e-Journal of Sociology* 5, no. 1 (2008): 21–41. It has been republished with permission.

3 Paradigms of Development and Their Power Dynamics

INTRODUCTION

Despite mounting criticism,[1] development is still a concept that remains indispensable in understanding human society. The concept of development was popularized through the expansion of colonization and underwent various transformations as the socio-political structure of the world changed over time. During the era of colonization, development was understood as *having colonies* and referred to the organizing of European societies, labor, and markets by disorganizing the non-European colonies (Hoogvelt 2001; McMichael 2008). After the end of World War II, a new phase of development emerged as the newly independent countries, whose leaders were seeking political legitimacy, adopted the Western notion or model of development. They had to depend on the technologies of their former colonial masters. The adoption of the European model across the formerly colonial world in the post–World War II era underpins what Philip McMichael (2008) calls "the development project." The U.S. was a powerful reality at that time. Asian and African decolonization started at the time when the U.S. was at the height of its power and prosperity and eager to reconstruct the postwar world to expand its markets and secure its flow of raw materials. Reconstructing a war-torn world was an international project, inspired by a vision of development as a national enterprise to be repeated across the world of newly independent states (McMichael 2008).

From the West, especially from the U.S., this development was viewed as a concept based on *democratic fair dealing* (McMichael 2008). For the Americans and their allies, this was a liberal vision projected globally—a vision of universal political opportunity to pursue national economic growth. Therefore, the discourse of development assumed additional meanings—understood more *as a natural process, with universal application*, than the colonial initiative. That is, development could be administered by non-Europeans. This new development paradigm, however, ignored and obscured the contribution of former colonies to European development. In short, the development project, as summarized by McMichael (2008:56), was understood as (a) an organizing concept to provide universal meaning (e.g., development as emulating Western living standards, rationality, and scientific progress); (b) a national framework for economic growth; (c) an international framework of aid (military and economic) binding the developing world to the developed world; (d) a growth strategy favoring industrialization; (e) an agrarian reform strategy encouraging agro-industrialization; and (f) central state initiatives to stimulate and manage investment and mobilize multiclass political coalitions into development alliances supporting industrial growth.

Whatever the outcomes, Western intellectuals formulated and accepted this Western notion of development as the only standard for the globe. An evaluation of the development projects leads us to at least three significant points. First, since the world has changed, the projects have been modified in various ways since the 1950s. Second, they are increasingly questioned, as some of their expectations have failed to materialize and thus gave rise to the emergence of the neo-Marxist dependency school; and third, the founding assumptions and practices of the development projects represented *historical choice* rather than an inevitable unfolding of human destiny. The development projects were organized strategies to overcome the legacies of colonialism. Development became an organizing principle to shape world politics and to determine relations—mostly power relations—between Third World and First World countries (McMichael 2008; M. S. Islam 2009).

Over the last few decades, the field of development studies has embraced a diverse range of intellectual pursuits, albeit with no sense of common purpose and direction. First, the field has fragmented into area studies, in which the success of East Asian 'developmental' states offers a promising focus for theoretical renewal, albeit more closely related to the field of comparative political economy than to the subject of development studies itself. Second, there have been meta-theoretical critiques of those theoretical constructs that had long constituted the toolbox of development theory. Dependency, exploitation, unequal exchange, modes of production, modernization, rationalization, progress—all these have come under the deconstructing axe of postmodernists, post-Marxists, and poststructuralists alike. Third, some development literature has merged with the literature of the international political economy. Fourth, the inclusion of gender and environment is increasingly evident in recent literature on development (Hoogvelt 2001). Finally, the pervasiveness of the notion of power inherent in the discourse of development has been uncovered by postmodern theorists. This chapter is a comprehensive survey of the literature and understanding of how power is understood in different theories and schools of development.

DEVELOPMENT AND POWER

Liberal/Modernization Framework of Development

'Modernization' is a theory of social and economic development that follows functionalist or consensus assumptions that societies need to have harmony among their components. This assumption leads to the belief that modern capitalist economies manifest special characteristics in their cultures and their structuring of social relationships (Cowen and Shenton 1996; Hoogvelt 2001). For example, family systems are assumed to change toward a narrow conjugal form, away from extended structure, in order to accommodate the individualism and occupational flexibility that is demanded by a modern complex economy undergoing continual transformation.

Modernization theory evolved from two ideas about social change developed in the nineteenth century: the conception of *traditional* vs. *modern* societies (*gemeinschaft* vs. *gesellschaft*), and *positivism*, which viewed development as a societal evolution through progressive stages of growth (Hoogvelt 2001; Rostow 1960). The unique characteristics of *modern* capitalist society, as viewed by Max Weber, are its 'formal rationality', the best means (rational calculation) to achieve given ends (profit), as opposed to the 'substantive rationality' of *traditional* society. For Emile Durkheim, *modern* society is characterized by 'organic solidarity', which is based on the recognition of difference, contractual laws, and individual rights rather than shared identity, as opposed to 'mechanical solidarity', which is based on homogeneity and collective consciousness characteristic of *traditional* society (Collins and Makowsky 1998).

In modernization theory, problems that held back the industrialization of poor countries were related to the 'irrational' way in which resources were allocated in a traditional society. Traditional societies became modern by rationalizing resource allocation and by eliminating the cultural, institutional, and organizational roadblocks that hindered development. Developing countries with traditional societies could evolve by starting in a stage with an *un*developed and traditional society and through an evolutionary linear process change its society by rationalizing it, reaching the stage of a modern and developed society. The theory identified different stages, variables, and processes through which a society develops. Positivist evolution implied that all societies would pass through the same set of stages that the Western society had completed in moving from a traditional to a modern society. The modernization stages were (1) the traditional society, (2) preconditions for take-off, (3) take-off, (4) the drive to maturity, and (5) the age of high mass consumption. These five stages of modernization were known as Rostow's stage theory (Hunt 1989; Rostow 1960). From a modernization-theory perspective, the degree of industrialization, urbanization, and cultural values is the main indicator of change in development in a country. Therefore, the level of use and access to information technologies within a society is captured by these indicators, but use is basically determined by the degree of rationalization of a society and cultural attitudes toward science and technology. According to modernization theory, changes in openness to ideas and a more global sense of belonging occur when changes in development occur. Modernization also implies that a society's culture, value system, and institutional configuration determine its potential for development. It places ideas and differing value systems, not material conditions, at the center in explaining disparities in development (Cowen and Shenton 1996; Hoogvelt 2001).

There have been various paradigm shifts or transformations within the modernization or capitalist framework. During the twentieth century, the two-sector (traditional vs. industrial) model vividly identified the capitalist or industrial sector as the engine of growth and development for the developing world. Capitalism in the mid–twentieth century was defined by an era known as Fordism, marked by intense relationships between governments, unions, and international capital; this type of economics is marked by high levels of state control. World War II gave a boost to industries that required mass production (chemicals, steel, etc.), and Fordism's heyday was between 1945 and 1973. Since the 1970s, Fordism has given way to post-Fordism, which is characterized by (1) transition from manufacturing-dominated to service-dominated economies; (2) new patterns of industrial distribution; (3) intensifying globalization: (a) large global capital flows defying attempts at state control (e.g., Black Wednesday[2]), and (b) fewer and fewer people controlling more and more production; (4) weakened power of trade unions, less-secure jobs, increase in low-paid jobs, and so forth; and (5) hyper-mobility and hyper-flexibility of capital (Hoogvelt 2001; Rist 2002). Post-Fordism is also known as neoliberalism, albeit negatively.

Behind the backdrop of the earlier theoretical development, a paradigm shift known as neoliberalism occurred during the mid–and late twentieth century. Neoliberalism has been designed, pushed, and implemented by some of the biggest and most powerful institutions in the world, such as the International Monetary Fund (IMF) and the World Bank (WB). The policies of neoliberalism include privatization, marketization, and globalization (Lefeber 2003). The story of neoliberal economics and globalization also includes the Kuznets (1955) 'Inverted U' hypothesis. The Kuznets theory says that when a country begins developing economically, its income inequality worsens. But after a few decades, when the rich begin investing more in the economy and wealth begins to 'trickle down', income equalizes, and people are wealthier than they would have otherwise been. The international financial institutions (IFIs) that have adopted this theory—namely, the IMF—enforce structural adjustment programs on heavily indebted Third World countries. These programs aim to get the state out of the economy through a number of measures known as *shock therapy* and at the same time create conducive environments for the forces of globalization to take off (Cowen and Shenton 1996; Hoogvelt 2001; M. S. Islam 2009).

The modernization framework of development was considered by some to be an oversimplified and generalized theory with strong racial stereotypes and cultural biases. It ignored specific historical experiences and phases of prosperity in societies that had not changed their 'traditional cultures'. Modernization theory was attacked as *ahistorical* (ignoring phases of prosperity from a broader historical review) and *ethnocentric* (assuming that only one culture and one path was *the* way to development) (Hoogvelt 2001; Pett and Hartwick 1999; Rist 2002). World systems theory emerged as a contestation to modernization theory by suggesting that development differences were largely explained by taking into account the initial conditions and the relations of dependency in trade relations among countries in a whole system, which was termed as the 'world system'.

According to world systems theory, the global digital divide is really a reflection of the divides already present. This divide is better explained by the degrees of *peripheralization* (a country's position in the core, semi-periphery, or periphery). Countries in the wealthy core were bound to forge ahead in the use of new information technologies, leaving behind countries in the deprived and dependent periphery. In consequence, the digital divide is a predictable consequence of the structure of the world system, in which less developed countries (LDCs) become more peripheralized when they are penetrated by interests located in the core: information and communication technologies are no exception to the core-periphery relation (Hoogvelt 2001; Rist 2002; Sklair 1995; Wallerstein 1995). Most importantly, modernization theory obscures the production and relations of power between developed and developing nations. Many have claimed that the obscured power relation poses a major hindrance for the development of 'traditional societies'. Paradoxically, others claim that the same sort of power relation is needed for the development of traditional societies. Power and development are both related dialectically and reciprocally.

Modernization Paradigm and Power

Power affects, and is affected by, development in complex ways that makes it interesting for us to understand how this relationship has been examined by scholars in the past and present. One of the first in-depth critiques of capitalism's power inequities was by Karl Marx. Marxism was a Hegelian-inspired philosophy that concentrated on political economy, calling attention to *unequal power relations* between classes in capitalist society. It was largely an economic-deterministic perspective of the world. Marx's base-superstructure theory (economic base provided for cultural superstructure) was later elaborated by such theorists as Antonio Gramsci,[3] who formulated post-Marxist theories of hegemony. Gramsci builds on Marx's base-superstructure theory (economic base provided for cultural superstructure) to arrive at his theory of hegemony, which states that in modern society, the subjugated classes willingly accept their exploitation by superordinate classes in society (Fontana 1993).

'Hegemony'—the willing acceptance of dominance and control of one social group by another and the dominating group's main vehicle of control—can be seen in terms of the more complex view of social structure, elaborated for the analysis of popular culture, developed in recent years within the Gramscian tradition and articulated by such theorists as Stuart Hall. However, an understanding of the more fundamental use of the term is also important. While it is difficult to find an adequate definition for hegemony, Todd Gitlin (2003:253) gives a sense of how the concept works:

> [H]egemony is a ruling class's (or alliance's) domination of subordinate classes and groups through the elaboration and penetration of ideology (ideas and assumptions) into their common sense and everyday practice; it is the systematic (but not necessarily or even usually deliberate) engineering of mass consent to the established order. No hard and fast line can be drawn between the mechanisms of hegemony and the mechanisms of coercion. . . . In any given society, hegemony and coercion are interwoven.

In the 1920s, the Frankfurt School developed as a German Marxist critique of capitalism in ideological terms (as opposed to economic terms). The Frankfurt School's position, broadly, was that people are easily fooled by capitalism and the culture of industry. The reality was that created by bourgeois society in capitalism—culture is processed through the culture of industry. This is quite different from Enlightenment ideas of affirmative culture, harmony, and authenticity that encompass the best of people when they are authentically free. The Frankfurt School viewed ideology as a distortion of reality, with the purpose of camouflaging and legitimating unequal power relations. The work of the Frankfurt School laid the basis for many more recent critiques of capitalist-inspired mass culture (Fontana 1993).

Proponents of the modernization paradigm, however, have a modest understanding of power, although no consensus among themselves. Unlike Marxian perspective, which views power as *limiting*, proponents of modernization view that power is something *contributing* to the entire social fabric. In their view, the mass population has the ultimate power: power to consume, power to boycott products, power to elect their leaders to govern themselves. Development is thus a *democratic fair dealing* (McMichael 2008) with power centered in the opinion of the masses. Some proponents of the modernization paradigm subscribe to the *elitist perspective of power*, which rationalizes the fact that in order for the survival and smooth functioning of a society, it must be run by a few *efficient* elites who are elected by the majority of its citizens. This model of understanding power and development pervaded till the early twentieth century. Another, mostly recent, cohort of proponents thinks that power is something prevalent in every stage of development, not centered in the 'bourgeoisie' as Marx claims. They subscribe to a pluralist model of power in development discourse. All involved—be they donors of the development project, researchers, activists, local populations, indigenous communities, or academic personnel—possess power of their own and can influence each other. Development is pursued through a complex web of power exertion, with one influencing the others. This model is generally presented in response to the postmodern critique of development discourse.

Dependency Theory

Dependency theory, like modernization theory, emerged during the post-war period and is based largely on the Marxian understanding of power. However, dependency theory has intellectual roots stretching into the past. Classical theories of imperialism had also addressed relations of domination and subjection between nations. According to the dependency school, underdevelopment is seen as the result of *unequal power relationships* between rich developed capitalist countries and poor developing ones. In the past, colonialism embodied the inequality between the colonial powers and their colonies. As the colonies became independent, the inequalities did not disappear. Powerful developed countries, such as the U.S., Western European countries, and Japan, dominate dependent, powerless LDCs via the capitalist global economy that continues to perpetuate power and resource inequalities (Hoogvelt 2001).

Dominant most developed countries (MDCs) have technological and industrial advantages that allow them to manipulate the global economic system to serve their own interest. Such organizations as the WB, the IMF and the World Trade Organization (WTO) have agendas that benefit the firms and consumers of primarily the MDCs. One of the main aims of the WTO is to free up world trade; this benefits the wealthy nations that are most involved in world trade. Creating a level playing field for all countries assumes that all countries have the necessary equipment to be able to play. For the world's poor, this is often not the case (Hoogvelt 2001; Khor 2001).

Unlike modernization theory, which blames the culture of the under-developed for its plight, dependency theory postulates that the responsibility for lack of development within LDCs rests with the MDCs. Advocates of dependency theory argue that only substantial reform of the world capitalist system and a redistribution of assets will 'free' LDCs from poverty cycles and enable development to occur. Measures that the MDCs could take would include debt cancellation and the introduction of global taxes, such as the Tobin Tax. This tax on foreign exchange transactions, named after its proponent, American economist James Tobin, would generate large revenues that could be used to pay off debts or fund development projects (Hoogvelt 2001; Khor 2001). There are however significant problems in this model as well; hence, it is very difficult to implement. First, power is not easily redistributed, as countries that possess it are unlikely to surrender it. Secondly, it may be that it is not the governments of the MDCs that hold the power but large multi-national enterprises that are reluctant to see the world's resources being reallocated in favor of the LDCs. Thirdly, the redistribution of assets globally will result in slower rates of growth in the MDCs, which might be politically unpopular.

Postmodern Critique: Development as a Regime of Knowledge/Power

The postmodern critique of development by such writers as James Ferguson (1990) and Arturo Escobar (1995) sees development discourse as nothing more than an apparatus of surveillance and control. Even although they do not identify themselves as purely Marxist or Foucauldian, they are highly influenced by the intellectual traditions of Marx and Michel Foucault. In order to maintain a focus on the notion of power and domination as well as on the most pervasive effects of development, they see development in terms of discourse. Escobar (1995:6), quoting from Foucault (1986), observes that discourse analysis creates the possibility of "stand[ing] detached from [the development discourse], bracketing its familiarity, in order to analyze the theoretical and practical context with which it has been associated." Escobar's view of development from the standpoint of discourse analysis is as follows:

> To see development as a historically produced discourse entails an examination of why so many countries started to see themselves as underdeveloped in the early post–World War II period, how 'to develop' became a fundamental problem for them, and how, finally, they embarked upon the task of 'un-underdeveloping' themselves by subjecting their societies to increasingly systematic, detailed, and comprehensive interventions. As western experts and politicians started to see certain conditions in Asia, Africa, and Latin America as a problem—mostly what was perceived as poverty and backwardness—a new domain of thought and experience, namely, development, came into being, resulting a new strategy of dealing with the alleged problems. Initiated in the U.S. and Western Europe, this strategy became in a few years a powerful force in the Third World. (1995:6)

Escobar nicely delineates how 'poverty' was discovered and 'problematized', how the 'Third World' was constructed in the discourse of development, and how two-thirds of the world population were put under the regime of control by discursive practices. "The poor increasingly appeared as a social problem requiring a new way of intervention in society" (1995:22), and "the treatment of poverty allowed society to conquer new domains" (23). The management of poverty called for interventions in education, health, hygiene, morality, and employment, and the instillment of good habits of association, savings, child-rearing, and so on. The result was a panoply of interventions that accounted for the domain of knowledge and intervention. Not only poverty but also health, education, hygiene, employment, and poor quality of life in towns and cities were constructed as social

problems. These problems require extensive knowledge about the population and appropriate modes of social planning (Escobar 1992). "The most
significant aspect of this phenomenon was the setting into place of apparatuses of knowledge and power that took upon themselves to optimize life
by producing it under modern, 'scientific' conditions" (Escobar 1995:23).

The result of such construction and practices was pervasive. The poor
countries started defining themselves in relation to the standard of wealth
of the more economically advantaged nations. This economic conception of
poverty (comparative statistical operation) found an ideal yardstick in the
annual calculation of per-capita income. Thus, "two-thirds of the world's
people were transformed into poor subjects in 1948 when the World Bank
defined as poor those countries with an annual per capita income below
$100. And if the problem was one of insufficient income, the solution was
clearly economic growth. Thus poverty became an organizing concept and
object of new problematization" (Escobar 1995:23–24).

If we delve deeply into this construction, we will find an inherent power
relation. The Third World is constructed by *distancing* it from the civilized
and developed West. This distance, which is not a simple marker of cultural
diversity, is constructed with connotations of inferiority and negativity (e.g.,
backward, underdeveloped, poor, lacking, traditional, and so forth). When
such negative images are constructed on a group of people, they automatically become subjects for certain treatments and interventions, and, thus,
the former justifies the latter. The construction of the Third World is such
that the power relation between the agency that constructs and the constructed subjects resembles that of "father-child" or "doctor-patient" relationships (Escobar 1995:159).

As Escobar argues, Third World construction was part of a wider scheme
by the rich countries of the West. The latter "created an extremely efficient
apparatus for producing knowledge about, and exercise of power over, the
Third World" (1995:9). New forms of power and control, which were more
subtle and refined, were put into operation. The poor people's ability to
define and take care of their lives was perhaps eroded more extensively
than before. The poor were now subjected to a variety of programs, which
involved more sophisticated practices, developed by the rich countries (39).
Various programs, institutions, and centers of power proliferated in the
West to study these 'poor subjects' and their conditions. The Third World
then witnessed "a massive landing of experts, each in charge of investigat-
ing, measuring, and theorizing about this or that little aspect of the Third
World societies" (45). To understand development as a discourse, one must
look not at the elements themselves but at the system of relations established among them. "It is a system that allows the systematic creation of
objects, concepts, and strategies. . . . [T]he system of relations establishes
discursive practices that set the rule of the game: who can speak, from what
point of view, with what authority, and according to what criteria of expertise. It sets the rules that must be followed for this or that problem, theory,

or object to emerge and be named, analyzed, and eventually transformed into a policy plan" (Escobar 1995:40–41).

However, not all those who claim to be experts have the authority to exercise power. "Some clear principles of authority were in operation. They concerned the role of experts, from whom certain criteria of knowledge and competence were asked; institutions, such as UN, which had the moral, professional, and legal authority to name subjects, and define strategies; and international lending organizations, which carried the symbols of capital and power" (Escobar 1995:41). The principle of authority also concerned the governments of the poor countries, which commanded the legal political authority over the lives of their subjects and the leadership positions of the rich countries. These leaders had the power, knowledge, and experience to decide on what was to be done. The exercise of power/power relations is evident between and within developed nations and poor countries. In Escobar's (1995:41–42) words:

> Economists, demographers, educators, and experts in agriculture, public health, and nutrition elaborated their theories, made their assessments and observations, and designed their programs from these institutional sites. Problems were continually identified, and client categories brought into existence. Development proceeded by creating "abnormalities" (such as the "illiterate," the "underdeveloped," the "malnourished," "small farmers," or "landless peasants"), which it would later treat and reform. Approaches that could have positive effects in terms of easing material constraints became, linked to this type of rationality, instruments of power and control.

Patriarchy and ethnocentrism, the obvious manifestations of power and control, are inherent in the development discourse. The indigenous people have to be modernized in line with the appropriate 'values' (Western, white). This process gives them an understanding of their own culture as 'backward', 'evil', or 'inimical to development' (McMichael 2008) and creates in them a racial and cultural inferiority complex. It has profound effects on their lives and way of thinking and becomes a sophisticated way of exercising power and control. As Larry Lohmann (1999:70) posits, "[R]acism is a process of social control, not a set of beliefs and feelings." The superordinate-subordinate power relation is normalized in such a way that it goes uncontested and accepted as usual. The subjugated people often accept that as their fate. History has witnessed the common situation of development planners (mostly economists—75 percent of the staff in the World Bank are economists) and engineers, by their economistic mind-set, create models, calculations, and formulate plans, which often have no relation to the actual population and reality on the ground, the subjects, and how they (the subjects) see their own problems and solutions. Due to this problem, most development projects become unsuccessful and therefore create tensions. Interestingly, when any project fails to materialize its target, the blame goes to the victims and their culture, not the planners. It is the organization that plans and creates categories—and finally also constructs the blame. For example, for ecological disasters caused by development programs, the poor are blamed and "admonished for their 'irrationality' and their lack of environmental consciousness" (Escobar 1995:195). Institutional ethnography is, as Escobar suggests, helpful to study these dominant organizations, especially their ideologies.

From the discussion, it appears that what development reveals is intended to hide or occlude something. It is constantly expanding its power by constructing new domains. The conspicuous process is (1) *problematization*, or creating knowledge in a very efficient way; (2) *institutionalization*, or bureaucratization and managerialism; (3) and finally *normalization of power*. This is what Foucault (1979, 1986) discovers and explicates regarding the relations and exercise of power in the modern society. One of the apparent implications of this extension of power is that it "privilege[s] certain actors, and marginalize[s] others" (Brosius 1999:38).

Apart from the above critiques, since the 1980s, another group has emerged that may be called 'ultramodernist'. It consists of economic theorists who insist that the laws of economics have been proven valid and that the 'invisible hands of the market' allocate resources optimally. Therefore, there is only economics, not development economics. When governments and outside agencies try to make the market work better, they introduce doctrines, which make it work worse. The free market does not guarantee equality of income, they say, but it produces as optimal an allocation of resources as is possible (see F. Cooper and Packard 1997).

THE DEVELOPMENT PROJECT AND POWER NEGOTIATION

Over the past few decades, the development projects and their proponents faced mounting criticism because of their failure to bridge the gap between developed and developing nations. One of the key criticisms was surrounding unequal power relations. The harshest criticism came from underdevelopment or dependency theorists. They not only unveiled the problems and flaws inherent in the capitalist paradigm but also advocated an alternative vision of development. But after the demise of the USSR and its eventual entry into the global capitalist club, followed by China's gradual penetration in and acceptance of the free-market world economy, their alternative vision lost market currency. The postmodern critics of development, despite their thoughtful explication to equate development with power exertion, failed to suggest any development agenda that constitutes an alternative to capitalist paradigm. As different criticisms emerge, the capitalist paradigm is now undergoing different transformations as agents of power try to adopt and show a pluralist model of power relations involving and empowering the locals. Here are some key models and current debates surrounding them.

'Empowering' Civil Society and Ensuring 'Good Governance': The Role of NGOs

Non-governmental organizations (NGOs) are more popular than ever in official circles these days. However, few decades ago, their popularity lay largely in their supposed efficiency in meeting the basic needs of the people at the grassroots level in 'tackling poverty'; today they are being trumpeted, according to the UNDP Human Development Report (1993), as representative *par excellence* of civil society in the so-called Third World. In the post–Cold War era, international institutions and donor agencies are turning their attention increasingly to concerns about democratization and popular participation. As the UNDP report dramatically puts it, "Greater people's participation is no longer a vague ideology based on the wishful thinking of new idealists. It has become an imperative—a condition of survival" (Keck and Sikkink 1998). But again, NGO involvement in the development projects and their influence over national politics raise numerous questions.

Many scholars, including Geoffrey Wood (1997), are skeptical regarding the proliferation of NGOs in developing countries. According to Wood (1997), for NGOs to operate, for markets to penetrate and hold authority, and for private organizations to take hold of the societies' power, the first necessary condition is to diminish the power and authority of the state by curtailing its role in providing services to its citizens and by reducing its control on resources. This is a neoliberal agenda, and to do that, NGOs advocate the rhetoric of 'good governance', which is paradoxical in meaning and operation. Wood calls this scenario the 'franchise state' (the state franchising its responsibility to NGOs).

In the West, 'good governance' is explained as a "democratic process with strong accountability between state and people, removing the prospects of dictatorial oppressive governments and underpinning, therefore, the protection of fundamental human rights" (Wood 1997:97). Wood calls it 'hypocrisy' embodied in the Western preoccupation of the theme 'good governance'. He argues that 'good governance' represents a revival of ethnocentric, modernizing ideology, attempting to make the myths of one society reality in another. Giving the example of the UK, he adds, "Good governance is more possible elsewhere than in those countries which purport to be the keepers of the discourse" (Wood 1997:80). When one talks about 'good governance', there arise many questions and problems, especially the problem of accountability. First of all, 'good' is not universal but rather relative and contingent upon cultural expectations and distributional outcomes. The paradoxes in the notion of 'good governance' are numerous. First, the thrust of policy is to undermine the monopoly of the state in service provision and allocation of resources, thereby creating more opportunity for exit choices and thus reducing the necessity for government to be good. Second, the prescriptions of privatization and markets on the one hand and good governance on the other do not easily sit side by side. Third, adherence to neoliberal views about the efficacy and the responsiveness of the market as an allocator of public goods crucially avoids the issue of responsibility. Markets tend to ignore responsibility and have been proven to be failures in distributing resources. Markets rather serve the capitalists for their relentless accumulation and legitimation (Panitch 1977). Fourth, 'good governance' is geared to improve 'participation'. It is very contradictory, as most NGOs are operated in an authoritarian manner. Finally, 'good governance' undermines and limits the capacity and power of the state, but the state remains responsible for defining, guaranteeing, and regulating entitlements on the one hand and delivery on the other. NGOs that are operating to improve 'good governance' are basically working to "break the state monopolies in both service and goods delivery and to remove regulations and licensing to allow markets to breathe" (Wood 1997:86).

Wood (1997) further argues that the 'franchise model' cannot be an alternative to states and markets, because markets have been proven to be inefficient allocators. Other skeptics argue that policies of the IMF and the WB in the developing countries virtually created more tensions and problems. East Asia, Russia, and Latin America are some examples (Grinspun 2003; Lefeber 2003; Stiglitz 2000; Weisbrot et al. 2001), and the skeptics think that NGOs have close links with donors and other capitalist institutions; hence, they are mostly operated by those outsiders. It is disempowering for the locals, as it substantially erases their ability to define themselves and take care of their own lives. As the experiences from the Orangi Pilot Project (OPP; Hameed 1997) and the Agroforestry Outreach Project (AOP; Murray 1997) show, the top-down approach is mostly ineffective.

Despite criticisms and skepticism, there remains significant empirical evidence that NGOs play a vital role in empowering locals, creating vigorous civil societies, ensuring participation of local communities in development activities, and making development more meaningful and acceptable for them (Keck and Sikkink 1998).

Community-Based Natural Resource Management

The exploitation of natural and human resources, including local people and forest or upland dwellers, results in severe environmental and social damage. In addition, it also results in the direct control and sometimes aggressive deployment of the 'development project' by development agencies. In response, scholars and activists have proposed the Community-Based Natural Resource Management (CBNRM) paradigm to improve the effectiveness and fairness of the 'development project'. The paradigm offers to (a) promote democracy and participation among the local people, including women, who are historically excluded; (b) create mechanisms for their empowerment; (c) claim for them the natural resources that are otherwise extracted mainly by the state elite; (d) reorganize local communities in legal entities/frameworks for the management of resources; (e) create networks from the local to the international level; and (f) make the development project more fruitful by ensuring the participation of the local people, thereby making it meaningful and acceptable to them (Brosius, Tsing, and Zerner 1998; M. S. Islam 2013; Li 2002; Lynch et al. 1995).

While CBNRM offers an excellent paradigm to create a voice for the historically excluded and oppressed local communities in the development project, it also poses significant questions, concerns, paradoxes, and some dangers that remain to be addressed. The key debates surrounding this model are as follows: first, Owen Lynch and his colleagues (Lynch et al. 1995) adumbrate a concern that the impoverished rural communities in the developing world are denied their fundamental rights to substantive participation in decisions that impact their well-being and livelihoods, and through CBNRM, their important participation can be ensured. The question arises: does participation really ensure democracy and make any impact on decision making? There is a need to look at how far their participation really affects decision making. The danger is that the state and the development agencies can cite locals' participation to claim legitimacy. The notion of participation is complex; for instance, community chiefs can be privileged, while majority people remain disempowered. J. Peter Brosius, Anna Lowenhaupt Tsing, and Charles Zerner (1998:164) raise important questions: "How are powerful institutions, including multilateral financial organizations, bilateral aid agencies, national and transnational conservation organizations, and private sector actors appropriating community based natural resource management projects and policies to advance their own diverse, sometimes intersecting, interests? What are the political, cultural, environmental, and economic consequences of these appropriations and manipulations?" By engaging local communities in development activities, the development projects get unquestioned acceptance, and if the projects fail, the burden of responsibility is usually put on the local people. That begs the next question: is CBNRM a legitimate instrument or an 'ideological device', in Marxist terms, to conquer the local terrain?

Second, the success of disseminating the paradigm of CBNRM has raised new challenges, as "the concepts of community, territory, conservation, and indigenous are worked into politically varied plans and programs in disparate sites" (Brosius, Tsing, and Zerner 1998:157). 'Indigenous' or 'native' is one of basic elements in the program of CBNRM, which is often used for resource claims. For example, Lynch et al. (1995) make a distinction between Hispanicized and un-Hispanicized ethnic groups in Philippines. However, the notion of 'indigenous' is subject to contestation, as human history shows that people are often mobile in hopes of a better future and are displaced by human and natural forces. Old and new migrants are often interspersed, and cross-marriage, hybridity, and so forth are common phenomena in almost every community (Li 2002).

Tania Li's (2000) argument is that a group's self-identification as tribal or indigenous is not natural or inevitable, but neither is it simply invented, adopted, or imposed. It is, rather, "a *positioning*, which draws upon historically sedimented practices, landscapes, and repertoires of meaning, and emerges through particular patterns of engagement and struggle" (2000:151). She elaborates that the conjectures by which some people come to identify themselves as indigenous, realigning the ways they connect to the nation, the government, and their own unique tribal places, are the contingent products of agency and the cultural and political work of articulation. The concepts of *articulation* and *positioning*, which she draws from Hall (1991, 1996), are central to her analysis. Moreover, in this era of a borderless world and transnational citizenry, the notion of 'indigenous' is gradually losing its market value. Incorporation and integration into a new society are very common phenomena in modern society. Market citizenship is a new concept that contests the notion of 'indigenous' (Strange 1996). The notion of 'indigenous' can also be used for exclusionary purposes. Malaysia is a good example, where the so-called 'bumi-putra' (indigenous), or alternatively known as 'sons of the soil', are granted privileged rights, while the discursively constructed non-bumi-putra are historically excluded in many respects. Claiming or constructing 'indigenous identities' may lead to more complexity and conflict. Palestinian and Israeli claims to 'indigenous' rights to land have resulted in cycles of violence for decades. Another danger lies when the CBNRM projects use ethnicity for land or resource claims. 'Ethnicity' is a problematic concept, and the construction of an ethnicity (for land/resource claims) may lead to an essentialized identity.

Third, one of the assumptions of CBNRM is that indigenous peoples' life is based on forest resources (Lynch et al. 1995). This kind of assumption is highly contested. "The characterization of indigenous people as forest resource dependent is more problematic" (Li 2002:267). The question follows: should forest dwellers remain traditional and forest-dependent? In this era of advanced technology, science, and communications as well as healthy and decent standards of living, one may wonder whether people should imagine a life in forest. CBNRM is concerned about the management of forests by the forest-dwellers, but in reality the "tribal people are not being asked if or how they want to manage their forests" (E. Brown 1994:59). Li (2002) explicates that many tribal people in Indonesia and elsewhere have denounced their tribal identities, as they do not want to pursue their future in the forests or hills.

Fourth, in CBNRM projects, we see that discursive terms, such as community, territory, indigenous, traditional, and so forth, are defined and constructed by outsiders. It entails a regime of control and authority or power over them. The local people are turned into an 'object of knowledge' and lose their ability to define themselves in their own terms and take care of their own affairs. The agencies decide who may speak and from what point of view. In Escobar's (1995) view, local communities are constructed and reconstructed through discourses and practices, often in the name of creating a voice for them or ensuring their participation in the development project. Such discourses and practices are motivated by the lucrative self-serving interests of the powerful development agencies. Escobar (1995) explicates, as alluded to earlier, how development expands by creating different domains of thought and discourses. The process includes, to use Foucauldian framework, creating knowledge in a very efficient way (*problematization*), bureaucratization and managerialism (*institutionalization*), and finally *normalization of power*, as elaborated earlier. One can argue that by deploying the regime of CBNRM, the local communities, who were outside the direct domination of development agencies, are now under their direct control, power, and surveillance.

Fifth, does CBNRM further lead to 'institutionalization' and 'managerialism' where the local communities become the 'objects of policies'? Richard Schroeder (1995) raises the concern that the language of community and conservation, on several occasions, has served to help shift resources away from local strategies for livelihood and empowerment toward resource management that has served powerful institutional (e.g., corporate, scientific, military-administrative, Western consumer–oriented) interests. There is a need to explore how CBNRM, if it goes toward institutionalization and managerialism, privileges a fortunate few and precludes others (Brosius 1999); how it affects the state government and the fate of the local communities; and how, if any, multilateral institutions and bilateral lending agencies have influenced national governments to enforce CBNRM by decree.

Sixth, the paradigm of CBNRM is based on a common assumption that the state is an oppressive regime to the local community, and in order to create a voice for the local community, the state power needs to be subverted (Li 2002; Lynch et al. 1995). Hence, we find various discourses that construct the state as an 'alien' to the local community. However, states may not always be aliens to local communities. One can argue that undermining states is necessary in order to create a vacuum for the market to penetrate and take over the activities previously done by the state. While we may not necessarily be convinced that we have to oppose the state in order to create a voice for oppressed communities, there is a need to keep in mind that states are still a legitimate organization or institution to organize the people, work for their well-being, and represent their interests. Viewing the state dogmatically as an oppressive regime is a kind of simplification. However, it would be equally unwise to ignore the fact that in many developing countries, local communities are oppressed, and many of them have already been displaced by states. For instance, hundreds of Penan people in Sarawak, Malaysia (Brosius 1999), the forest-dwellers in Thailand (Lohmann 1999; Vandergeest and Peluso 1995), and so-called Hispanicized people in Philippines (Lynch 1995) and others are in a condition of acute manipulation by their respective states. Nonetheless, McMichael (2008) shows that displacement and oppression are largely because of the aggressive deployment of the development projects, and it is not the state alone but also the powerful bilateral and multilateral development agencies that deployed the development projects that should equally share responsibility and blame. For instance, the agony of the highlanders in Thailand is mainly due to the Asian Development Bank's aim to "reduce the population of people in mountainous areas and bring them to a normal life" (Lohmann 1999:70). Rather than viewing states as a separate entity and hence subverting their power, we can envision democratic states with equal and meaningful participation from all communities. Both state and community can be mutually constitutive. Li (2002:281) explicates:

> A core concern of CBNRM has been to strengthen the capacity of the communities to protect their natural resource base from the more destructive and rapacious activities of ruling regimes, among others. The model envisages a shift in power from states to communities, conceived as separate entities. Instead, as I have argued, states and communities are mutually constitutive. CBNRM offers state systems an opportunity to rearrange the ways in which the rule is accomplished, while also offering the communities an opportunity to realign their position within (but not outside) that system. Where citizens are indeed up against "vicious states," the potential of CBNRM to empower them is very limited. Older vocabularies about peasant struggles, class conflict, and democracy are better able to name the problem, and to indicate the forms of collective action through which it might be addressed.

The above are some critical points relating to CBNRM. Scholars of CBNRM, the donor or development agencies, and state governments need to keep all these in mind. We can envisage a fruitful collaboration and mutual sharing of power between these three groups: communities, donor agencies, and nation-states. That should be the goal of CBNRM as well as its associated development projects. We conclude by quoting Li (2002:270): "CBNRM serves as a vehicle for negotiating the responsibilities and rights of the citizenship. It is not, however, the only possible vehicle and its strengths and weaknesses need therefore be evaluated in relation to the alternatives."

CRITIQUE OF THE POSTMODERN CRITIQUE

Frederick Cooper and Randall Packard (1997:2) rightly point out that "[t]he development process has from its inception been self-critical and subject to critiques." From the discussion of development and power above, we can discern different accounts of history and analysis. In conventional analysis, development can be seen in terms of evolution of theories and ideas or as the succession of more or less effective interventions (Leys 1996). For political economists, the same history reflects different ideological responses to allegedly deeper contradictions, dictated by capital accumulation and circulation or by capital accumulation and legitimation (Panitch 1977). This history, however, can also be seen from the perspective of the discursive regime, with its changes and transformations, even if these changes are circumscribed by discursive practices tied to political economies, knowledge traditions, and institutions of ruling (Escobar 1995), wherein lie the notion of power.

Hence, critics of the postmodern critiques argue that development is, in no way, a monolithic discourse. As it has different accounts of outcomes and gains, so it has criticisms from different perspectives. It is accepted by a wide range of people, and simultaneously contested by many as well, while some adopt an ambivalent position. The prevalence of different accounts on the discourse of development certainly shows that *development may not be all about power* (or the knowledge/power/regime theory), as propounded by Escobar (1995) and his colleagues. From our analysis, we can safely say that development is, rather, both empowering and disempowering—it operates and functions through complex and interwoven relations of power. It empowers certain actors, spaces, and species, while disempowering others.

The arguments of the dependency school as well as postmodernist critics are framed so persuasively as to lead many to think that development is all about top-down power exertion, to the exclusion of other possibilities. These schools are therefore criticized as overly reductionist. Unlike postmodernist critiques of development (knowledge/power/regime), theorists of 'underdevelopment/dependency' propose a more radical alternative. Rather than closing the door by deploying the discourse of 'dependency' or 'knowledge/power/regime' on development, liberal reformists are arguing for moving further. Cooper and Packard (1997:4), for instance, propose "neither to bury development, nor to praise it." They explain that over the past few decades, development encountered some passionate confrontations and criticisms, although in a limited scale, which to some extent provided some kind of 'checks-and-balances' to development projects and endeavors. The debates continue: the postmodernists criticize developers for imposing undesired modernity, while developers reject postmodernists' nihilism and statism. Postmodernists criticize developers for not interacting with the target people when making calculations, creating client groups, and preparing models for development, which eventually results in failure; while people engaged in development projects constantly insist that they are doing practical work interacting with the local people and need models and more practical frameworks to make the progress more coherent and fruitful. In Cooper and Packard's words, "no side in these tussles has a monopoly of virtue, and all have something to gain by a more introspective, contingent view of the terrain upon which these battles have taken place" (1997:4).

Amid this milieu of arguments and counter-arguments, critiques and counter-critiques, it will be somewhat overly simplistic to be caught up on a single discourse, like the discourse of 'knowledge/power/regime' of 'dependency' or even the 'modernization' hype. Sugata Bose (1997), with a positive vein, elucidates India's historical experience of development in a comparative manner and mentions that the development that India experienced over the century is neither simply a knowledge-making apparatus nor enhancement of dependency. Development there created lot of possibilities and has had numerous achievements. Consequently, India, being powerful enough, not only is capable of managing its own economic affairs but also has provided the world with eminent experts in development economics. Akhil Gupta (1997), on the other hand, explains that development in India gave rise to different social movements among the poor, who demanded for reform and, sometimes, opposed projects, such as building a dam, that would have been hazardous to their communities. Based on Indian experience, both Bose (1997) and Gupta (1997) argue that development is more than the relation of power in an extreme hierarchical order, such as what Escobar (1995:159) calls "father-child" and "doctor-patient" relationships. To them, it is rather a complex web of power exertion, with all parties influencing and being influenced, popularly expressed as a 'pluralist' model of power exertion.

The scholars of the pluralist camp argue that the power relations and the regime of control as explicated by Escobar (1992, 1995) and Ferguson (1990) seem one-sided and vertically monolithic; the developers are at the top and the Third World is at the bottom, and the development projects strengthen this power relation in a deeper manner, while in reality power is dynamic and exercised in different angles and in a variety of ways. They add that development does not always make the Third World powerless; rather it can help these countries regain power. Women, beset by patriarchy, for example, have gained a considerable amount of power due to development (Packard 1997). Cooper (1997) shows that the image of the African farmers' survival is evidence of innovation and the Africans' gradual struggle to reclaim power. Moreover, "within the world of development, power is distributed in a highly uneven manner" (Cooper and Packard 1997:20). It is, to the pluralist camp, important to see how institutions from the WB to local-level financial and development organizations operate. They present evidence showing how local-level community networks (social movements) have been able to evade, reject, or reform development projects (see, for example, Akhil Gupta 1997). Therefore, communities are not just the passive recipients of the development projects imposed by the developers; they also possess choice and power.

According to Escobar, the production and dissemination of development knowledge is always top-down—from the WB to the Third World/local—where institutions such as the WB or UN have the "legal authority to name subjects, make client groups, and define strategies" (1995:41). To the pluralist camp, it is a simplistic explanation that does not tell the whole story, since it "overlooks the specific networks of communication through which ideas circulate internationally. The power of an institution like the World Bank is based as well on its position within overlapping global networks of research, communication, and training. The bank recruited internationally from developing and developed countries . . . and projects' review documents . . . are disseminated globally" (Cooper and Packard 1997:21). The pluralist camp also contests the notion that the production and dissemination of development ideas are always unilinear, as perceived by Escobar, by providing instances in which the local people have provided knowledge to the WB. Gupta (1997), for instance, argues that the development knowledge prevalent in India was not entirely produced and disseminated by the WB. India refined and restructured the development knowledge provided by the WB and produced some unique knowledge on development through its own local experts. These local experts in turn contributed to development projects elsewhere in the world. Therefore, the production and dissemination of development knowledge in this case was not unilinear but rather reciprocal, contextual, and subject to revision.

Furthermore, as Cooper and Packard (1997) explain, the successful transmission of ideas emanating from the powerful development organizations has also been fostered by global political shifts. The end of the Cold War narrowed development options by discrediting socialist alternatives. It is perhaps historically significant that the earlier postwar push for market-led development was short-circuited by the rising 'fear of communist expansion' and the need for more interventionist development, while the second coming of market-driven development—and the willingness of the leaders of the U.S. and elsewhere to accept whatever consequences the market may have—became politically feasible, in part, through the demise of communism.

The pluralist camp, however, cannot afford to deny the predominance of global governance, power, and control held by the development organizations. But they argue that it is because of the fluidity of the market. The nature of the present-day market system demands more control and surveillance. Interestingly, one of the shifts of the development organizations is remarkable: from 'good economics' to 'good government'. Despite concerns and criticisms, they think that this move is directed toward a positive outcome. Cooper and Packard (1997), for example, note that the insistence on 'good government' reproduces much of what was previously said about 'good economy': a bland assertion that the West has defined objective standards for others to meet, a generalized set of categories (elections, multiple parties) that define those standards, irrespective of the actual debates that might be going on in specific contexts over how more people might acquire a meaningful voice in their own lives.

Escobar (1995) claims that all development projects are economistic, as economics have the monopoly of authority in the area of development, which excludes other disciplines of social science. "About 70 percent of the World Bank's professional staffs are economists; a good portion of the remaining 30 percent are engineers" (1995:165). To counter this, the pluralist camp argues that in recent years, there has been a remarkable shift, as researchers from various other disciplines (such as sociology, anthropology, political science, and environmental studies, among others) have ventured into the field of development economics—both as critics as well as contributors. Hence, the delineation of the field of development studies is blurring. The field of development studies is now interdisciplinary in nature. While the area of development is still dominated by economists and engineers, this domination is increasingly being subverted and contested. The pluralist camp argues that many development activists, who are not economists, are working to ensure that the voices of local people are heard.

What is clear from the discussion above is that both development and power are pervasive, yet complex, phenomena in our society. The complexities of both concepts as well as ideological orientations of scholars have led them to view these concepts from different perspectives. Rather than rejecting one and accepting another, comprehensive analysis and debate of all perspectives are likely to provide us with a better understanding of the interwoven relations between these two very important concepts in our society. But how and with what effects does development with its power dynamics operate within the broader nexus of the environment? In other words, what are dynamic relationships between society and nature? How does a social system with its development and power dynamics interact with an ecosystem? The following chapter explores these crucial questions.

ACKNOWLEDGMENTS

The earlier version of this chapter was published in *Journal of Sustainable Development* 2, no. 2 (2009): 24–37. It has been reproduced with permission.

4 Theorizing Nature-Society Relationships

INTRODUCTION

Social theories are narratives about social order and social change, explaining how and why changes in society occur and the ways in which societies are organized. Theoretical approaches to understanding the interactions between environment and society seek to explain how social changes are related to environmental changes and provide narratives to explain the causes and impact of environmental changes on society. It is beyond the scope of this chapter to provide an in-depth discussion of all of them. Many scholars have dedicated entire books to that task, creating a rich literature of work on the topic (see for example Barry 1999; Buttel 2000, 2002, 2003, 2004; Dickens 1998; Dunlap et al. 2002; Goldblatt 1996; Hannigan 2006). This chapter instead examines a few key theoretical approaches, such as treadmill of production, world-systems theory, the metabolic rift, ecological modernization, and the risk society to understand the relationship between society and the environment.

Michael M. Bell (2009:35) argues that causality is rare in social life, and rightly so. Biological determinism is as dangerous as social determinism in our attempts to understand social order and social change. So is environmental or ecological determinism in our attempts to understand the environment-society relationship. The environment interacts with social processes in what Bell calls an "ecological dialogue"—i.e., the interactive causality between social forces and environmental change (Bell 2009:35). The theories reviewed here shed light on that complex relationship, specifically examining the effects of development and social change on the environment and how such effects rebound on social relations and organizations.

THE RELATIONSHIP BETWEEN CONSUMPTION AND THE ENVIRONMENT

Before reviewing the theories, let us first examine the relationship between consumption and the environment. Consumption drives the engines of production and economic growth in modern industrial society. Accordingly, social processes within modern industrial society are structured to encourage consumption, influencing our perceptions of our needs, desires, and wants. We are living in a consumer society, where the need to consume is sometimes akin to that of a civic duty. As Jean Baudrillard (1970) argues in his work *The Consumer Society*, we can think of consumption as a language—a way of communicating power and social status.

We are all consumers. We all consume food, clothes, accessories, and other material goods. Most of us, aside from the poor, consume more than we need, and for some of us, a lot more. The need to consume, the desire to do so, and the availability of a wide array of consumer goods for us to choose from to match our lifestyle choices are shaped by social forces and the way our social and economic systems are structured. However, we must not forget that consumption in modern industrial societies has a dialogic relationship with the environment. In other words, consumption has direct and indirect impacts on the environment, while the environment is the ultimate source of all consumer goods. More importantly, the effects of society's present consumption levels on the environment will significantly influence society's future consumption options.

In *The Theory of the Leisure Class*, Thorstein Veblen ([1899] 1967) writes about how people in modern society display social power through practices of *conspicuous consumption*, *conspicuous leisure*, and *conspicuous waste*. 'Conspicuous consumption' refers to the visible displays of wealth through possession of goods, such as expensive cars, luxurious homes, computers, the latest cell phones, and so forth. It is often expressed in terms of the volume of consumption as well. 'Conspicuous leisure' refers to the more subtle practice of non-productive consumption of time, in which one displays one's distance from environmental needs as a sign of empowerment. These practices may include going on vacations, playing sports, taking self-development classes, and learning skills that demonstrate the amount of free time one has. All show how one is distanced from having to engage in laborious productive work. They also include employment choices that do not require one to be closely and productively engaged with the environment, such as lawyers and corporate managers. 'Conspicuous waste', in turn, refers to the practice of excessively consuming more and more goods, discarding old ones, and getting new ones instead of repairing or reusing the original goods. An example from modern lifestyle habits includes the tendency to change cell phones frequently and to constantly buy new clothes instead of wearing old ones that may have only been worn once or twice. By showing that one can afford to waste, conspicuous waste also signals one's power. While conspicuous display is mainly intended to show off wealth, there is an environmental dimension here. Human society meets its material needs by appropriating nature and, through the process of labor and technology, transforming raw material from nature into products for society's needs. Those who are wealthy do not have to engage in productive activities with the environment. They do not need to use their own labor to appropriate nature and transform the material from nature into products for their needs. They are able to command others and use others' labor to meet their needs. Veblen thus argues that conspicuous consumption, leisure, and waste are convincing statements of power, because they show that an individual is not constrained by the brutal necessities of material life and the environment (Bell 2009:40).

Consumption, leisure, and waste are environmentally damaging, as the production of consumer goods continues to remove materials from nature while returning damaging waste to it. The usefulness of Veblen's work for understanding the environmental and societal relationship lies in the implication one can draw from his work about the competitive and comparative character of conspicuous consumption, leisure, and waste. Simply put, individuals in society are competing against one another in displaying such practices in a bid to acquire more social power and higher status. As individuals are caught in the race to make conspicuous statements of power, levels of consumption rise, as does the level of environmental impact from resource depletion and pollution generated through the production processes of goods.

Veblen identified consumption as the key driver of societies back in the nineteenth century, in the same period that Karl Marx's works focused on production in industrialized Europe as the key to understanding social change and social relations. Having examined the relationship between consumption and environmental degradation, we now direct our attention to the treadmill of production theory. This focuses on production as the key process explaining increased environmental degradation in modern industrialized societies and also in developing countries that may not have reached similar stages of industrialization but nevertheless suffer environmental degradation as a result of production demand from affluent developed countries.

TREADMILL OF PRODUCTION

The treadmill of production theory constructs a narrative of how economic expansion in advanced industrial societies conversely causes environmental and ecological damage. Environmental sociologist Allan Schnaiberg develops and popularizes the idea in his book *The Environment: From Surplus to Scarcity* (1980). The treadmill of production refers to the endless cycle of production processes inherent in our current economic system— i.e., the capitalistic mode of production in modern industrial society. This cycle of endless production processes generates large quantities of oft-toxic waste, which is usually dumped back into the environment. The resultant degradation affects the natural ecosystems and human well-being. Natural resources are increasingly being exhausted when raw materials are extracted at exponentially increasing rates to meet production demands. When natural resources are exhausted in one area, capitalists and politicians do not reduce consumption levels and encourage lifestyle adjustments. Rather, new areas for exploitation are sourced, and production continues. Proponents of the treadmill of production theory believe that the treadmill is unsustainable, as the *carrying capacity* of our planet is finite, and natural resources and raw materials will soon be exhausted at current rates of extraction. Advertising and marketing drive the treadmill in current consumer societies. Demands for consumer goods are fueled by the creation of desires and wants as opposed to practical needs through advertising, which convinces people to purchase more and more consumer goods for lifestyle enhancement and luxurious enjoyment. The treadmill of production theory predicts a pessimistic future for humanity and a planet Earth doomed for environmental destruction should current unsustainable practices be continued. Ecological and environmental damage is blamed on the causal forces of economic growth directed by human-created social, economic, and political systems.

The concept of a societal-environmental dialectic is important to understanding Schnaiberg's critique of the irrationality within modern capitalistic societies. Through *withdrawals* from the environment, natural resources and raw materials are transformed into products. *Additions* are returned to the environment in the form of waste, sometimes toxic and pollution. To aid production processes, new technologies may be used to increase productivity and replace the dependency on human-labor input. Machines and new technologies often use more energy and chemicals, increasing the amount of both resource *withdrawals* from and toxic *additions* to the environment. As economic growth continues, the treadmill constantly generates environmental degradation and the destruction of ecosystems.

Investments in new technologies may, however, allow production to be more efficient and maximize profit generation. These investments are made possible through the profits generated by workers' labor and productivity. Ironically, their input helps the firms purchase technologies that replace their labor. "Influenced by the corporate-framed ideology of modernization, growing world competitiveness, and free trade, workers have been indoctrinated to accept automation and the transfer of jobs overseas" (Barbosa 2009:34). The heart of the treadmill is "occupied with monopoly sector firms consisting of several hundred transnational firms and non-unionised workers" (Humphrey, Lewis, and Buttel 2002:52). These transnational corporations look for cheap labor in less developed countries (LDCs), and sometimes whole operations are shifted to these developing regions to exploit the readily available cheap labor.

Under such conditions, would it be reasonable to expect that workers and trade unions will rise up against their governments and the corporations? Unfortunately, the mechanisms of the treadmill are lubricated by the social institutions of modern industrial societies. States—specifically welfare states—provide safety nets for workers who are unemployed and retraining to help them reenter the job market. As mentioned earlier, the state promotes economic growth so as to fund welfare benefits while ensuring job creation and stability for workers. Labor unions are generally supportive of the treadmill, since growth provides jobs for the workers. Moreover, in consumer societies, the creation of wants and desires ensures that families take it upon themselves to consume goods, ensuring the endless demand for production and the turning of the treadmill. Education as a social institution ensures the indoctrination of consumer ideologies and tendencies, while co-opting future workers into the system. In short, capitalists, workers, and politicians alike are caught in the web of the treadmill, unable to escape its clutches throughout modern industrial societies.

The role of the government ought to lie in balancing the facilitation of capital accumulation and economic growth on the one hand and regulating environmental protection on the other. However, more often than not, governments have to prioritize economic growth as an indicator of national progress and development; they also depend on economic growth for tax revenues to fund social and other administrative services. To appease calls for environmental protection and criticisms of environmental negligence, governments usually adopt ambiguous or weak policies and frameworks that do little to impede the engines of economic growth. Governments legitimize their political power through ensuring economic growth, often at the expense of environmental protection.

In the context of the LDCs, the treadmill of production helps us understand the increased vulnerabilities these countries face in their pursuit of development. The demand for consumer goods in developed countries leads to an intensification of production processes. Many transnational corporations (TNCs) move their production and operations to the developing countries so as to exploit the raw materials and cheap labor available. While the production factories and operations are shifted to the developing countries, thus offering employment for local populations, the intensification of such processes and operations also means increased environmental degradation. The governments of these developing countries and LDCs are dependent on Western models of development, which involve attracting foreign investment and encouraging industrialization—i.e., the intensification of production processes. They may also be under pressure because of their debts to such international financial institutions (IFIs) as the World Bank and the International Monetary Fund (IMF), which require these countries to take steps to promote economic growth as part of their loan agreements. To attract these foreign investments, environmental regulations may also be loosened. As a result of the treadmill of production's effect in these LDCs and developing countries, environmental damage is intensified. These countries suffer increased vulnerabilities from the environmental hazards caused by unregulated dumping of chemical and toxic waste, the by-products of the industrial processes. While the developed world gets to enjoy the luxury of consumer goods, the environmental hazards are redistributed and diverted unfairly to the developing world, where communities suffer more environmental and social vulnerabilities.

In sum, the treadmill of production theory has the advantage of locating the causes of present environmental problems in human economic and political systems. Developed countries' consumption needs influence production expansion while rendering developing countries more vulnerable to the environmental hazards generated by the production process. As Allan Schnaiberg and Kenneth Gould aptly summarize: "Both domestically and internationally, not only are production decisions controlled disproportionately by a small number of decision-makers, but also consumption capacity is increasingly being allocated to a smaller share of the world's consumers" (2009:59).

Critics of the treadmill of production theory point out that it is too pessimistic and does not allow for the possibilities of gradual reform and improvement even without radical changes to the economic and political structures in societies. They remain convinced of the adaptive and transformative ability of capitalism in the face of environmental challenges and argue that small steps, such as recycling programs, still provide hope for ameliorating environmental conditions. As we discuss later, some other theories, such as ecological modernization theory, do indeed suggest that better technology can fix the situation and that we do not need to radically change our economic and political structures.

WORLD-SYSTEMS THEORY

Complementing the treadmill of production theory, the 'world-systems theory' provides us with a useful tool in understanding the global stratification system underlying the unequal distribution of environmental and social vulnerabilities. World-system scholars (see for example Caldwell 1977; R. Clark 1998; Gereffi and Korzeniewicz 1994) generally argue that wealth (in the form of raw materials and energy) flows from the resource-rich periphery regions to the industrialized core, while the waste generated from the industrialized core (including the waste generated from its consumption) flows back to the periphery regions (Frey 2001b:106).

Immanuel Wallerstein (2004) argues that the world we live in today, the modern world-system, originated in the sixteenth century. Expanding from Europe and the Americas, this world-system now covers the whole globe. According to Wallerstein, the world-system today is that of a capitalist world economy. So what exactly is this capitalist world economy, and how does it explain the environmental exploitation and degradation experienced across the globe? A world economy refers to a "large geographic zone within which there is a division of labor and hence significant internal exchange of basic or essential of basic or essential goods as well as flows of capital and labour" (Wallerstein 2004:23). A capitalist system refers to the mode of production in a society that gives priority to the *endless* accumulation of capital through the value produced by wage-laborers. The emphasis here is on '*endless*' accumulation of capital that is characteristic of a capitalist system. People and firms are engaged in a production cycle that generates profits for the purpose of accumulating more capital to generate more profits, an endless and continual process. For Wallerstein, the world economy and the capitalist system are held together by a special relationship between capitalist economic producers and the holders of political power. "Capitalists need a large market (hence mini-systems are too narrow for them) but they also need a multiplicity of states, so that they can gain the advantages of working with states but also can circumvent states hostile to their interests in favor of states friendly to their interests. Only the existence of a multiplicity of states within the overall division of labor assures this possibility" (Wallerstein 2004:24).

The ability to favor states that are friendly to their interests is crucial in our discussion of how capitalist TNCs can influence the unequal distribution of environmental and social vulnerabilities between developed and developing countries. Markets are important to the functioning of a capitalist world economy. However, Wallerstein labels the belief in the existence of free markets as nothing more than a myth. He is convinced that free markets cannot exist for capitalism to function. Since the conditions of perfectly free markets would mean that buyers choosing between competing producers could force down the prices of goods and hence lower profits to levels that would render it impractical for capitalists to continue production, only partially free markets exist. These partially free markets are dominated by quasi-monopolies and oligopolies. Oligopolies make the desired high rates of profits possible.

The spread of the capitalist world economy created a global division of labor comprising three zones—namely, the core, periphery, and semi-periphery. The core zones include Western Europe and the U.S., with Japan joining in the late twentieth century. The core exploits the periphery for raw materials, labor, and new markets. There is a third zone, one that lies in the middle of the core-periphery relationship—the semi-periphery zone. This zone includes countries that experienced relative decline out of the core or that managed to rise from the periphery. They are careful not to fall back down to the periphery, while constantly working toward entering the core. Examples include Brazil, South Korea, and Mexico (Barbosa 2009). In addition, there is an unequal exchange between the core and periphery. There is a constant flow of surplus value from the producers of peripheral products to the producers of core products (Wallerstein 2004:28); this is where the profits flow to the capitalist TNCs and their affiliated firms.

Stephen Bunker (1988) argues that First World's exploitation and extraction of natural resources from the Third World represents a permanent loss for the latter. 'Underdevelopment', and not development, results in these

Third World countries as irreplaceable transfers of assets occur from the periphery to the core. The Third World countries are plunged into poverty and economic instability as a result. The core is responsible for increasing affluence and consumption levels and placing demands on increased production, which inevitably lead to increased extraction of natural resources and pollution in the periphery states where production takes place. As R. Scott Frey observes, periphery countries have little choice but to allow exploitation of their resources and "to accept hazardous wastes from the core even though they have limited expertise in treating, storing, and disposing wastes" (2001b:111). The pressure for their consent to such exploitation comes from their need to deal with poverty, debt, and a world-system that produces global economic and political inequalities. In addition, weak and corrupt national governments often mean they find themselves in a weak bargaining position against the powerful TNCs overseeing the hazardous-wastes exchange. These countries often find themselves caught in the vicious cycle of environmental exploitation and degradation as a result of a lack of political will to formulate and implement stronger environmental regulations and restructure their economic policies.

The semi-periphery states are the ones in the most difficult position. Careful not to slip back into the peripheral category, they are under pressure to develop their economies at a rapid and unsustainable pace. In making themselves more competitive, countries may loosen environmental regulations and throw open regulatory doors for foreign firms and local firms alike to exploit natural resources and labor under the banner of 'economic growth and development'. As Barbosa aptly observes, "Environmental degradation is limited in the periphery by lack of development, and intense environmentalism in the core has led to passage of strict environmental laws. On the other hand, semi-peripheral countries sacrifice their environments for the sake of development. In Thailand people have to wear surgical masks due to heavy traffic pollution" (2009:37).

The world-systems theory explains how the stratification system within our capitalist world economy contributes to the unequal distribution of environmental and social vulnerabilities experienced by different countries. We now move on to discuss another neo-Marxian theory that attempts to explain the relationship between human societies and the environment, focusing on how economic relationships within a capitalistic society underlie the nature and magnitude of environmental degradation.

THEORY OF METABOLIC RIFT

Classical sociology and early theorizing efforts have been charged with neglecting the close and interdependent relationship between human societies and the natural environment. Such scholars as William R. Catton and Riley E. Dunlap (1978) claim that sociology, during the discipline's founding years, followed a "human exemptionalist paradigm" (HEP) where human societies were studied as if nature did not matter. It has been argued that classical sociological theories were resistant to the study of nature and its relationship to society, with scholars fearing biological determinism in theorizing social processes if they were to assign causal powers to nature in effecting social changes. Sociology legitimized itself by focusing on the analysis of social processes and social institutions, unwilling to cross the boundaries into the study of environmental processes and natural changes.

In recent times, the subfield of environmental sociology has developed significantly, and environmental analysis is increasingly incorporated into mainstream sociological scholarship. Efforts are also made by practitioners to reinterpret the works of classical theorists, such as Marx, Emile Durkheim, and Max Weber (widely accepted as the founding fathers of modern sociology). Much literature exists now arguing that the classical theorists are not totally blind to environmental concern and analysis in their works. Popular in the classical tradition are Marx's works, which offer a well-developed critique of the capitalistic mode of production and its attributing of production in modern societies as being the chief culprit for the causes of ecological degradation. John B. Foster (1999) develops Marx's theory of metabolic rift through reinterpreting Marx's works, specifically emphasizing his later works in political economy found in his three volumes of *Capital*.

Foster argues that "Marx had provided a powerful analysis of the main ecological crisis of his day—the problem of soil fertility within capitalist agriculture—as well as commenting on the other major ecological crises of his time (the loss of forests, the pollution of the cities, and the Malthusian spectre of overpopulation)" (1999:373). Marx was able to develop a critique of the environmental degradation during his time and anticipated much of present ecological thought, including the question of sustainable development. Rebecca Clausen aptly describes the concept of metabolic rift, following Foster and Marx: "The metabolic rift describes how the logic of accumulation severs basic processes of natural reproduction leading to the deterioration of ecological sustainability" (2009:426).

There are two meanings of 'metabolism' as used by Marx. The first meaning is concerned with the interaction between humans and nature governed by regulatory processes, specifically in relation to nutrient cycles. The natural nutrients found in the soil are exhausted at high rates due to intensive agricultural practices, usually aided by technological advancements in the utilization of machines to increase productivity. As a result, the natural regeneration process of these nutrients in the soil is no longer viable. Rather, nutrients and fertilizers for the soil have to be acquired elsewhere. Urbanization processes resulting in migration from rural areas to large cities and towns also create a rift in the metabolism of nature-society relations, as nutrients from crops are transported away from the farms in which the crops were produced, and the waste from crop consumption accumulates in distant cities and towns. Applying the analogy of metabolism to the practices of agriculture, the main process of production in his times, Marx points out that capitalist agriculture creates a metabolic rift in the natural cycles of soil fertility and waste accumulation.

We have just discussed the meaning of the term 'metabolism' in the ecological sense. The second, wider meaning of the term has to do with the social meaning of metabolism, where there is a rift between humanity and nature as a result of the relationship between wage labor and capital. Extending the analogy of metabolism from biology, the process by which people take nutrient matter and energy from their environments, digest it, and return waste material is called social metabolism (Salleh 2010:206). Clausen explains the social metabolism in capitalist societies: "Private property in the earth's resources, the division between mental/ manual labour, and the antagonistic split between town and country illustrate the metabolic rift on a social level. In capitalism the rift is manifest in many ways, such as the primacy of corporate speculation in real estate, the loss of autonomy of subsistence farmers to the knowledge of 'expert' technicians, and the demographic transition from rural farms to urban centres" (2009:427). "The rift in social metabolism of food production under capitalism is aggravated by private ownership of land, the strict division between mental and manual labour, and the unjust distribution of the fruits of labour" (2009:435). Marx was deeply influenced by the works of Justus von Liebig (1859) on the relationship between agriculture and chemistry. Mindi Schneider and Philip McMichael aptly sum up Liebig's views on the impact of agricultural processes on the environment during the nineteenth century: "Justus von Liebig, Germany's leading agricultural chemist, along with agronomists in Britain, France, and the U.S., argued that by shipping food and fibre from the countryside to cities, soil nutrients were being lost. Whereas in 'traditional' forms of agriculture nutrients were recycled back to the soil, because modern crops were being transported long distances between the sites of production and consumption, nutrients instead ended up in urban sewage that became an important source of pollution in early industrial cities" (2010:462).

Drawing upon Liebig's works, Marx was convinced that capitalist agriculture was unsustainable and that there was an "irreparable rift in the interdependent process of the social metabolism prescribed by the natural laws of life itself" (1981:949–950, cited in Foster 1999:379). The development of the capitalist mode of production results in the extraction of natural resources, such as soil and wood, from the environment at an unsustainable rate that is damaging to the reproductive and recovery abilities of these resources. Capitalism impoverishes and exploits labor and nature alike. Marx's understanding of the labor process is key to his concept of metabolism: "The worker can create nothing without *nature*, without the *sensuous external world*. It is the material on which his labour is manifested, in which it is active, from which and by means of which it produces" ([1844] 1972:58; emphasis original). To elaborate:

Labour is, first of all, a process between man and nature, a process by which man, through his own actions, mediates, regulates and controls the metabolism between himself and nature. He confronts the materials of nature as a force of nature. He sets in motion the natural forces which belong to his own body, his arms, legs, head and hands, in order to appropriate the materials of nature in a form adapted to his own needs. Through this movement he acts upon external nature and changes it, and in this way he simultaneously changes his own nature. . . . It [the labour process] is the universal condition for the metabolic interaction [*Stoffwechsel*] between man and nature, the everlasting nature-imposed condition of human existence. (Marx 1976:283–290, cited in Foster 1999:380)

Human lives from nature and is part of it. Human society relates to nature through the process of labor. Nature, then, is as much a source of wealth as is labor. The metabolic interaction between humans and nature is regulated by society through the governance of labor and its development within historical social formations (Foster 1999:383). Marx's analysis identifies an environmental contradiction within capitalism: as capitalist societies develop and produce ever-increasing volumes of goods, environmental degradation will correspondingly reduce prospects for sustainable development and the continued production of goods, as current rates of extraction deplete dwindling natural resources. According to Bell, "[T]here are many ways that societies can arrange material production from the environment, and these arrangements have great consequences for how we live, even how we think. Our ecology is our economy, and our economy is our society" (2009:35).

So how can the theory of metabolic rift help us understand the relationship between development, power, and the environment in contemporary capitalist societies? The global metabolic rift (B. Clark and Foster 2009) emerges with the development of a capitalist world economy (Wallerstein 2011). As consumption levels and demands in the core states increase, more resources are extracted from the periphery regions at the expense of increased environmental degradation. Production requirements to meet that demand increase the exploitation and extraction of natural resources and raw materials from the developing regions:

The economic development of capitalism has always carried with it social and ecological degradation—an ecological curse. Moreover, ecological imperialism has meant that the worst forms of ecological destruction, in terms of the pillaging of resources and the disruption of sustainable relations to the Earth, fall on the periphery rather than the centre. Ecological imperialism allows imperial countries to carry out an 'environmental overdraft' that draws on the natural resources of periphery countries. As the material conditions of development are destroyed, Third World countries are more and more caught in the debt trap that characterizes extractive economies. (Clark and Foster 2009:329–330)

Brett Clark and John B. Foster rightly point out that Third World countries' development efforts become derailed as the developed regions continue to exploit and extract their natural resources. In sum, the development needs of the North and the rich countries are met at the expense of increasing the metabolic rift between Third World societies and their natural environments, seriously degrading the latter. Third World countries are left with little choice as they continue to depend on the loans provided by IFIs and foreign investment from the rich countries. They become more vulnerable to the environmental and social risks brought about by increased extraction of natural resources from their environments. The processes of ecological imperialism, the global metabolic rift, and the treadmill of production, so characteristic of the capitalist mode of production in modern industrial societies, generate unprecedented levels of risk for the global environment and the societies it supports.

ECOLOGICAL MODERNIZATION

In contrast to the neo-Marxian theories discussed above, a prominent neoliberal theory has been raised—the ecological modernization theory, or EM in short. EM theory may be seen as a response to the treadmill of production theory that was popular during the 1980s. Specifically, EM theory is an attempt to rescue and defend the capitalist modernization project against the claims of neo-Marxian theories that environmental salvation can only be achieved through radical structural changes to capitalistic economic structures. Proponents of EM theory believe in reforming rather than radically changing existing systems.

The founders and proponents of EM theory include Joseph Huber, Martin Jänicke, Arthur Mol, and Gert Spaargaren. The main premise of the theory is that capitalism is flexible enough as a system to find solutions to the environmental issues and evolve toward 'sustainable capitalism'. They argue that more modernization is needed to find solutions to the environmental crisis, as opposed to radical ecologists' suggestions of abandoning the modernization project altogether. Huber (1982, 1985) posits the idea that industrial society develops in historical stages. He believes that modern society will eventually arrive at the third stage, involving the process of 'superindustrialization'. This 'superindustrialization' is a process of an "ecological switchover of the industrial system" (Hannigan 2006:24). Technology plays an important role in this process, with proponents of EM theory suggesting that better and more environmentally friendly technologies can be developed to deal with environmental problems.

Another tenet of EM theory is that 'reflexive modernization' (within modern societies) will transform capitalism to become more environmentally friendly. "Reflexivity involves the individual and society constantly re-examining their own circumstances—beliefs, social practices, etc.—in light of new information or knowledge" (Barbosa 2009:38). This reexamination involves a heightened awareness and prioritization of environmental concerns among consumers, whose demand will drive gradual changes at the institutional level for governments and corporations. These will incorporate environmentally conscious knowledge and technologies into their policy formulations and *modus operandi*, respectively. In this way, free-market mechanisms will ensure that firms and corporations transform themselves to be more environmentally friendly. Competition, availability of capital, and other market factors will accelerate the competition between firms to develop and adopt new, better, and environmentally friendlier technologies and practices. In short, EM theory posits that modern capitalistic society will be able to self-regulate and move toward 'sustainable capitalism' or 'sustainable development'. While EM theory has become a popular approach in environmental sociology, posing a strong challenge to the treadmill of production theory, we can also discern some similar tenets in 'natural capitalism' developed in the field of economics. In their book *Natural Capitalism: Creating the Next Industrial Revolution*, economists Paul Hawken, Amory Lovins, and L. Hunter Lovins provide four central arguments, which are similar to those in EM theory. The arguments, as summarized by Barbosa (2009:39), are as follows:

- *Radically increase the productivity of resource use.* Fundamental changes in technology and design can lead to substantial savings.
- *Shift to biologically inspired production (bio-mimicry) with closed loops, no waste, and no toxicity.* Natural capitalism seeks to eliminate waste altogether.
- *Shift the business model away from the making and selling of "things" to provide the services that the "things" deliver.* The natural capitalism model delivers value as a continuous flow of services.
- *Reinvest in natural and human capital.* Any good capitalist reinvests in productive capital.

EM theorists criticize neo-Marxian theorists' approach to environmental issues as being too 'economically deterministic' and pessimistic regarding human society's ability to adapt and transform itself without radical structural changes. On the other hand, EM theorists themselves are charged with being overly optimistic about the positive power of technology to fix things, forgetting that 'clean technologies', such as nuclear power, have their own risks and undesirable features. The superindustrialization process also reminds us of the silicon-chip revolution, which was not entirely environmentally neutral, as EM theory would have us believe.

Nevertheless, the EM theory is an admirable attempt to bridge the gap between the radical structural changes proposed by some groups, such as the deep ecologists, and the business-as-usual approach implied by some capital apologists (Sutton 2004:146). The faith of EM theorists, such as Mol and Spaargaren (2003), in 'responsible capitalism' points to some hope that while capitalism may be blamed for the environmental problems we face today, it is flexible and resilient enough to offer the best hope for a solution that will allow human societies to continue enjoying development while ensuring that the environment is protected and sustained for future generations.

RISK-SOCIETY THESIS

According to Ulrich Beck's well-cited works (1992, 1999, 2009), we are now living in a 'world risk society'. Beck observes that under conditions of globalization, scientific and technological progress do not necessarily reduce risks. Rather, paradoxically, developments in technology, science, and industrialism lead to more risks for our environment, health, and overall well-being. For Beck, post-traditional society is full of uncertainties as a result of the technological developments and their application: "technology has resulted in the need to cope with risk situations which are different in character from those of the past" (Denny 2005:29). In his characterization of the post-traditional 'risk society', Beck presumes that a 'value consensus' exists in society and that mass concerns about survival make way for concerns about risks and insecurity. While the value of structural equality used to be the main concern for traditional class-based societies, in post-traditional society it is the value of safety that has become the main concern: "The place of the value system of the 'unequal' society is taken by the value system of the 'unsafe' society. Whereas the utopia of equality contains a wealth of substantial and positive goals of social change, the utopia of the risk society remains peculiarly negative and defensive. Basically one is no longer concerned with attaining something 'good' but rather preventing the worst" (Beck 1992:49).

Social movements around the world championing for environmental protection, organic food, and a return to nature, which have become powerful vehicles of political mobilization for change, suggest society's recognition of the limitations of scientific progress and economic growth. Indeed, these movements reflect the increasing suspicion, fear, and distrust of the risks generated by scientific and technological developments and their profit-driven outcomes. For Beck, a process of social restructuring has taken place; in traditional class-based societies, conflicts occurred over the distribution of goods (i.e., money and other material resources), but in the modern risk society, conflicts occur over the distribution of 'bads' (i.e., pollution, technological hazards, and other forms of environmental degradation). In class society, it was your material position (i.e., your income, employment, and place of residence) that determined who you were. In risk society, it is your ideas and beliefs that matter most (Bell 2009:227). Worries about security issues and reliance on technology and social systems characterize a life of risk.

The idea of 'reflexive modernization' is as important for the risk-society thesis as it is for the ecological modernization theory. While some have argued that Beck's risk society is filled with too much pessimism, he does see hope through 'reflexivity'. 'Reflexive modernization' for Beck is the second stage of modernization, where society is able to collectively reflect upon the meanings of science, modernity, and rationality. David Denny, following Beck, "describes reflexive modernization in terms of changing patterns of social experiences in which old certainties provided by traditional institutions like the Church and the professions are being fundamentally challenged" (Beck 1998, quoted in Denny 2005:31). Environmentalism is a result of such 'reflexivity' where the individual and society reflects on its institutions and consumption practices while confronting the role and impact of science and technology in light of new information about the environment and its relationship with human societies.

Beck makes a distinction between risks and hazards. Hazards, for him, are the potential harm that may arise from naturally occurring events. Risk, in contrast, is the calculation of the potential and possibilities of harm (to individuals, society, economy, ecology) from the utilization of science and technology for wealth production. According to Beck, hazards were most evident during the pre-industrial era. Those were the times when hazards arose most often from non-human activity, being naturally occurring events, such as floods, famines, and earthquakes. He believes these types of hazards have been largely overcome with the arrival of the modern industrial society.

Industrial society, for Beck, saw the reduction in hazards accompanied by the generation of risks from industrial production and the distribution of wealth. Risks now originated mostly in human activities and were the results of conscious decision-making processes. He observes that industrial modernity was able to produce systems and responses not so much to eradicate natural disasters but to greatly increase society's capabilities to predict, control, and manage naturally existing hazards through regimes of control, disaster-relief measures, warning systems, and emergency-management systems. Through scientific and technological application, risks were measured, assessed, managed, and controlled.

For Beck, since the middle of the twentieth century, the risk society has been a break from the industrial society of the past. Individuals living in the risk society are waiting for the latest technological developments to catch up with the negative consequences of previous innovation (Denny 2005:30). As technology and science advanced, it provided society with the technical means and ability to control and reduce risks. Social, political, ecological, and individual risks became manageable through such instruments as insurance and state-funded departments for emergencies (e.g., paramedic and firefighting services). Engineers, to state another example, could use sophisticated models to calculate and manage the risks of the automobiles and machinery they built.

Yet in a risk society where such powerful developments as nuclear, genetic, and chemical technologies, among others, have great potential for danger along with their potential for good, insurance itself is becoming increasingly unreliable, as these developments are more unstable and unpredictable than the risks of the past. In short, there has been a change in the nature of risks, and an increase in its magnitude for individuals. Within the dynamism of modernity, the move from the industrial society to the risk society is a result of 'unintended consequences'. Social order is threatened not just by the increase of these risks but also by societies' technical means and ability to control and manage these 'mega-risks'; the orderly control and distribution of risk across and within communities becomes unviable and meaningless.

Beck (1999) recognizes that modern risks to the environment are distinct from what may have occurred before, in that these risks are by-products of technology and are examples of what he calls 'manufactured uncertainty'. He argues that such risks to the environment, as opposed to those in the past, are increasingly only detectable through science; such threats as spillages and accidents now "require the sensory organs of science—theories, experiments, measuring instruments—in order to become visible and interpretable as threats at all" (1992:162). According to Denny, individuals in risk society "constantly seek to come to terms with uncertainty, through a contested form of scientific rationality" (2005:39).

Beck has been criticized for his failure to take into account the fluidity of risk (see M. Brown 2000). He has also been charged with being pessimistic about risk and failing to recognize that different people may experience and explain risk in different ways, even though such differences may be subtle. People in the past also had to deal with the unknown and the uncertain. They did so in different ways from modern societies, such as rituals of religion and magic. So we see that societies throughout history have always been concerned, in varying degrees, with the management of risk and security. Pat O'Malley (2000) has argued that risk is but one aspect of the social world and that Beck focuses too heavily on it. As Bell points out, the difference between present-day risks and those of the past lies in the "language we use to think and to talk about our worries, a language that, in keeping with the spirit of our time, is highly rationalistic" (2009:218).

While Beck has correctly pointed out that global environmental issues affect us all, as compared to such issues as poverty, which are hierarchic, he has little to say about the unequal distribution of environmental degradation, which specifically affects poor countries more seriously, as they lack the wealth of the developed countries to avoid the worst consequences of environmental problems. In short, material inequalities—which are supposedly the basis of traditional class societies—are still important in understanding the unequal distribution of risks in the present day, which Beck sometimes calls the 'second modernity'. Wealth, in Bell's words, "remains an important cleavage in environmental politics" (2009:227). Uncertainties and risks brought about by poverty and socio-economic inequalities are still prevalent in both developing and developed countries.

The theories discussed above offer both competing and complementary understandings of the relationship between nature and society. Despite variances and tensions between the theories, all of them try to understand the environmental and social risks endemic in our societies. All the theories—more or less—address fundamental issues of our societies, such as development, power, and the environment, with a greater focus on the Global North. However, the complexity of modern societies—with their unique issues and challenges that humanity has never experienced before (such as globalization, climate change, the neoliberal food regime, the post-9/11 neoliberal security regime, the rise of the BRIC states (Brazil, Russia, India, and China), increasingly assertive identity and cultural politics, etc.)—calls for an integrated theoretical analysis. The growing complexities of interaction and intersection between development, power, and the environment have produced many paradoxes and clear sets of winners and losers. Chapter 5 explores some of these paradoxes.

5 Neoliberal Paradox
Connection through Disconnection

UNDERSTANDING NEOLIBERALISM

Neoliberalism refers to an economic model or paradigm that rose to prominence in the 1980s (Steger and Roy 2010). Perhaps it is more appropriate to discuss 'neoliberalisms' given the diverse strands of neoliberal manifestations in countries and regions of various social, economic, cultural, and political conditions or environments. However, scholars (see for example Gamble 2001; Harvey 2005; Mudge 2008; Steger and Roy 2010) have argued that across these strands and variations of neoliberalisms, we can still identify some core tenets of an economic paradigm that has been adapted to suit the needs and conditions of different geopolitical territories. In this chapter, I discuss some of the core tenets of neoliberalism.

'Neoliberalism' is a term that was coined during post–World War II Germany by scholars from the 'Freiburg School'. It is also often linked to the 'Washington Consensus', a label advanced by John Williamson (2004) in a conference paper for the Institute for International Economics in which he proposed a list of ten policies of what he thought could be commonly accepted by institutions in Washington D.C., such as the World Bank and the International Monetary Fund (IMF), as necessary for developing countries, in particular the Latin American region. David Harvey contends that "the capitalist world stumbled towards neoliberalization as the answer (to the crisis of capital accumulation in the 1970s) through a series of gyrations and chaotic experiments that really only converged as a new orthodoxy with the articulation of what became known as the 'Washington Consensus' in the 1990s" (2005:13).

To understand the neoliberal model and its historical basis, we have to first trace the development of classical liberalism and Keynesian liberalism, the theoretical predecessors of neoliberalism. Classical liberalism rose in prominence in nineteenth-century Europe and the U.S., drawing on the economics of classical liberals, such as Adam Smith (1723–1790) and David Ricardo (1772–1823). These two thinkers advance the ideals of the 'free-market' economy, believing that the role of the state should be limited to facilitating and preserving an open economic exchange, with limited intervention into the economic activities of self-interested citizens. Classical liberalism was a development in opposition to the mercantilism of monarchs from the eighteenth century onward. In addition, it was opposed to protectionist policies, such as the Corn Laws in England[1] during the nineteenth century. Its core tenants were the protection of private property, the legal enforcement of contracts, and the unwavering belief in the 'invisible hand' to ensure efficient and effective allocation of resources. In short, classical liberalism promoted the idea of a 'free-market' economy with limited state intervention in which the role of the state was limited to the facilitation of economic activities. In times of economic hardships, classical liberalists would blame excessive state interference in the 'free market' as the cause of economic crises and any imbalances (Harvey 2005; Smart 2003; Steger and Roy 2010).

Economist John Maynard Keynes ([1936] 2008) critiques classical liberalism for its deficiencies in putting full faith into 'free-market' principles. While keeping faith in 'market' principles, he believes the state should take a more active role in the economy to ensure the well-being of all. Keynesian economics took over as the dominant paradigm of economic governance in the early twentieth century, especially after the 1930s economic depression in the U.S. and during the immediate construction period following World War II. Keynesian economists advocated a higher degree of state involvement in steering economic policies and activities; government expenditure was encouraged as a strategy to stimulate the economy during times of crises and to achieve full employment, creating new jobs and lifting consumer spending. Keynes challenges classical liberalism's belief in the ability of market mechanism to naturally correct itself without state interference (Smart 2003; Steger and Roy 2010).

The economic crisis during the 1970s led to another paradigm shift. As Keynesian economics lost its popularity, an entirely new breed of liberal economists sought a way forward by reviving the old doctrine of classical liberalism under the novel conditions of globalization. It is arguable that this period marked the birth of neoliberalism. Such scholars as David M. Kotz (2009) observe the break from regulated forms of capitalism during the post–World War II period and the emergence of neoliberal capitalism. For Kotz, capitalism periodically goes through systemic crisis. He traces the history of capitalism through the systemic crises that occurred during the 1930s depression period, and the 1970s when regulated capitalism stopped working effectively. From the late 1970s and early 1980s emerged the neoliberal form of capitalism, and Kotz is convinced that the financial crisis that started in 2008 will yet again transform capitalism.

According to Manfred B. Steger and Ravi K. Roy (2010), neoliberalism is identifiable through a common set of ideological and political principles dedicated to the worldwide spread of an economic model emphasizing the 'free market' and 'free trade'. John L. Campbell and Ove Kaj Pedersen's definition of neoliberalism captures the 'free market' and 'free trade' as fundamental tenets:

[A] heterogeneous set of institutions consisting of various ideas, social and economic policies, and ways of organizing political and economic activity. . . . Ideally, it includes formal institutions, such as minimalist welfare-state, taxation, and business regulation programs; flexible labour markets and decentralized capital–labour relations unencumbered by strong unions and collective bargaining; and the absence of barriers to international capital mobility. It includes institutionalized normative principles favouring free-market solutions to economic problems, rather than bargaining or indicative planning, and a dedication to controlling inflation even at the expense of full employment. It includes institutionalized cognitive principles, notably a deep, taken-for-granted belief in neoclassical economics. (2001:5)

Stephanie Lee Mudge finds that Campbell and Pederson's definition of neoliberalism lacks a historical basis, choosing to define it as "an ideological system that holds the 'market' sacred, born within the 'human' or social sciences and refined in a network of Anglo-American-centric knowledge producers, expressed in different ways within the institutions of the postwar nation-state and their political fields" (2008:707). Mudge's definition emphasizes neoliberalism as an ideological system, alluding to the dominance of a neoliberal mentality or frame of thinking in shaping the conduct of economic activity and social relations in the current social order. According to neoliberal principles, the market order is to be held together by governments, both national and local. The role of governments is limited to the facilitation of market order through sustaining strong political and legal foundations (Gamble 2001). In other words, governments are to refrain from intervening excessively in economic activities, removing those regulations that may inhibit the ease of doing business. Such scholars as J. Ronald Stanfield and Michael C. Carroll observe that "[u]nder the guidance of the so-called Washington Consensus, there has been instituted a neoliberal governance regime [around the world], which has removed many social and political controls of market economic forces" (2009:1).

For analytical purposes, neoliberalism can be categorized into two distinct waves. The first wave was in the 1980s, guided by the political leadership of Ronald Reagan and Margaret Thatcher. The second wave in the 1990s was guided by the administrations of Tony Blair and Bill Clinton. I examine briefly the two waves of neoliberalism and the corresponding spread of neoliberalism to Asia and Latin America, taking on various strands each according to its idiosyncratic social, economic, and political conditions.

The first wave of neoliberalism is associated with the administrations of Thatcher of Great Britain and Reagan of the U.S. during the 1980s. These two leaders put into practice the ideas of neoliberalism and monetarism as advanced by Friedrich Hayek and Milton Friedman. The first wave succeeded in shattering the Keynesian paradigm that had dominated economic policies since the Great Depression and that remained in effect during the postwar reconstruction period. In addition, the first wave of neoliberalism in the 1980s was "interlaced with the geopolitical imperative to stop the spread of communism and socialist developmentalism in the Third World" (Steger and Roy 2010:47). The 1980s enshrined the neoliberal principles of deregulation, liberalization, and privatization as a formula for promoting economic growth and progress, setting the stage for the second wave of neoliberalism.

The second wave of neoliberalism continued in the 1990s. Associated with the leadership of Blair of Great Britain and Clinton of the U.S., this wave continued with neoliberal policies but added a socially progressive agenda. Keen to attend to the neglected social and ecological issues from the 1980s, Blair and Clinton enhanced social and welfare programs in their policies. The aim was to promote what Steger and Roy call "a socially conscious market globalism" (2010:51). The second wave produced a period of rapid economic growth and an increase in transnational trade through regional free-trade agreements. World leaders led by Clinton and Blair were "united in their attempts to liberalize trade relations and continue towards integrating national economies into a single global market" (51). This period of neoliberalism was also linked with the common acceptance of the Washington Consensus, a ten-point program for structural adjustment that international financial institutions (IFIs), such as the IMF and the World Bank, impose upon governments in exchange for much-needed loans and debt-restructuring schemes. The ten-point program manifests the neoliberal vision of establishing an integrated global free-market economy and the principles of deregulation, liberalization, and privatization to guide policy formulation. While Part II of this book (especially Chapter 6) examines impacts of these neoliberal policies through various case studies, to foreground that, I first discern here some inherent paradoxes of the neoliberal globalization project.

PARADOXES OF NEOLIBERALISM

Empowerment and Powerlessness in an Age of Reflexive Modernity: Connecting to the 'Postnatural World' through Disconnecting from the 'Traditional World'

One of the paradoxes of neoliberal globalization can be derived from Anthony Giddens's discussions of late modernity (1990, 1991). I discuss two characteristics of late modernity posited by Giddens—high-consequence risks and reflexivity—and analyze how these two characteristics contribute to the paradox of empowerment and powerlessness in contemporary social life.

For Giddens, environmental and ecological threats are examples of the 'high-consequence risks' (1990) experienced in late modernity. We are now living in a 'postnatural world' (1991, 1994), which means that 'nature' is no longer 'natural' but rather 'socialized' through the use of science and technology and the intertwining of natural and social systems. The uncertainties of ecological threats are manufactured uncertainties arising from human intervention and action. For instance, the development of nuclear energy and nuclear power plants has resulted in the manufactured risks of a nuclear disaster; the impact of such an event is equally damaging to human life as it is to the rest of nature. Humanity has transformed the natural world to such an extent that it is no longer possible to clearly demarcate what is natural and what is social. The risks we face in late modernity have led to a disruption of our ontological security. Ontological security is a psychological state where an individual experiences low and manageable levels of anxiety in relation to autonomy of bodily control with predictable routines. Ontological insecurity is heightened in late modernity. To manage this insecurity, people now turn to abstract systems, with a corresponding transformation of 'trust' in contemporary social life.

Abstract systems are bodies of expert or specialized knowledge. In premodern orders, traditional institutions dominate social actors' sources of meaning and information on what to do and how to live. With 'time-space distanciation' (Giddens 1995), such institutions increasingly lose their grip on social actors' everyday lives. A process of *deskilling* takes place. For example, social actors in premodern orders would know how to build their own shelters, using materials from the environment and skills transmitted by their parents, or what was to them 'common sense'. But in modern orders, and especially in later stages of modernity (i.e., high modernity), we are losing these 'commonsense' skills. Instead, abstract systems prevail, where experts claim technical expertise over areas or fields. To build a house today requires the appropriation of construction principles through engaging a contractor (an expert). The specialization of tasks creates a huge variety of abstract systems. In reaction, there has emerged a huge body of literature in the area of self-help to teach people how to be happy and how to conduct their lives. A *reskilling* process occurs when social actors (re) appropriate these abstract systems to manage their everyday lives.

Following Karl Polanyi (2001), Stanfield and Carroll conceive of the market capitalist economy as "disembedded and socially destructive" (2009:9). The market capitalist economy during the neoliberal era emphasizes the prioritizing of individualistic self-interested economic behavior: "The concept of the disembedded economy refers to a tendency for economic relationships to become superior to the social relationships of kinship and polity" (2009:9). For Giddens, this is reflective of a transformation of trust. To trust in abstract systems today is different from trusting in the premodern orders. In the past, trust was part of personal relations, such as when someone could trust that a fellow villager would keep his side of the bargain in a barter exchange. Today, we have to trust in the impersonal relations of paying online through the credit-card system and trust that our goods will be delivered from a distributor that might be overseas. Other neoliberal financial mechanisms in late modernity, such as pension securitization,[2] also require workers to put their trust and money into formal instruments and into professional and technical knowledge presented as infallible, valid, and true. Workers are led to trust in these abstract financial systems, such as the credit system, to maintain their basic living standards. They experience empowerment as shareholders of these schemes that promise to be infallible. However, this empowerment coexists with powerlessness when workers are faced with the realities of capital accumulation crises.

Trust in these systems is not without risks—indeed, the risks are far higher than in premodern orders. The impersonal nature of abstract systems means that even though risks and dangers are now more calculable, counterfactual thinking (i.e., 'what-if' scenarios) is limited in providing full predictability of the development of knowledge. The 2008 global financial crises demonstrated the high risks accompanying the development of abstract financial systems. Other prominent risks we face today are the threats of global warming, nuclear disasters, and natural disasters, among others. Amid these uncertainties, we still have to manage our ever-increasing levels of anxiety and ontological insecurity.

Giddens's 'late modernity' is characterized by the dialectic between powerlessness and empowerment. From the need to trust abstract systems for our daily routines, we may feel a sense of powerlessness and a high level of anxiety from the lack of control we have over our lives. In facing environmental threats, we can only rely on the current prediction systems put in place to warn us of any potential disasters. More often than not, these systems and the current scientific community's findings produce much more manufactured uncertainty than before. But at the same time, the diminishing influence of premodernity's rigid rules and regulations means we are more empowered than before to make choices for our lives. In this age of the Internet, we are offered access to knowledge of almost anything and everything, from how to make bombs to the purpose of life; in this sense, we are empowered to choose what we want to be reskilled in. Giddens's use of dialectics helps us understand the complex nature of our social reality where there are dualities of trust and risk, opportunities and danger, powerlessness and empowerment, and so forth, in which uncertainty and promise come hand in hand.

It is in the empowerment that social actors receive in modernity that agency is to be located. Modernity is characterized by the breaking away from traditions and with it, social actors' identities that were once derived from those traditional institutions, such as religion and family, are now fragmented. The self finds itself with no meaning to hold onto as concrete. But this also means that there is opportunity—indeed, it is necessary—to reconstruct this self, an example being the construction of multiple selves through consumption culture, where one constantly switches between lifestyles and identifies with the products one appropriates. A process of self-reflexivity takes place where an individual is aware of his or her own conditions in modernity and uses this consciousness to bend backward on and to change those conditions. Giddens (1994) also believes that this self-reflexive project extends to modernity's reflexivity as well. The task of sociology for him was to characterize and to examine the nature of modernity as a historically contingent epoch. Through sociology and other academic disciplines, modernity understands its own condition and is able to (re) appropriate this knowledge to effect change.

This reflexive project is demonstrated by the outburst of environmental movements in late modernity. As Peter Dickens argues, "[E]nvironmental movements are envisaged by Giddens as an attempt to recover moral, existential and aesthetic relationships with the natural world, relationships which were allegedly extant in pre-modern societies but that have been subordinated by imposed manners and etiquettes" (1999:101). In sum, late modernity is characterized by reflexivity and high risks. These two characteristics lead to a paradox of empowerment and powerlessness. Neoliberal globalization is arguably the driver behind this late modernity. With advancements in science and technology, humanity can manipulate the natural world in ways previously unimaginable in traditional societies. But with this capacity comes higher risks associated with the manufactured uncertainties as a result of massive human intervention in the natural world. Neoliberal globalization results in the empowerment of human capacity and his/her ability to manipulate nature, but it also leads to higher uncertainties that threaten our own existence. In the face of these manufactured uncertainties, we are often found to be powerless.

Unequal Development: Connecting the Global North through Disconnecting the Global South

While we are led to believe through television commercials that we live in a world of people everywhere consuming global commodities, statistics show that 20 percent of the world's population consume up to 86 percent of all the goods and services. The poorest 20 percent only consume up to 1.3 percent of goods and services (McMichael 2008:1). Developed countries are empowered by advances in science and technology to manipulate nature and are equipped to manage natural disasters. Developing countries are sometimes powerless in that they cannot afford the same access to these knowledge and technological innovations and are left to face the full wrath of sometimes-human-induced natural disasters.

Wealthy nations located in temperate regions are less vulnerable to ecological changes and have resources to protect citizens from natural disasters (such as flooding, droughts, and temperature extremes). In the 1990s, while 90 percent of natural-disaster fatalities resulted from hydro-meteorological events (such as droughts, floods, hurricanes, and windstorms), 97 percent of natural disaster–related deaths occurred in the Global South (McMichael 2008:2).

The empowered rich world, in the process of transforming nature, is increasingly contributing to environmental degradation. However, it is the powerless who are most vulnerable to the risks these environmental threats pose. Developed countries possess the capacity to reduce global carbon emissions through green technology and thus hold more sway in decision-making processes during international negotiations, but developing countries, such as Ethiopia, whose carbon emissions are only a 300th of the levels generated by the U.S., are left powerless to ensure that more measures are taken to address climate-change issues. There is clearly an unequal distribution of power and risk under the present conditions of neoliberal globalization (details in Chapter 9, this volume). Why is it that some countries and groups of people are more empowered than others? I turn to this question in the next section through examining the neoliberal tendency to restore the class-based power of economic elites.

Winners and Losers of Neoliberal Globalization: Accumulation by Dispossession

The rhetoric of neoliberalism claims it is the best way to advance the well-being of all, but neoliberalism in practice only serves to restore or to create the power of a few global elites while disempowering and dispossessing the masses of their rights and well-being. The neoliberal doctrine holds the belief that personal freedom can be preserved if society adheres to the free-market institutions, the rule of law, and a belief in the principle of private property. The basic elements of personal freedom are the freedom of thought and expression. Extending personal freedom to the economic actions of individuals, people should be free to trade with other people and to accumulate wealth through their ability and effort, albeit within legal constraints. Harvey points out that the theoretical framework of neoliberalism is not entirely coherent, especially when one considers the contradictions between the theory and actual pragmatics: "The scientific rigour of its neoclassical economics does not sit easily with its political commitment to ideals of individual freedom, nor does its supposed distrust of all state power fit with the need for a strong and if necessary coercive state that will defend the rights of private property, individual liberties, and entrepreneurial freedoms" (2005:21).

According to Pierre Bourdieu, the neoliberal ideology in theory is divorced from the reality. Neoliberalism tends on the whole to favor severing the economy from social realities and thereby constructing, in reality, an economic system conforming to its description in pure theory—that is, a sort of logical machine that presents itself as a chain of constraints regulating economic agents (Bourdieu 1998). Harvey argues that the 1950s and 1960s were dominated by processes of capital accumulation through "expansion of wage labour on industry and agriculture" (2005:178), which produced embedded liberalism. In contrast, accumulation by dispossession is fragmented and particular—"a privatization here, an environmental degradation there, a financial crisis of indebtedness somewhere else" (178).

"Dispossession entails the loss of rights" (Harvey 2005:178). The loss of rights may lead to individuals' turning to non-governmental organizations (NGOs) to protect them and to provide for social services. This allows neoliberal states to further withdraw themselves from their responsibilities for social provision. In many cases, these NGOs are privatized and operate according to neoliberal principles as well: "They tend to be elitist, unaccountable, and by definition distant from those they seek to protect or help, no matter how well-meaning or progressive they may be" (177). When advocating for 'universal' rights, such as environmental rights, these NGOs may be blindly pursuing these rights just as capitalists blindly pursue profits. While environmental groups may have good intentions when fighting for international agreements to cut emissions or increased regulations to protect the environment, these actions and decisions may ironically result in increased injustice to local populations, indigenous groups, and developing countries. The imposition of regulations, or the closing off of certain areas for nature reserves, may cause indigenous populations to lose their means of subsistence. The imposition of environmental regulations on the developing world by the developed and rich countries has also been seen as attempts to maintain the status quo of an unequal system benefitting only a few.

Redistribution rather than the generation of wealth and income has been the main outcome of neoliberalization. For Harvey, the (capital) accumulation practices of neoliberalization rely on a corresponding process of dispossession. There are four main features of this process. First, accumulation of capital works through the mechanisms of corporatization, commodification, and privatization of public assets. These public assets includes public utilities; social-welfare provisions, such as education and health care; public institutions; and even warfare (Harvey relates to the security contractors hired in Iraq to protect foreign investors). The commodification process extends to global environmental commons (land, air, and water), which are global public assets. The capitalists appropriate the value and profits generated by these public assets. The neoliberal state plays a key role in facilitating this dispossession through enacting policies to weaken or to destroy the power of organized labor and environmental-rights activism, often using instruments of coercion and abusing their monopoly on the means of violence. Common property rights won after long periods of class struggle are also lost through privatization policies.

The second feature of the accumulation by dispossession process is *financialization*, which since the 1980s has been marked by its 'speculative and predatory style'. Speculation, predation, fraud, and thievery have increased along with deregulation of the financial system. Credit and stock manipulation and speculative raiding carried out by hedge funds increasingly have dispossessed whole populations of their assets (e.g., pension funds). What is supposed to be a positive benefit—'spreading risks'—is really a system of redistributing and 'stratifying risks', where the risk of collapse and losses is borne by the masses. In short, the financial system accumulates capital and wealth to a few through manipulation and speculation in the market, dispossessing the masses of their livelihood and pension rights in the process.

The third feature of the accumulation by dispossession process is *the management and manipulation of crises*. Harvey observes that when a global capital accumulation collapse occurs, financial institutions, such as the IMF, the World Bank in collaboration with the U.S. Treasury, and Wall Street institutions, would organize 'bailouts', offering loans to the poorer countries. Such loans were in fact tickets to pillage the poor countries' economies, leading to a debt crisis. Harvey argues that "these debt crises were orchestrated, managed, and controlled both to rationalize the system and to redistribute assets" (2005:162). Accumulation is achieved by the richer countries through dispossessing the poorer countries of their assets, including natural resources. Deliberate management and manipulation of crises sometimes creates high unemployment as part of the strategy to produce a labor surplus for further accumulation. Such practices may result in uprisings and unrest, and the function of state intervention is to prevent or to deal with the revolts to allow the process of accumulation by dispossession to continue.

The fourth and final feature of the process of accumulation by dispossession is *state redistribution*. Through privatization of social and welfare services, the state dissolves and divests itself of the responsibility to ensure a safety net for the poor and needy in society. Provision of important services, such as public housing, once privatized, disadvantages the lower classes in society over the long run. For example, when Thatcher allowed social housing in Britain to be privatized, housing speculation, especially in the prime locations, led to lower classes being either bribed or forced out of these areas. Some lost their homes, while others were forced to live in the outskirts given their low wages. In this way, through the redistributive policies of neoliberal states, the upper classes or economic elites are able to accumulate profits and capital by dispossessing the lower classes of their most basic needs and assets, such as housing and health care. These services that were previously the responsibilities of the state are now privatized and controlled by corporations whose only interest is to accumulate profits. In addition, the state provides tax incentives, subsidies, and other benefits for these corporations, effectively becoming an agent for redistributing wealth from the marginalized masses to the powerful economic elites. The accumulation of wealth is achieved at the expense of dispossessing the masses of their common asset—the natural environment and its resources.

Sowing the Seeds of Neoconservatism

Neoconservatism, which is now predominant in many countries, including the U.S., is another side of the same coin as neoliberalism. The uncertainties and risks of social disintegration and disorder brought about by neoliberalization create an opposing culture in neoconservatism. Neoconservatism is an answer to the contradictions of neoliberalism. Neoconservatism's core principles are still in line with those of embedded liberalism, but it is different from neoliberalism in that neoconservatism is concerned with order and espouses the application of state intervention to restore or to create social solidarity. It is concerned that neoliberalism's emphasis on individualism may lead to a chaos of individual interests and the breakdown of social solidarity, resulting in anarchy and nihilism. To avoid this, neoconservatism turns to militarization—as this process allows for the promotion of nationalism and patriotism, it will unify the masses in a fight against an often-created threat, usually foreign, as in the case of the U.S. uniting its citizens against external 'terrorists'. Neoconservatives also turn to religion as a moral glue while legitimizing the regime. Often, appeals to militarization and religion are used together; for example, calls for recruits to join in the fight against 'terrorists' are also presented as a calling to fight for God against evil (more details in Chapter 12, this volume). As Harvey points out, "[Neoconservatism] in no way departs from the neoliberal agenda of a construction or restoration of a dominant class power. But they seek legitimacy for that power, as well as social control through construction of a climate of consent around a coherent set of moral values" (2005:83–84).

Neoliberal Environmentalism

Following Ramachandra Guha, environmentalism is defined as "a social program, a charter of action which seeks to protect cherished habitats, protest against their degradation, and prescribe less destructive technologies and lifestyles" (2000:3). Environmentalism as we know it today took off under conditions of neoliberal globalization. While the early neoliberal period during the 1980s—under the leadership of Thatcher and Reagan—paid little heed to environmental movements, environmental concerns increasingly took on importance in the main agendas of international negotiations and agreements from the 1990s. For Noel Castree, "free-market environmentalism" (2009:186) guides governments' approach in dealing with environmental concerns under conditions of neoliberal globalization.

Communities around the world are increasingly aware of environmental challenges being the main threat to humanity going into the twenty-first century. Technological progress, especially the development of the Internet, has led to the increase in environmental consciousness as it has provided the means of spreading the message of ecological interdependence across boundaries. Access to information, including expert views on climate change, the loss of biodiversity, and instant updates through social-media platforms (e.g., Facebook and Twitter) on the impact of natural disasters, such as the 2004 and 2011 tsunamis in Asia, have elevated the environmental insecurities of the global community. Environmental social movements have used the Internet (Chapter 10 as a case study, this volume) to raise awareness of the urgency of such issues and to mobilize environmental groups from various societies toward a common cause through direct political pressure on both state actors and private enterprises. The 'world-risk society' (Chapter 4, this volume) that Ulrich Beck talks about is now a shared experience of all human societies. "The threat posed to environmental and cultural continuity by the innovations and resource reallocations of the market economy has led to organizations dedicated to environmental protection and historical preservation" (Stanfield and Carroll 2009:10). Tammy L. Lewis (2009:250) observes the positive impact of globalization on the environment, pointing to the 'greening' of most organizations, including states, international NGOs, intergovernmental organizations, and IFIs. Globalization has produced more environmental legislation, both locally and internationally. Concomitantly, there has been much growth of national environmental ministries, international environmental NGOs, and UN focus on environmental issues. Lewis also argues that 'local' environmental groups have benefited through gaining "support from global environmental actors to win locally" (2009:251). In short, environmentalism has positively benefited under the conditions of neoliberal globalization, with increased awareness of, and action on, the environmental challenges of the twenty-first century.

However, environmentalism under conditions of neoliberal globalization may have also produced 'neoliberal environmentalism', which is paradoxically impeding efforts at bringing about more radical but necessary structural changes to our economic and political structures, over and above the superficial lifestyle changes advocated by business actors who encourage 'green consumerism'. The emergence of 'green consumerism' and 'ecological modernization' is arguably representative of neoliberal views of environmental domination governing the human-nature relationship of modern societies. While such movements advocate for environmental concern and sustainability through technological adaptation, some critics have pointed out that they do not have the same effects as radical structural changes to the global economy and political systems would have, and which are deemed necessary. Critics of 'ecological modernization' have pointed out that the belief in science and technology to provide solutions for the environmental problems created by science and technology itself is "at best accommodationist and at worst a rhetorical ruse to allow the current power structures in society to have their merry way, perhaps with a few minor reforms" (Bell 2009:177). 'Green consumerism' and 'green advertising' have also been criticized for being hypocritical attempts by corporations to encourage consumption and to sell their products by playing on the environmental concerns of consumers. Such corporations as The Body Shop and Ben and Jerry's portray themselves as being concerned about sustainability and 'green' products over simple profit; other companies have emphasized their contributions to environmental causes through corporate donations and incorporation of recycling programs into their operations. Bell points out that such 'green consumerism' is a "new form of sentimental hook" (2009:48) that these major corporations use to increase their products' attractiveness and to legitimize their operations.

Rapid technological advances have been the driving force behind the economic progress brought by the industrial revolutions spreading across the world until today. The pursuit of economic progress and capital accumulation have become the *raison d'être* for most if not all national governments to legitimize their political power and to ensure their participation in the process of globalization. James O'Connor's (1998) discussion of capitalism's 'second contradiction' elucidates the impact of unchecked environmental externalities during the neoliberal era of capitalism, leading to the problems of resource depletion and environmental degradation. The over-exploitation and extraction of natural resources by capitalists, whose self-interests are mainly profit driven, would, over time, result in a crisis when other stakeholders—for whom the natural world is a source of spiritual meaning, aesthetic pleasure, and other non-profit-driven values—retaliate and struggle in a conflict against the capitalist class.

As Bell (2009) has observed, there are ideologies at work that influence our understanding of the value of the environment. For Bell, "ideologies of environmental domination" (2009:137) explain the state of environmental degradation around the world today. The neoliberal ideology skews our perspective of the environment toward an exploitative view and has probably helped legitimize ideologies of environmental domination. Development under conditions of neoliberal globalization appears to be favoring the valuation of nature as a commodity: "Not only does the development paradigm privilege monetary relations and measures, often at the cost of non-monetary resources, but also it is busy encouraging the conversion of resources like water (in bottles), air (tradable pollution permits), survival networks of the poor (micro-credit), and even love (the global care industry) into commodities" (McMichael 2008:2). Nature is viewed in terms of its extrinsic value—that is, the use value it provides for human well-being. The exploitation of nature for natural resources, legitimized through the development and growth imperative, is an outcome of the neoliberal drive for capital accumulation. The neoliberal project forces developing countries to open up their physical environments and natural resources to transnational corporations (TNCs) as part of the conditions for receiving loans from IFIs, such as the IMF, and also for practical economic reasons (i.e., the foreign investment would at least solve the short-term urgency of alleviating severe hunger and other poverty-related needs). The unregulated exploitation of these resources by TNCs exacerbates for a long term the degradation process and intensifies environmental problems, including deforestation, pollution, and loss of biodiversity.

The neoliberalization of the human-nature relationship results in a mentality of plundering, as argued by Claudia von Werlhof (2008):

Social, cultural, traditional and ecological considerations are aban-
doned and give way to a mentality of plundering. All global resources
that we still have—natural resources, forests, water, genetic pools—
have turned into objects of "utilization". Rapid ecological destruction
through depletion is the consequence. . . . Climate, animal, plants,
human and general ecological rights are worth nothing compared to
the interests of the corporations—no matter that the rain forest is no
renewable resource and that the entire earth's ecosystem depends on it.
If greed—and the rationalism with which it is economically enforced—
really was an inherent anthropological trait, we would have never even
reached this day.

Despite the talk of crisis on the backdrop of the 2008 financial meltdown,
the international community appears to ironically continue to place its faith
in the market principle in dealing with environmental issues, such as climate
change, specifically through the push for international pollution-trading
schemes. While neoliberalism has produced increased environmental degradation, the heightened environmental awareness and growing environmental movements are also turning to neoliberal principles to regulate the
human-nature interaction in the hope that market principles will encourage green sustainability and promote the use of energy-efficient technology.
Apart from the 'market-centric' characteristic of such developments, what
makes them recognizable as neoliberal adaptations is that these schemes
benefit the interests of a few economic elites. For instance, the developed
countries, having had their industrialization programs come to maturity
before the imposition of such regulations, have an advantage over the developing countries, which will now have to contend with the new regulations
and may have to trade their emissions permits for short-term financial
loans or credits. In short, the emergence of 'free-market environmentalism'
demonstrates the resilience of neoliberalism and neoliberal capitalism; in
the face of crises, neoliberalism continues to adapt itself and still works
to preserve the class power of a few economic elites. The evidence of such
resilience as shown in the face of environmental challenges puts to rest the
claims of such scholars as Jamie Peck, Nik Theodore, and Neil Brenner that
the "free-market project is on the ropes" (2009:94). Instead, environmentalism—which perhaps started as a critique of economic globalization—is
now, ironically, increasingly neoliberalized.

THE END OF THE NEOLIBERAL PROJECT?

While neoliberalism may be undergoing a crippling crisis since the 2008
financial meltdown, this crisis may not necessarily bring about radical
changes to the social order. Some scholars (see for example Peck, Theodore, and Brenner 2009; Wallerstein 2008) have argued that the era of

neoliberalism has come to an end. According to this camp of thought, it is yet uncertain what will replace neoliberalism. The suggestions of these scholars point to the internal contradictions of neoliberal globalization. However, the crisis facing neoliberalism would not necessarily result in its complete destruction. As Castree notes, "A social order does not crumble overnight—unless there's a revolution led by well-organized dissidents, preferably with popular support. . . . Even when 'crisis talk' becomes mainstream, it [is] as likely to result in the application of palliatives rather than root-and-branch reform" (2009:200). A new form of capitalism may emerge, with hopes of a radical overhaul of capitalism remaining nothing but naive optimism. Just as capitalism is deeply rooted in our modern times, it appears that neoliberalism is also a deeply rooted paradigm that will continue to influence the modes of governance and economic policies—albeit under an increasingly state-regulated framework.

Part II
Case Studies

6 Development Dynamics in the Global South

From Colonization to Globalization

DEVELOPMENT: FROM COLONIZATION TO GLOBALIZATION

During the era of colonization, development was understood as having colonies and the organizing of European societies, labor, and markets by disorganizing the non-European colonies. European civilization was to develop by extracting and exploiting human (e.g., slavery, forced-labor) and natural resources in the occupied colonies (McMichael 2008). The 'problems' of the colonies were addressed through methods of extermination, suppression, and containment. Colonial masters took on the burden of spreading their 'superior' civilization all over the globe, a responsibility known as the 'white man's burden' (Hoogvelt 2001; McMichael 2008). Philip McMichael further elaborates:

> Development thus became an extension of modern social engineering to the colonies as they were incorporated into the European orbit. Subject populations were exposed to variety of new disciplines, including forced labor schemes, schooling, and segregation in native quarters. Forms of colonial subordination differed across time and space, but overriding objective was either to adapt or marginalize colonial subjects to the European presence. In other words, *development was a power relationship.* (2008:26; emphasis original)

The notion of development during the colonial era had debilitating effects on the colonized subjects, such as the creation of a huge resource gap between the colonized and the colonizers, the dismantling of the political and social structures of the colonized territories, and a cultural genocide or marginalization of the indigenous populations. The extraction of labor, cultural treasures, and resources in turn enriched the colonial powers, their private interests, and public museums. Colonizers used different ideologies in justifying colonial rule, such as racism and modernity. These subsequently led to the creation of 'colonial subjectivities', with diverse responses ranging from submission and an internalization of inferiority to a variety of forms of resistance—from everyday manifestations to sporadic uprisings to mass political mobilization (McMichael 2008).

After the end of World War II, a new phase and meaning of development emerged. To legitimize their political authority, the newly independent nation-states adopted Western notions of development, which was then heralded in the form of 'modernization'. Because of the long period of subjugation, dismantled political and social fabrics, and an absence of indigenous social principles to organize their societies, the nation-states in the Global South had little or no option other than to accept the Western model. Development now became a globally focused national enterprise. Newly independent states in the postcolonial world had to operate in an international framework that was not of their making; but dependence on that framework became necessary for their governments' political legitimacy. In the first place, their newly independent states were materially impoverished and required economic stimulation. Second, the acceptable model of economic stimulation was the European model of development. Third, the source of stimulation was European economic aid. In short, the framework within which political independence was realized was that of the European conception of development. The adoption of the European model across the former colonial world in the post–World War II era underpinned what we call the 'development project' (McMichael 2008).

The pursuit of economic growth by newly independent countries across the globe required international support. Foreign aid, technology transfer, exchange-rate stability, and robust international trade were all deemed necessary to sustain national development policies. The dominant roles were played by different international agencies and organizations, such as the United Nations, the World Bank, and the International Monetary Fund (IMF). The U.S. spearheaded two initiatives to reconstruct the world economy: the Marshall Plan and the Bretton Woods program. The Marshall Plan was a vast, bilateral transfer of billions of dollars to the European states and Japan, serving U.S. geopolitical goals in the Cold War. The Bretton Woods system managed an international exchange between the First and Third Worlds that resembled the colonial division of labor. The patterns of development assistance contradicted the universalism of the development project, as U.S. aid programs to some countries were oriented toward their function as military outposts in securing the perimeters of the so-called Free World and in preventing a 'domino effect' of Third World realignments toward the Soviet bloc. For the U.S. and its First World allies, then, the development project was more than a transmission belt for Western technology and economic institutions to the Third World. So long as the Third World, a vital source for strategic raw materials and minerals, was under threat from an alternative political-economic vision, such as socialism, the survival of the First World was at stake. Not only that, development and survival of the West was articulated as the under-development of the non-West (McMichael 2008). This view was clearly articulated by Walt Rostow, an influential development economist: "our military security and our way of life as well as the fate of

Western Europe and Japan are at stake in the evolution of the underdeveloped areas" (quoted in McMichael 2008:62).

Until the 1970s, development was understood primarily as a *national process of economic and social transformation*, but by then two trends were becoming clear. First, the First World was not waiting for the Third World to catch up; indeed, the gap between these world regions was expanding. Second, a strategy emerging among some Third World states was to attempt to reduce the gap by aggressively exporting manufactured goods. Accordingly, in the 1970s, 'development' was further redefined by the World Bank as *successful participation in the world market*. The prescription was that Third World countries should now follow the example of the newly industrializing countries, such as Korea and Taiwan, pursuing a strategy of export-oriented industrialization and making a dramatic shift toward specialization within the larger world economy rather than specializing economic activities within their own national frameworks (Hoogvelt 2001; McMichael 2008).

The 1980s' debt crisis consolidated two distinct trends that had been emerging in the 1970s: (a) the unfolding of the Third World as a collective entity, as economic growth rates diverged among states; and (b) global managerialism, in which the world economy was managed through coordinated, rules-based procedures—the debt regime. The debt regime, which ultimately led to neoliberal globalization, provided further patterns of meaning to 'development'. The rise of the global banking system, matched by international financial liberalization, laid the foundation of what is now termed 'globalization'. Because of the sheer influence of the U.S. economy and the centrality of the U.S. dollar in the money markets, the global economy became U.S.-centric. Global managerialism, for its part, is the reformulation of economic policy making according to global rather than national considerations. Under the conditions of the debt regime, the multilateral institutions compelled states to adopt policies privileging global over national economic relationships. The states had no choice but to collaborate and surrendered their powers to manage their own economies. Sales of public enterprises and reductions of social subsidies effectively remade Third World states and restructured their societies, shifting economic burdens onto the lower classes, especially women in these lower classes. A considerable extent of states' autonomy and sovereignty was lost to the global managers (the IMF, the World Bank, the World Trade Organization [WTO], the General Agreement on Tariffs and Trade [GATT], and the U.S. administration). A disconnect arose between the governments and their publics as the governments had to give priority to the global market over their people; and their publics, largely uninformed about the inherent dynamics of globalization and development, increasingly become frustrated with their governments. This led some governments to respond in oppressive ways, a striking consequence of the relationship between Third World oppressive regimes and neoliberal globalization. The globalization project that succeeded the 'development project' builds on the latter as a way of organizing economic growth that corresponds to the growing scale and power of inter-national financial institutions (IFIs) and transnational corporations (TNCs). The increasing volumes of economic exchanges and the greater mobility of money and firms require forms of regulation beyond the reach of the nation-state. Neoliberal globalization is therefore a form of crisis management stem-ming from the demise of development (McMichael 2008).

DOMINANCE OF NEOLIBERAL GLOBALIZATION

Neoliberal globalization involves the liberalization of markets and the rapid expansion of trade and capital flows. Economic growth is driven by technological progress. However, it is also a highly uneven process; there is an unequal distribution of the benefits of globalization between and within countries, creating distinct groups of winners and losers. As Ziya Öniş postulates, "[T]he paradox of neoliberal globalization is that it unifies and integrates while it fragments and marginalizes" (2000:284). Neolib-eral globalization processes dislocate individuals from social relations and uproot them from their communities. Yet they also strengthen the develop-ment of civil societies around the world and lead to a proliferation of trans-national non-governmental organizations (NGOs). Some of these groups promote democracy and demand a more equitable distribution of resources and opportunities: "Neoliberal globalization is an inherently inegalitarian process that undermines the redistributive capacities of the state, but para-doxically tends to promote democracy" (Öniş 2000:305).

Inequality is structured into the neoliberalization process, as David Har-vey (2005) has argued through examining the neoliberal project in Chile, alleged to be an experiment supported by the upper classes in the U.S. who were looking for a viable solution to their gradual loss of class power and dominance of economic wealth. This neoliberal project proved to be a res-toration of class power, with a large proportion of the revived capital accu-mulation being redistributed back to the foreign investors, ruling elites, and upper classes. In other words, the neoliberal project has increased the income gap: the rich become increasingly and ludicrously richer at the expense of ordinary workers.

However, it should be noted that in discussing the concept of 'class', we are dealing with an extremely problematic term. What do we exactly mean by 'class' here? "Class is not a stable social configuration" (Harvey 2005:31). Class, in the Marxist tradition, is defined in relation to the own-ership of means of production. But the neoliberal project aptly calls for a new definition of this term. Max Weber has also discussed 'status groups' to replace the term 'class' so as to capture, perhaps more correctly, the com-plex hierarchies and power relations in society. An upper class, redefined under the neoliberal project, may include managers, CEOs, and successful entrepreneurs. These new groups of people are additions to the 'traditional' strata of upper classes, some of whom may increasingly lose power in the new configurations brought about by neoliberal policies. Harvey sums up aptly: "While neoliberalization may have been about the restoration of class power, it has not necessarily meant the restoration of economic power to the same people" (2005:31).

Neoliberalization produces a pool of 'disposable labor'. Sweatshop conditions are found in many poorer countries with a cheap and docile supply of labor. The workers are subjected to harsh and demeaning conditions, with low pay (sometimes no pay), exposure to health risks, long hours, and abuse (sometimes sexually) by managers. Women are subjected to some of the harshest conditions and abuse, as Harvey argues: "Accumulation by dispossession typically undermines whatever powers women may have had within household production/marketing systems and within traditional social structures and relocates everything in male-dominated commodity and credit markets" (2005:170). The process of dispossessing labor power and social protection is further exacerbated by the neoliberal state's policies of privatizing or cutting expenditures on social-welfare services, such that these services become available only to those who can afford them.

While neoliberalism relies on innovation from entrepreneurs, it does not treat ordinary wage laborers with equal respect. Given its hostility to all forms of social solidarity, it seeks to destroy or to diminish the power of labor unions. The source of capital accumulation, labor, is increasingly alienated. While neoliberal states strengthen the social solidarity of business interests and lobby groups, they weaken the solidarity of ordinary workers. Furthermore, the accumulation of wealth is at the expense of depleting the most important source of wealth mankind has—i.e., the environment. Environmental degradation has greatly soared since the 1970s. Global environmental issues, such as the depletion of natural resources, pollution, and global warming, that are increasingly threatening the long-term sustainability of humanity coincided with the administrations of neoliberal leaders, such as Ronald Reagan, Margaret Thatcher, and, in more recent times, George W. Bush and even Barack Obama. China, another rising global economic powerhouse, has seen its contributions of carbon emissions and energy consumption rise exponentially over the last few decades. Thatcher's administration was arguably more active than the Reagan or Bush administration in promoting environmental causes through negotiating for the Montreal Protocol, but her environmental policies may not have been entirely disinterested. Through advocating for environmental causes, she indirectly also legitimized the closure of coal mines and the breaking up of miners' unions. Growth, in the cases of India and China, has often been accompanied by increased environmental degradation. In opening up their economies to foreign investment as one of the conditions to receiving international aid and loans from IFIs, such as the World Bank and the IMF, developing countries have to allow TNCs from the developed countries access to their natural resources. Often, these foreign corporations will exploit the resources unsustainably, destroying the natural habitats and ecosystems and taking away land from the local populations, who traditionally depend on the land and its resources for subsistence. The local population usually does not have the political or economic means to resist these foreign influences, which are often supported by national governments. The accumulation of wealth is achieved through dispossessing the masses of their common asset, the natural environment and its resources.

With increasing inequality, there emerges a growing tension between winners and losers. Consequently, the underprivileged in society increasingly demand more welfare policies, and ruling parties have to give in or compromise in order to preserve their political legitimacy through securing electoral votes (Öniş 2000). Andrew Gamble (2001) argues that from the 1990s, the revival of the U.S. economy served to strengthen the neoliberal message and aided its spread to other national economies around the world. According to him, "neoliberalism became assimilated within globalization and the policies of international agencies such as the IMF and the World Bank in pushing neoliberal agendas" (2001:133). What could be identified as neoliberal globalization is a historically contingent process where economies around the world increasingly adopt neoliberal ideas and beliefs, culminating in the emergence of an integrated global market economy.

Neoliberal globalization constitutes to be the dominant trend in the world economy at the present juncture. It is driven by a widespread push toward trade and capital account liberalization, the increasing internationalization of corporate production and distribution strategies, and an intensification of technological change that is rapidly dismantling barriers to the international tradability of goods and services and extraordinary mobility of capital (Öniş and Aysan 2000). Others (such as Castree 2009; Harvey 2005; McMichael 2008) have observed that the neoliberal era emerged from the financial crisis of the 1970s and is closely related to the economic globalization processes of the 1980s.

The 'neoliberal era' has been marked not only by economic 'globalization' but also 'the financialization of everything', backed by powerful ruling parties that captured the state apparatus at the end of the postwar boom (Castree 2009; Harvey 2005). Neoliberal globalization could be simply understood as the spread of neoliberalism and its ideals through globalization processes around the world. In this context, neoliberalism is also an economic project inasmuch as it is a political project that has involved the imposition of Western development models upon Third World countries since the late 1970s. The influence of IFIs, such as the IMF and the World Bank, plays a central role in the promulgation of neoliberal economic policies. Many developing countries, in desperate need of loans and debt-restructuring schemes, turn to the IMF and the World Bank. Among the instruments of neoliberal globalization are the Structural Adjustment Programs (SAPs) offered by the IFIs, making it mandatory for the governments to adopt neoliberal reforms in exchange for the loans. The national governments are generally given a ten-point program, commonly known as the Washington Consensus, involving policies centered around the key principles of deregulation, privatization, and liberalization (of trade and industry). I now turn to the spread of neoliberalism to other parts of the world, examining in brief the examples of Asia and Latin America, two developing regions where neoliberalization was imported through SAPs.

NEOLIBERAL GLOBALIZATION IN ASIA

The central tenet of neoliberal thought—that of the 'free-market' principle under conditions of globalization—was adopted in Asia, where it had to contend with strong traditions of state interventionism and economic centralism. As Manfred B. Steger and Ravi K. Roy observe, "[P]olitical leaders such as Prime Ministers Ryutaro Hashimoto and Junichiro Koizumi of Japan, Chinese Presidents Jiang Zemin and Hu Jintao, and Indian Prime Minister Manmohan Singh have embraced certain aspects of neoliberalism in an effort to enhance the economic performance of their respective countries" (2010:78). The spread of neoliberal globalization to Asia is far from uniform; various Asian governments adopted neoliberal reforms to varying degrees of success in attaining high growth rates. High levels of state intervention in the economy and close private-public sector cooperation also remained a consistent hallmark of Asian development.

In Japan, neoliberal reforms were met with resistance from the traditional elites, many of whom were stakeholders of the large national firms, unwilling to take huge risks in privatizing publicly owned assets. While Prime Minister Junichiro Koizumi's attempted neoliberal reforms (called *kozo kaikaku*) and their success level were not of the same scale as those effected by Tony Blair in Great Britain and Bill Clinton in the U.S., "the impact of his neoliberal reforms on Japan's economy is evident in its global integration . . . introducing new market-based approaches and practices, thus altering Japan's traditional state-managed model" (Steger and Roy 2010:83). Harvey (2005) describes the neoliberalization of China's economy as 'neoliberalism with Chinese characteristics'. After Mao Zedong, Deng Xiaoping led China on a gradual economic and social transformation from the late 1970s with the adoption of neoliberal principles of a market economy and varying degrees of deregulation, privatization, and liberalization. As Steger and Roy note, "The transformation of China's economic system was a gradual process but the spread of Western neoliberal ideas, particularly among urban elites, occurred much more quickly" (2010:83). The privatization of state-owned enterprises (SOEs) picked up speed in the 1990s and 2000s, with the opening of some SOEs to foreign ownership. This period coincides with the leadership of Presidents Jiang Zemin and Hu Jintao. Jiang adopted neoliberal reforms that manifested a shift toward objectives of economic growth and profit maximization—a break from

Deng, who had proceeded more cautiously. When Hu came to power in 2003, he expanded neoliberal reforms into the areas of science and technology, intellectual-property rights, and trade policy. The Chinese state continues to exert influence and to directly regulate the value of the yuan, refusing to relinquish its control over capital flows. Much to the ire of the U.S. and the European Union (EU), the Chinese state continues to manipulate its exchange rates so as to increase its global-export competitiveness. Neoliberal reforms in China have produced mixed outcomes: wealth accumulation has been accompanied by a widening income gap and increasing social and economic inequalities.

In India, Prime Minister Rajiv Gandhi started mild neoliberal reforms during the 1980s, including easing government restrictions on some industries and liberalizing some export regulations, slowly shedding the economic nationalism of his mother, Prime Minister Indira Gandhi. In the 1990s, Finance Minister Singh was tasked with rebuilding India's hobbling economy. Singh, trained in Economics at Oxford, was tasked with implementing the neoliberal reforms required by the IMF bailout package. Since 1991, under the leadership of Singh, neoliberal reforms have been carried out at a rapid pace. During this period of time, India welcomed foreign investment, liberalized its trade and industry, and privatized key state-run industries (Steger and Roy 2010). India also initiated closer collaboration with the U.S. for economic reasons and as a counterweight to the threat—both political and economic—posed by a rising China. As in the case of neoliberal globalization in China, such reforms in India led to massive economic growth and exchange-rate stability. With them came the cost of a widening income gap and discontent from those left behind.

In sum, the spread of neoliberal globalization to Asia has been remarkable in the last two decades. Neoliberalism had to adapt to existing political and socio-economic systems that vary from country to country; hence, there is no one uniform model of the transformation process different countries have taken. As Jamie Peck, Nik Theodore, and Neil Brenner argue, "Establishing 'market rule' was never a matter of imposing, from above, a singular regulatory template" (2009:107). One common challenge in the experience of neoliberalization across Asia was the resilience of high state-intervention and state-centric models of economic management that are, theoretically, in tension with the neoliberal drive toward deregulation and privatization. Neoliberal policies are blamed for thousands of farmer suicides in India (McMichael 2008).

NEOLIBERAL GLOBALIZATION IN LATIN AMERICA

The spread of neoliberalism in Latin America is often associated with the imposition of the ten-point policy program that is the Washington Consensus. Neoliberal reforms in this region were undertaken after the 'development project' (or developmentalism) of the 1950s and 1960s, which advocated state-directed economic development, centralization, and nationalization of key industries. As Emir Sader observes, Latin America was a "laboratory for neoliberal experiments" (2009:171). Here, I briefly examine the neoliberal projects of Chile and Argentina.

In 1973, a CIA-supported coup resulted in Augusto Pinochet's taking over power in Chile. He began to "impose neoliberal policies at breakneck speed while clamping down on his political opponents" (Steger and Roy 2010:100). This was a period known as the 'Chile Project'—Chile was seen as a testing ground for neoliberal policies. The outcome was a stabilization of Chile's economy; inflation was brought under control, and gross domestic product (GDP) growth increased. However, this was at the cost of rising inequalities and massive human-rights violations under an oppressive and somewhat dictatorial regime.

In Argentina, neoliberal reforms took off under the leadership of Carlos Saul Menem. While he was elected into office based on populist promises of reviving Latin American developmentalism, Menem quickly changed direction once he was in power. He gave in to the demands of the IMF to adopt structural adjustment policies in exchange for much-needed loans and debt-restructuring schemes. State-owned industries were privatized amid more sweeping neoliberal reforms, including "severe cuts to public spending and [liberalization of] capital controls" (Steger and Roy 2010:103), which attracted an increase in foreign investment. While becoming more integrated into the global economy allowed Chile to enjoy high growth rates in the 1990s, opening the domestic market to cheap imports from other countries led to high unemployment as local industries were undermined. Argentina's integration into the global economy also made its economy vulnerable to financial crises happening in other parts of the world, such as the 1997–1998 Asian financial crisis and the 1999 currency crisis in Brazil. Such events weakened the Argentinean economy gradually, and it collapsed in 2002. Peck, Theodore, and Brenner aptly sum up neoliberal globalization in Latin America: "While Latin American experiences can and should spur the postneoliberal imagination, the region's lessons are also sobering ones. Here, audacious forms of neoliberalized accumulation by dispossession inadvertently prepared the ground for widespread social mobilization and radical resistance politics" (2009:111).

The neoliberal globalization project produces two realizations. First, neoliberal globalization across national boundaries has never been one of direct imposition of a singular regulatory template from the West to the East or from developed countries to developing countries; rather, each nation-state adopts neoliberal principles that suit its unique set of social and economic conditions and its existing political and institutional framework. That is why it is more appropriate to speak of strands or varieties of neoliberalism. Second, neoliberal globalization across different countries often produces initial rapid economic growth, but this is also at the expense of a widening income gap and ever-increasing socio-economic inequalities. I now turn my attention to the chief agent of neoliberal globalization, the IFIs.

INTERNATIONAL FINANCIAL INSTITUTIONS AND NEOLIBERAL GLOBALIZATION

IFIs continue to be the key agents in the global expansion of neoliberal thought, policies, and institutions. The GATT, created in 1948, was engineered by the U.S. with the aim of facilitating trade expansion between countries. In the 1980s, at a time of recession and declining industrial leadership, the U.S. initiated the Uruguay Round, with the aim of liberalizing agriculture and services (banking, insurance, telecommunications), sectors in which the North held a competitive advantage. The liberalization movement was supported by an activist lobby of 'free-trader' agro-exporting states (the Cairns Group); TNCs, such as IBM and American Express; and agri-businesses, such as Cargill, Ralston-Purina, General Mills, Continental Grain, RJR Nabisco, and ConAgra, which were looking to reduce trade barriers, domestic price supports, and supply-management policies restricting demand for farm inputs, such as fertilizer and chemicals (McMichael 2008).

The Uruguay Round led to the creation of the WTO on January 1, 1995. As McMichael posits, "[T]he WTO is arguably less about trade rule consistency than about governing member states via liberalization. *Free trade* [italic in original] is a misnomer for the reach of WTO rules. In combination, they challenge national democratic processes, removing decision making to non-transparent tribunals located in Geneva, Switzerland, using "market logic" to override individual government policy where it interferes with "free trade"" (2008:167). The WTO has the power to enforce its rulings on member states. Often, these rulings go beyond issues of 'free trade' to intervene in national governments' jurisdictions over labor, immigration, and environmental legislations and policies. TNCs are key beneficiaries of the WTO, as rulings often require member states to remove trade barriers and to reduce trade tariffs. The WTO expresses the essence of the globalization project, in particular the neoliberal globalization project, in which the principles of 'free trade' and 'free market' are promoted above national governments' social and environmental considerations.

Free Trade Agreements (FTAs) manifest the neoliberal adherence to 'free-market' and 'free-trade' principles under conditions of globalization. FTAs facilitate cross-border flows of capital, labor, technology, and so forth. Regional FTAs have been the trend, with the North American Free Trade Agreement (NAFTA), the EU, and the Asian-Pacific Economic Cooperation (APEC) representing powerful and influential mega-regional FTAs in the global economy. These three mega-regional FTAs produce about two-thirds of world manufacturing output and three-quarters of world exports (McMichael 2008:182).

The World Bank and the IMF are key agents of the neoliberal globalization project. They are leaders among the IFIs, with extensive power and influence over the direction of neoliberal globalization. An important objective of the World Bank and the IMF is to attend to the welfare of the world's poor. Instead of offering direct aid, the World Bank and the IMF offer loans to help poor countries restructure their economies and participate more actively in the global economy. Recipient countries are required to formulate and to implement policies targeted at promoting global trade and foreign investments that often marginalize local priorities, such as food security and long-term environmental sustainability.

To legitimize their operations, IFIs co-opted NGOs into the system to coordinate the provision of social services, while national governments of the poor countries use IFI loans for the construction of infrastructure to attract foreign investment and to improve productivity. Social-welfare provision is often neglected or cut along the way. In short, the IFIs repackage neoliberal policies in "participatory rhetoric" (McMichael 2008:187). The Poverty Reduction Strategy Papers (PRSPs) was another financial mechanism developed to relegitimize the IFIs in light of their original mission: to provide assistance for the poor and vulnerable who may have been left behind in the drive toward economic globalization. PRSPs require governments to liberalize their policies and to privatize state-owned corporations that provide essential services, such as utilities and education. National governments are forced to sell off these public assets to prepare for the implementation of PRSPs. "Within the terms of neoliberalism, since governments are no longer directly responsible for the poor, responsibility falls on the poor themselves. Most PRSPs, despite emphasizing pro-poor growth, exclude policies to redistribute wealth and promote equality" (McMichael 2008:188).

In sum, IFIs have enormous influence over the development of Third World nation-states. In exchange for loan facilities, IFIs require Third World governments to restructure their economies along neoliberal principles. This makes it easier for TNCs to access the Third World's domestic markets and natural resources and ensures that those countries repay their debts and obligations. Meanwhile, current inequalities structuring the world economy are maintained, as national governments are forced to privatize essential public services and to rely on NGOs to provide social-welfare services.

WHITHER DEVELOPMENT?

From this discussion, it appears that development was perhaps a 'master' concept of the social sciences. It is, however, no longer clear whether this continues be the case, for the concept now appears to be in crisis. It has now been repackaged as the 'globalization project', which metaphorically is little more than old wine in a new bottle, raising more questions than it answers. It remains a selective enterprise that favors a fortunate few and marginalizes others. In retrospect, the legacies of the development project are as follows: (a) it represented a fork in the historical road, favoring the Western model over alternative models in the non-Western world; (b) this fork included a strong dose of economistic thinking, which threatens to overpower all other conceptions of social organization; and (c) because of the combined impact of these two forces, the world faces an uncertain future, and the concept of development itself is under considerable questioning (McMichael 2008).

During the era of colonization, development in the metropolis meant the underdevelopment of the colonies. The former was organized by disorganizing the latter. After World War II, when the 'development project' was introduced based on the Western model, the outcome was problematic. It created huge environmental and social costs, and the development was highly selective. There was an inherent power relation in the project of development, empowering few while disempowering the masses. The question arises: does 'development' mean a concomitant 'underdevelopment'? Is there necessarily any exploitative correlation between development in one place and underdevelopment in another? Neoliberal globalization seems to show that the answer is yes.

7 Green Revolution
Transformation, Optimism, and Reality

INTRODUCTION

'The Green Revolution' refers to a dramatic transformation of agriculture that began in 1943. It is associated with technically packaged, bioengineered hybrid seeds that require chemical and mechanical inputs for their creation and use. These seeds were designed to raise the agricultural productivity of such crop species as corn, wheat, and beans. Originally developed by the Rockefeller Foundation of Mexico to feed the rapidly growing population of the country, the package was aimed at developing more varieties of wheat in order meet Mexico's food demand (McMichael 2008). At first, it was extremely effective. In 1943, before this package was introduced, Mexico had to import half its wheat to feed its population. In only twelve years, Mexico became self-sufficient. By 1964, Mexico was even able to export 500,000 tons of wheat (Dewar 2007). As a result of successful and continuing agricultural research and infrastructural development, the associated agricultural transformation has been advancing constantly ever since.

A crucial characterization of the Green Revolution was a transfer of agricultural technologies from 'developed' countries, such as the U.S., to the 'developing' countries of Latin America, the Middle East, and Southeast Asia. These technologies included chemical fertilizers, pesticides, irrigation infrastructure, and new crop varieties developed with modern scientific methods. In the 1960s, the Green Revolution received support from the Ford Foundation in the Philippines, followed by tropical centers in Nigeria and Colombia. The success of the Green Revolution culminated in the formation of the Consultative Group on International Agricultural Research, partnered by the United Nations Development Program and the World Bank, in 1971. The Green Revolution has been the principal median through which the U.S. chemical agriculture model was introduced to less developed countries (LDCs), especially the Third World (McMichael 2008). Promoted by the U.S. land grant university system and capitalism, it instigated significant changes in Third World agricultural practices. Once these new technologies were introduced to the Third World, local farmers rapidly accepted them, and agricultural production increased dramatically. The environmental and social repercussions began to emerge somewhat later.

The Green Revolution boosted global food production. Cereal production in the world tripled within twenty years after the beginning of the Green Revolution. Yields of wheat, rice, and maize also increased during this period (Paddock 1970). Advocates of the Green Revolution claim that without the Revolution, there would have been greater worldwide famine and malnutrition. From their perspective, the increased production fostered by the Green Revolution has fed billions of people and helped avoid world hunger. To support their claim, they point out that today's average person in developing countries consumes about 25 percent more calories per day than before the Green Revolution.

While the Green Revolution modernized agricultural practices, it did not resolve the problem of global famine. It is clear that the Green Revolution has substantially increased the supply of food, but conversely, this boost in crop yields has encouraged further world population growth, which could soon become problematic. In recent years, advancements in grain yields have slowed down considerably, with plant scientists attributing it to the physical limits of the plants' rate of growth. On the other hand, global population growth shows no sign of stopping, which means never-ending increasing demands for higher food productivity. Agricultural economist Lester R. Brown, president of the World Watch Institute, an environmental advocacy group, puts it this way: "The problem is that population growth hasn't stopped, so the Green Revolution has to happen all over again. And that won't be easy" (quoted in Mann 1997:1038).

The Green Revolution also resulted in adverse social consequences. The lowering of food prices brought by the Green Revolution had a negative impact on traditional farmers' income, especially in the Third World. The Revolution turned traditional agriculture, in which inputs are generated on the farm, into modern agriculture, which requires the purchase of manufactured inputs. This has led to the widespread establishment of rural credit institutions. As a result, class disparities have increased considerably, since wealthier farmers had better access to credit and land. Many small farmers have lost their farmland, and many more have gone into debt due to the Revolution (Pray 1981). Additionally, after the arrival of the Green Revolution, a significant decrease in the size of rural populations has been observed. The number of slum-dwellers (in the outskirts of urban cities) increased by 50 percent in the Third World (McMichael 2008).

The Green Revolution has also had terrible effects on the environment. The new high-yielding varieties of hybrid seeds used in the Revolution, called 'miracle seeds', were heavily dependent on chemicals for disease and pest protection. Large doses of fungicides and pesticides, which are highly damaging to the environment, had to be used for the Green Revolution to succeed. Extensive irrigation and fertilization measures became necessary. Furthermore, the high-yielding varieties displaced time-tested agro-ecological methods of crop rotation by promoting industrial farming. The hybrid seeds disrupted the ecological cycle of natural regeneration and renewal, resulting in many long-term ecological problems. The aggregated social and ecological impacts of the Green Revolution have allegedly caused some 100,000 farmer suicides in India alone between 1993 and 2003 (McMichael 2008; Newman 2006).

The Green Revolution has also done devastating damage to economically LDCs. To dependency theorists, this is hardly surprising. According to their theory, resources flow from poor and underdeveloped states to wealthy states. In this manner, rich nations get richer and richer at the expense of poorer ones, which can only survive if they resign themselves to massive debt by incorporating themselves into the world system. The mass production of food brought about by the Green Revolution led the economically less developed nations to import three times as much cereal from the developed countries as before (TSR 2006). Ironically, although the Green Revolution was supposed to promote agricultural self-sufficiency in the Third World, it made these countries increasingly dependent on foreign imports. Furthermore, because implementing new agricultural technologies requires large amounts of chemical fertilizers, machines, and irrigation, the Green Revolution also created new markets for the industrialized countries but further plunged the Third World into debt and greater dependency. Consequently, the Green Revolution has accelerated the pace by which poor states are impoverished and rich ones are enriched. In the following case studies, I examine how the Green Revolution has affected various developing countries. The common theme that emerges throughout is that although the Green Revolution was undertaken with good intentions and some positive effects did emerge, overall the Green Revolution has further worsened global inequalities of social, ecological, and economic power between the First and Third Worlds.

China

Pollution problems in China are serious and becoming more so. As the country industrializes, more and more pollutants are released into the air and water, notably from coal-fired power plants, paper production, and other industrial processes. In a survey of over 10,000 citizens, more than 75 percent of them were concerned about pollution and thought that pollution has accelerated over the past decades (Sun 2009). One study shows that organic matter, acids, alkalis, nitrogen, phosphate, phenols, cyanide, cadmium, mercury, and chromium were found in dangerous levels in bodies of water near drinking-water sources (Wu et al. 1999). Industry is certainly responsible for many of these pollutants, but another significant contributing source is agriculture—specifically, some of the agricultural techniques that have been integral to China's Green Revolution and its participation in global food markets.

In the 1980s, the Chinese government deregulated its agriculture industry, allowing farmers to sell excess grain on the open market. Previously, the Communist government, following the principles of central planning, had set both quotas and prices for grain production and on the whole absorbed any losses that were incurred. The profit that farmers were now able to make from selling their grain provided an incentive for them to embrace Green Revolution technologies, including fertilizers, pesticides, plastic sheeting, and hybrid seeds. Nationally, the area of arable land decreased between 1978 and 1996, primarily due to industrialization and population expansion, but grain output skyrocketed from 200 million tons to 505 million tons. The increase was not restricted only to grain. Food production in China greatly diversified during this time, with a huge expansion in the variety and volume of vegetables produced and an ever-larger growth in meat production. Economically, in the initial phase, these changes were enormously positive for many small farmers in China. Notably, Jiangsu, a province in western China, has witnessed record yields as a result of changes in technology and production techniques. Unlike many other areas in China, the Jiangsu province is not prone to flooding. These favorable conditions have enabled its farmers to accumulate enough capital—undisrupted by flooding problems—to buy fertilizers and hybrid seeds. Families have indicated that they now have enough money for their sons to move away and to establish their own households as opposed to staying in multigenerational family homes, as was usually the practice. However, a 1995 survey shows that these financial gains came at the cost of serious environmental and social problems (Veeck and Shaohua 2000; Wu et al. 1999).

Fertilizer use rose from 26 million tons in 1990 to 33 million in 1994. However, it is estimated that only 30 percent of that increase was used effectively. Usually it was overapplied, causing major runoff pollution that led to eutrophication of water bodies. Algal blooms sometimes became so bad that some drinking-water sources—notably Taihu, the third-largest freshwater lake in the country—had to be shut down temporarily. In addition, research has shown that toxins emitted by the types of algae prevalent in China have been found responsible for increased rates of liver cancer. Pesticide use has also increased dramatically, and little research has been done on what the possible effects might be beyond the incidence of accidental spills. The effects of normal use as well as the possibility of bioaccumulation or the interactions among the slew of chemical compounds involved have not been well studied (Wu et al. 1999).

Another problem present in Jiangsu is decreased soil fertility and increased salinization (Rozelle, Veeck, and Huang 1997). These problems have been caused by numerous factors. Farmers in Jiangsu began to use plastic sheeting to cover their fields between rows of crops, or in the off season, in order to retain moisture and soil fertility and to reduce weed growth. However, when the plastic needs to be retrieved, it is difficult to recover all of it, and it is eventually tilled into the soil. There, it restricts drainage, so the salt dissolved in the irrigation water is deposited into the soil (Veeck and Shaohua 2000). Additionally, although the use of fertilizer is increasing, soil fertility is decreasing. This is the result of soil erosion, the practice of double-cropping—planting the field back to back without a 'rest' period—and the decreased use of natural manure and compost on land for grain production. Manure and compost are valuable resources, and the use of them is now being concentrated where it will have the greatest economic return—vegetable production. This causes grain land to become less and less fertile over time, especially in areas that are double-cropped to increase yields (Veeck and Shaohua 2000). Some use this phenomenon to explain the decrease in the rate of growth of grain production in the late 1990s. Critics argue that while advances in production have prevented a national and global food shortage that many thought was looming, those same advances may also be leading to the environmental conditions that will eventually cause a shortage (Rozelle, Veeck, and Huang 1997). As a staple product, grain is exceedingly important in the global food market, but currently in Jiangsu, as well as other parts of China, the area of arable land is decreasing. This means that production costs are going up for a product that was not very profitable to begin with and that fewer and fewer farmers are planting (Veeck and Shaohua 2000).

Currently, there is little incentive for farmers to practice more environmentally sustainable farming techniques. Most land contracts are short term, leaving farmers with little interest in preventing environmental degradation. According to the study in Jiangsu, many farmers recognize the negative environmental consequences and are interested in organic farming, but consumers are too skeptical to pay higher prices for the food. Also, as tiny players in the vast global market, individual farmers are hard to hold accountable when economic success or failure is on the line. Gregory Veeck and Shaohua Wang (2000) explain that farmers have little power to influence broader and inaccessible policies related to interest rates, prices, land tenure, land use, or environmental protection. Instead, they primarily respond, and quickly, to fresh commercial opportunities and new prices.

What appears clear is that while the Green Revolution and global food markets have brought vast economic success to many small farmers in China, they have also brought challenges, many of them environmental as well as social. The solutions will most likely have to be national or even global, and largely have yet to emerge; but they are immensely important to pursue on behalf of the health and economic security of the people living in China as well as for the security of global food markets.

India

India's Green Revolution began with a national tragedy that began in 1943 and lasted throughout the remainder of British rule in India. The Bengal Famine, which claimed more than four million lives in its first year, was a combination of widespread food shortages and unethical food-hoarding practices used by merchants throughout the country. Matters were worsened by the distraction of World War II. The colonial and local administrations became preoccupied with the war, and addressing the food-supply shortage fell sharply on their list of political priorities. The economy was left relatively unregulated, and markets spiraled out of control. Given public hysteria over food-supply shortages, merchants realized that consumers would be willing to pay outrageous sums of money for even the smallest amounts of food. They began hoarding the small amounts of food that were being produced and sold them off at extremely high prices to those who could afford them. Needless to say, lower-class citizens made up a large portion of the four million people who died during the first year of the Bengal Famine (Ganguly 2006).

Four years later, in 1947, British colonial rule ended. Although the nation's attention focused on its newfound sovereignty, memories of the Bengal Famine remained close. Determined to make sure that nothing like it ever happened again, legislators began formulating policies that led to a period of what is now referred to as India's Green Revolution. Until 1967, agricultural experimentation throughout the country was largely unsuccessful. Food production could not keep up with the rapidly increasing rate of population growth, so starvation deaths were still a pressing issue throughout the country. It was not until 1967 that India's true Green Revolution began. Marked by a trifecta of new agricultural methods, India's Green Revolution was arguably among the most successful in the world. Farmers throughout the country increased their crop yields exponentially using these new methods (Ganguly 2006). So what were they?

The first area of agricultural experimentation was the new technique of double-cropping farmland. This required a change from one crop season per year to two crop seasons per year. There were natural limitations to this change, however; since only one monsoon watered the land each year, an artificial monsoon had to be created to supply the water necessary for a second crop-cultivation season. Dams were created to collect water from the first monsoon so that it could be used to water the lands later in the year. The next experimental agricultural method used during the Green Revolution was the use of genetically engineered super-seeds. First created by Dr. M. P. Singh of the Indian Council for Agricultural Research, these high-yield value seeds (HYV seeds) were engineered to develop larger crops and in greater numbers. The strains of HYV seeds used in India were wheat, rice, millet, and corn. HYV seeds were the most important factor leading to the success of the Green Revolution. The last aspect of the Green Revolution in India was the continued expansion of farming areas throughout the country. Although the country had greatly expanded its cultivated areas since 1947, in order to meet the demands of its growing population, land area under cultivation increased exponentially beginning in 1967 (C. Baker 2009; Ganguly 2006).

From Saby Ganguly's (2006) analysis, there were manifold implications stemming from the Green Revolution in India. Economic benefits included growth in the nation's industrial and manufacturing sectors. To supply the pesticides, fungicides, fertilizers, and HYV seeds that were the foundation of the Green Revolution, those sectors created thousands of new jobs. There was a striking increase in the country's gross domestic product (GDP) from these new markets. The creation of an artificial monsoon through dams and reservoirs also introduced hydro-electric infrastructure around the country that improved the quality of life in India. India's success also caught the eye of other struggling countries, and experienced Green Revolution farmers came to be in demand around the world. Their earnings abroad helped improve India's foreign-exchange earnings and provided new incomes for previously struggling agriculturally based families. Economically, the Green Revolution helped India transform from a struggling and starving Third World nation to a powerful exporter. Politically, it also provided the basis of success for the Indian National Congress and allowed it to become a dominant party in the country.

The positives of India's Green Revolution were certainly impressive; unfortunately, the negatives were more profound. The Green Revolution embodied a seductive appeal for India: new seeds that would triple the annual amount harvested per year, solving the problems of hunger, desperation, and feeding the growing population. However, this Revolution involved the use of dangerous pesticides and fertilizers not widely understood at the time. In 1969 alone, USAID financed $200 million worth of chemical fertilizer on a loan basis for India. We now know that such huge amounts of chemicals would have caused considerable environmental damage. But at that time, global warming and environmental problems that now face our planet were not well understood. Most people only saw the benefits; as William Gaud, an administrator for USAID, said in 1968, "The world is on the brink of an unprecedented opportunity. The critical food problem of the next 20 years can be solved" (Gaud 1968). Today, the people of India are faced with the same problem that the world was faced with half a century ago. With the growing population and anticipated shortages in food production, many people feel that it is necessary to introduce another Green Revolution—or as Peter Rosset (2000) terms it, 'Green Revolution II'. Even though Indian granaries are overflowing now, more than 5,000 children die each day from malnutrition—and this is in a country where the Green Revolution was considered a success. Despite increased agricultural production in India, many remain unable to afford the food they need. Food that is priced beyond the affordable range goes to waste, and many poor people starve. The problem is therefore not simply an issue of productivity, but one of access and income inequality. Economic control and power ensure the ability to afford food and access to it. The Green Revolution provided a convenient avenue for the extension of neoliberal power and control in India, creating a petty bourgeoisie through the corporatization of agriculture. However, it generated a massive 'depeasantization' across the nation.

The Green Revolution has had negative impacts on the environment as well as on the people of India. The most lasting social impact of the Revolution was the emergence of corporate farming, accelerated later by neoliberal globalization. Today, many small farmers struggle to compete with these large corporate farms and are left in extreme poverty. There is a strong correlation between this farming transformation and the thousands of small farmers who commit suicide every year (McMichael 2008). It is also important to note that India continues to fail to completely satisfy the demand for basic sustenance for many among its expansive population. Many areas of the country are still in a famine-like state, and thousands of people die of hunger every year. With regard to the environment, the new techniques used during the Green Revolution are destroying India's land in the long run. With the change in planting patterns (two seasons), land quality has deteriorated greatly. What was once fertile land is now tired and worthless. Furthermore, high levels of chemicals in fertilizers have hardened the ground, and carbon levels within them have decreased to dangerously low levels. There is also a colossal issue with the chemical runoff that has reached important sources of water, such as lakes and rivers. Another key point is the fact that pests have become resistant to many of the pesticides developed during the Green Revolution. Their mutations have made them stronger, and pest infestation around the country is a significant problem. The last major environmental impact is the loss of biodiversity. Chemical fertilizers, pesticides, and insecticides have killed off many species in the Indian ecosystem, including various bird and insect species.

The immediate positive impacts of the Green Revolution in India blinded many officials to its negative long-term impacts. As more and more of these problems surface, it is becoming difficult for scholars to assess India's Green Revolution and to deem it as a complete success. It may have improved agricultural production in the country, but people continue to starve, and the environment has been severely affected.

Jamaica

Jamaica is another country that has been impacted by the Green Revolution. When the Green Revolution's new farming techniques were being transferred around the world to increase agricultural production capabilities, the Jamaican government decided it should adopt them in hopes of stimulating the country's agriculture. This has had lasting effects on both Jamaica's society and economy.

At the time of the Green Revolution, the Jamaican government supported the importation of chemical pesticides and subsidized their use. Since the cost of these chemicals became relatively low compared to the costs of hiring labor to do the job, such as weed removal and insect control, the farmers chose to use these chemicals in their farming. As a result, widespread over-use of pesticides occurred. The use of these pesticides subsequently had adverse consequences on crops and the surrounding environment. Pesticide use produced pesticide resistance, in which many of the pests adapted successfully to withstand the chemicals being used. This resistance resulted in farmers' inability to ward off the intended pests and also produced secondary pests. The secondary pests came during the time when the intended pests were vulnerable to the chemicals being used. After resistance was built, the farmer then had to contend with the adapted original pests as well as these new secondary pests (A. Wood 2011).

The environment in Jamaica also suffered from the adoption of Green Revolution techniques. Pesticides contaminated water supplies, due to chemical runoff from farmers' fields. The inability of local farmers to contain the spread of their chemicals harmed people as well as the surrounding flora. Once the health and environmental risks were established, the Jamaican government took steps to move away from using pesticides and chemicals in the country's agriculture. The government decided to stop subsidizing pesticides and instead tried to encourage organic farming. When this occurred, farmers found themselves in a quandary. Using pesticides, despite the negative effects on the environment, led to higher yields. When the government stopped providing incentives to use pesticides, farmers were forced to go back to natural farming methods. This badly affected the yield of their crops as well as the size, which led to Jamaica's eventual inability to compete credibly in international agricultural commodity markets.

Furthermore, without the larger crop yields, the Jamaican market for agricultural goods diminished. Due to larger countries' greater ability to successfully use Green Revolution techniques as well as to tolerate their consequences, Jamaican goods became inferior to the goods in demand around the world. When the Jamaican economy went into recession during the late 1970s and the 1980s, the local market for Jamaican grown foods was also reduced. The government's decision to impose price ceilings, on advice from the World Bank, made it such that the more expensive locally grown foods could not compete with the cheaper imported food goods from developed nations, such as the U.S. This, perhaps, was the World Bank's intention all along. Thus, the Jamaican farmers were unable to sell their goods locally and globally, leaving them to produce at an almost subsistence level. An exception to this example lies in Jamaica's banana industry, which has a market in Europe due to Jamaica's colonial past.

The results that occurred from the adoption of Green Revolution farming techniques in Jamaica partly reflect the ideas found in the dependency theory. The concept that larger countries profit from the incorporation of smaller countries through globalization is reflected, on a macro-scale, in the effects of the Green Revolution in Jamaica. The integration of pesticides and chemicals was done in the hope of sparking an agricultural revolution in Jamaica in an attempt to replicate the successes of the Green Revolution in larger countries. Once the side effects on humans and the environment were realized, however, the move away from pesticides resulted in Jamaican farmers' being unable to compete globally. With its economy in a recession, Jamaica was forced to take loans from such institutions as the World Bank, which came with the stipulation that the country discontinue its emphasis on national development by opening its doors to cheaper imported goods together with such measures as free trade zones. These stipulations benefited First World nations, especially the U.S., by giving them a market in Jamaica for necessary goods, such as food, their more successful use of Green Revolution techniques having produced an agricultural surplus, the export of which proved very profitable. The loan stipulations also took advantage of a cheap labor force to work in producing manufactured goods in the free trade zones. With Jamaica unable to sustain itself, it became dependent on foreign aid—much to its own disadvantage.

On hindsight, one might also argue that Jamaica would have been better off had it decided not to incorporate pesticides and chemicals into its farming to begin with; however, Jamaica's economic problems did not entirely rest on its agricultural problems. Jamaica's colonial past opened the doors for its exploitation by developed nations. Two observations follow this analysis of Jamaica's experience of the Green Revolution: first, Jamaica would most likely have been better off if it had been able to develop on its own without being pressured to take part in the world economy; and second, the Green Revolution has played a large part in shaping the global economy into what it is today as well as providing Jamaica with the aid it receives.

The Philippines

Another country that has experienced both the benefits and costs of the Green Revolution over the past several decades is the Philippines. The Green Revolution took off in the Philippines starting in 1966 when modern varieties (MVs) of rice were introduced with high-yielding capacities. In that year, the International Rice Research Institute (IRRI), located in the Philippines, released its first MV strain of rice, called IR8. Upon its release, many IR8 seeds were distributed to farmers of the East Laguna Village, which is located near the IRRI. These farmers almost immediately benefited from this new MV technology. Over the next decade, farmers began to see the average rice-paddy yield per hectare per crop season increase to at least double what farmers had never seen before the MVs were introduced. Nearly 100 percent of farmers throughout the Philippines were using the MVs within ten years of its being introduced. Along with the mass diffusion of the MVs came the increased use and application of chemicals and fertilizers. The input of fertilizers increased to more than four times the amount used by farmers prior to the start of the Green Revolution in the Philippines (Hayami and Kikuchi 2000).

The rapid increase in yields of rice during the first decade of the Green Revolution proved greatly beneficial for farmers, because the price of rice remained high during this time period. This was especially the case in the early 1970s, due to the world food crises occurring at the time. During this time, Filipino farmers were also able to obtain new mechanized inputs with relative ease as the government enacted a program called Masagana 99 in 1973, which significantly eased the credit constraints of farmers. This allowed them to purchase modern inputs and other new technologies associated with MVs. Although extremely beneficial for Filipino farmers, it had to be shut down by 1980 because of the massive costs borne by the government. Also, in the 1970s, land reforms began to take place where properties in private ownership were confiscated and redistributed to tenants and workers who did not own any land (Daquila 2005; Hayami and Kikuchi 2000). Tenants and non-landowners were now able to receive part of the economic return generated by the land used for rice farming. Also, agricultural laborers were able to gain from land reform, in addition to farmers' gains, in the form of increased wages (Hayami and Kikuchi 2000). These examples suggest that the first two decades of the Green Revolution in the Philippines could be considered a success in terms of the amount of good it did for farmers and agricultural workers of the time.

However, in the 1980s, the initial gains of the Green Revolution began to diminish in what is known as the 'Lost Decade' in the Philippines. Initially, it looked as though the Philippines would continue to prosper economically throughout the decade due to major improvements in transportation infrastructure, which was thought to increase non-farm employment and the income of Filipino villagers. Also, the national irrigation system for rice-paddy fields had been drastically improved upon, and the expected outcome of this was a sustained increase in productivity levels for rice farming. However, this was not the case at all; these expectations were interrupted by the economic recession brought about by political instability prior to and after the downfall of Filipino President Ferdinand Marcos in 1986. Non-farm employment wound up shrinking during this period, as did the real wage rate for rice growers. Also, the project that was intended to rehabilitate the Filipino irrigation system failed during the 1980s, with interruptions in the project as well as shortages in the supply of water due to construction's hindering farming in rice-paddy fields. Finally, the National Irrigation Administration in the Philippines had a financial crisis during this time that forced it to cut back on operating and maintaining the irrigation system; this crisis was at its worst in the 1990s (Hayami and Kikuchi 2000).

In addition to these problems faced by the Philippines in the 1980s, the increases in rice productivity experienced during the 1960s and 1970s were no longer nearly as high. The increase in rice productivity was decelerating partly due to the fact that the irrigation system in the Philippines was deteriorating, but mainly due to the declining influence of new MV technologies on rice productivity. This meant that the total factor productivity

(TFP), which was the output of rice per unit of input, was declining in the 1980s. Also, there was a drastic decline in the price of rice during this time period, which seriously affected Filipino farmers and agricultural laborers. As a result of these events, by the 1980s, the initially positive effects brought about by the Green Revolution were diminishing. In the 1990s, the Philippines began to see its economy recover, partly because non-farm employment opportunities for Filipino villagers had greatly expanded compared to during the 1970s and 1980s, and many workers were moving into the manufacturing sector (Hayami and Kikuchi 2000). However, during this time period, rice farming continued to suffer due to the failing irrigation systems of the Philippines and budget cuts from the National Irrigation Administration. The negative effects of the Green Revolution are still being felt by the Philippines today.

On balance, the Green Revolution has brought both benefits and costs to the Philippines. One obvious benefit was that the increase in the production of rice helped the country toward attaining agricultural self-sufficiency. Other benefits included more employment opportunities, increased family incomes, and foreign-exchange earnings. In certain cases, only large-scale farmers and landowners benefited from the Green Revolution, because only they had direct access to the basic capital and other resources needed to farm MVs, and they could buy smaller patches of land in order to achieve economies of scale. However, in many other cases, beginning in the 1960s, land reforms and support from the government helped smaller farmers and tenants also benefit from the Green Revolution. These land-tenure and redistribution programs were subsequently halted in 2005 for reasons of inefficiency and inequality, as large tracts of land are owned by a few rich families.

The Green Revolution in the Philippines has created multiple problems, such as a situation in which many small-scale farmers do not have access to the modern inputs needed to produce MVs. Also, the Philippines suffers the usual environmental costs associated with the use of chemicals and pesticides, such as the depletion of nutrients in soil and a reduced number of frog and fish species around rice-paddy fields. Moreover, the costs of the Green Revolution in the Philippines have been very high in terms of the large infrastructure costs of the failed irrigation system and the cost to the government of helping farmers adopt the use of MVs (Daquila 2005; Hayami and Kikuchi 2000). To sum up, it remains unclear whether the benefits of the Green Revolution have outweighed the costs for the Philippines on the whole; but it seems clear that the benefits over time have diminished as the costs have become more and more apparent.

GREEN REVOLUTION AND AFTER

With the Green Revolution, the agricultural systems in the Global South became integrated with global commodity networks, generating complex intersections and sometimes tensions (M. S. Islam 2008). Farmers have become increasingly aware of the changing diets of consumers, especially those from developed countries, and have been compelled to switch from basic grains to the production of high-value foods (HVFs) to meet global market demands. HVFs or agricultural products are defined as agricultural goods with a high economic value per kilogram, per hectare, or per calorie, including fruits, vegetables, meat, eggs, milk, and fish (Gulati et al. 2005). This transformation is sometimes called the 'Silent Revolution'. The global fisheries' experience of this revolution is particularly remarkable.

From the 1960s onward, the global aquaculture sector embraced a shift akin to the Green Revolution known as the 'Blue Revolution'. Similarly, it aimed at increasing global aquatic production considerably in order to stave off widespread hunger in the tropical nations. By 1985, the World Bank, the Asian Development Bank, and a variety of other international aid agencies were providing $200 million a year to aquaculture projects. Mangrove forests in the Philippines, Thailand, Bangladesh, and Ecuador were cleared to make way for shrimp ponds. Carp and tilapia farms were staked out on the flood plains of the Ganges, the Irrawaddy, and the Mekong rivers. As a result, the production of pond-raised fish has boomed (Boychuk 1992; Md Saidul Islam 2013; Public Citizen 2005).

Despite its ostensible aims of fighting hunger in the tropical Third World, the Blue Revolution was also driven and accelerated by neoliberalism to feed, and to profit from, the appetite of the wealthy consumers in the North. Either way, it has come with a price. The current Blue Revolution has been characterized by many writers in disturbing terms: a carving up of agrarian landscapes in the South into large farms in few hands, ecological devastation, displacement of rural subsistence farmers, rural tensions and violence, peasants' movements and resistance, exploitative labor relations, and so forth (see Boyd and Clay 1998; Md Saidul Islam 2013; Shiva 1995, 2000; Stonich and Bailey 2000). In Thailand, as Rick Boychuk (1992) has reported, the poor living in coastal communities actually took up arms to prevent corporations from seizing commonly owned mangrove forests for shrimp ponds. In this context, questions arise whether export-oriented high-value aquacultural and/or agricultural production brings displacement, violence, and food insecurity to producers and local communities; and whether food security for affluent consumers in the Global North through the global food market has to depend upon a foundation of social and ecological devastation.

CONCLUSION

The Green Revolution is, in theory, a good plan to reduce the problem of hunger. The problem, however, is that far too many people who need the available aid do not have the means to obtain it. Such companies as

Monsanto, DuPont, Novartis, and other chemical-cum-bio-technology companies state in their marketing efforts that they can help increase crop production and alleviate starvation. Yet it remains questionable whether the sufficiency of food produced will eventually reach the starving and whether the risks to the environment have been properly addressed (Colaneri 2006). In both emerging global superpowers, such as China and India, and relatively small global actors, such as Jamaica and the Philippines, Green Revolution technologies and practices have left a palpable mark. A remarkably consistent pattern has emerged in all these nations, despite their vastly different economic, social, and cultural contexts. That pattern is one of initial socio-economic benefit due to modernized Green Revolution technology and techniques, followed conversely by periods of decreased social and economic benefit, if not outright detriment. The reasons for this are varied; pest adaptation, environmental degradation at the hands of pesticides and chemical fertilizers, and economic overdependence all played key parts in each nation's diminishing Green Revolution returns.

The fundamental concepts and theories that tie all these negative effects together are the dependency approach and, to be more specific, the theory of the treadmill of production. Both ideas deal with the unequal power relations that exist among actors in the global community. The unequal global-power distributions that exist today can be directly traced back to capitalist ideologies that rule over modern markets. It is such philosophies of profit seeking over all else that saddle the Green Revolution with its shortcomings. Although well intentioned, the Green Revolution ultimately could not escape the global markets' need for profit and consequently became just another capitalist tool. Consequently, positive effects of the Revolution—such as increased food production and the independence of local farmers—have become minimized, while negative effects of the Revolution—such as land exhaustion, environmental degradation, local farmer displacement, and economic overdependence—have been maximized. We can observe very similar patterns in the Blue Revolution. As long as profit remains the chief concern of all global markets, advances that benefit all tiers of society and the environment will continue to be incredibly difficult, if not impossible, to effectively enact.

8 Food and Power
The Mirage of the Food-Aid Regime

THE FOOD-AID REGIME IN CONTEXT

Throughout the 'Development Project' in the postwar era and into the era of the 'Globalization Project', food has been an important political and economic tool for the world's advanced countries and global managers. Together, these global forces combined to use food supply to pursue geopolitical strategies and goals. Eventually, this program was termed the 'food-aid regime' and defined as "a substantial transfer of agricultural resources to Third World urban-industrial sectors" (McMichael 2008:70). This definition implies that while the context of the international food-aid regime may be presently characterized by political opportunism and strategy, it did not necessarily begin in this manner. To understand the present context of the food-aid regime within globalization, it is important to grasp its previous historical contexts and uses.

The food-aid regime originally derived from a regime defined as the international 'food order'. Harriet Friedmann describes it as "a stable set of complementary state policies whose implicit coordination creates specific prices relative to other prices, a specific pattern of specialization, and resulting patterns of consumption and trade" (1982:248). The international food order was founded largely as an economic institution. It began in the 1870s, when trade was relatively free and conducted through the gold standard. Fertile soil and efficient farm structures (family farms) caused the price of food to fall (Friedmann 1982). As the price of food dropped, "imports [of wheat] to Europe sextupled between 1870 and 1929" (Friedmann 1982:257). In response to increasing imports to Europe, such countries as Australia, Argentina, Canada, and the U.S. specialized in the production of wheat. Output tripled, and these countries became major traders in the international food order. These states and others within the order were positioned according to "patterns of wheat movement," marginalizing certain other wheat exporters, such as Russia, Austria-Hungary, India, and Romania (Friedmann 1982:255).

The establishment of the food-aid regime resulted from political pressures on the international food order at the end of World War II and during the Cold War. Restrictions on global trade, the task of restoring agriculture in Europe, and the agricultural surpluses accumulated by the U.S. farm-subsidy program of the 1930s revealed the need for a system designed to deal with these global problems simultaneously. The American Marshall Plan initiated just such a system. It allocated a significant amount of support to the restoration of agriculture in such places as Europe. Evidence also exists of food's taking on a political context, in addition to an economic one, in the main points of the Marshall Plan. These points included (a) the short- and long-term expansion of trade, (b) the restructuring of Europe and Japan with the purpose of containing socialist movements, and (c) food aid's being sent to Europe (Friedmann 1982, 1990; McMichael 2008).

Through the Marshall Plan, aid worth $13.5 billion was sent to Europe between 1948 and 1952. Twenty-nine percent of that aid consisted of food, feed, and fertilizers (Friedmann 1982). Such massive volumes of aid were an important step in the 'politicization of food' and in the creation of a food-aid program in the U.S. The bipolar structure of the postwar world allowed the U.S., as one of the two major world powers, to get rid of its agricultural surpluses for politically strategic outcomes, which also made economic sense. The U.S. did so by sending the surplus to countries in need. Therefore, food aid was, according to Friedmann, "the combined solution to American surpluses and to further integrating Third World agrarian societies into the capitalist sphere of the world economy" (1990:16). For example, in the postwar era, some of the initial purposes of food aid were providing immediate war relief, implementing the Marshall Plan, the Korean War, and sending food aid to underdeveloped countries. These political uses for U.S. agricultural surpluses proved enormously helpful to American interests and were later built into the food-aid regime (Friedmann 1982). However, the uses of food aid as defined in the Marshall Plan eventually became unsustainable.

Food aid became a fully realized and arguably political regime for the first time in 1954 with the passage of Public Law 480 (PL-480; Friedmann 1982), which elevated food aid from policy to legislation. PL-480's sole purpose was to help the U.S. remove excess farm surpluses, as it was 'suffering' from 'epidemics of overproduction' (McMichael 2008). The law contained three components or 'titles'. Title I called for ridding the U.S. of agricultural surplus through "commercial sales on concessionary terms— discounted prices in local currency"; Title II used "famine relief" to support suffering nations, and Title III provided "food bartered for strategic raw materials." PL-480 was aimed "[at increasing] the consumption of U.S. agricultural commodities in foreign countries, to improve the foreign relations of the U.S., and for other purposes" (McMichael 2008:70). This law demonstrates the simultaneous use of political and economic aid. Between 1954 and 1977, 70 percent of global food aid came from Title I sales. During the mid-1960s, 25 percent of global wheat exports came from food aid. As a result of an increase in global trade, food aid began to determine the price of food trade (McMichael 2008), as constant agricultural surpluses depreciated the price of food (Friedmann 1982).

The new political and economic implications of food aid are important to consider when analyzing food aid in the context of Third World countries in the postwar era. The discounted prices in local currency provided by Title I of PL-480 meant that countries could buy cheap food for their populations without depleting their foreign currency. The distribution of cheap food to Third World governments, which included no plans for improving agriculture in the recipient countries (Friedmann 1982), created food dependency in recipient nations (Friedmann 1990; McMichael 2008). While U.S. food aid helped build European self-sufficiency in wheat, its effect in the Third World during the next two decades was just the opposite: "It undermined local agriculture, creating new proletarians dependent on commercial food, and new nations dependent on imports" (Friedmann 2009:17).

It is interesting to note that there have been constant changes in the goals and the language of PL-480 over the twenty-five years following its inception (Schubert 1981) and even into the current period (Uvin 1992). One of the turning points in PL-480 came in 1962, when the law appropriated money toward non-profit school-lunch programs. Furthermore, in 1966 policymakers amended PL-480 by changing its name from the 'Agricultural Trade Development and Assistance Act of 1954' to 'Food for Peace'. Its main goal revolved around the prevention of hunger and malnutrition. Even into the 1970s, when both the amount of food and economic aid to Third World countries declined, the Food for Peace program maintained its goals (Schubert 1981). Other scholars further argue that when the perspective of food aid shifts to include other donor countries alongside the U.S., food aid is motivated by not only political but also economic self-interests. This claim is supported by a change to Title III of PL-480 in 1990, which distributed food aid to "low income, food-deficient countries," with the goal of increasing food security or allowing "access by all people to sufficient food and nutrition for a healthy and productive life" (Uvin 1992:294). For the majority of countries that participate in the food-aid regime, only 5 to 10 percent of their food production is given in aid. An increasing amount of food aid (more than 10 percent in 1992) is triangular, meaning that the donor buys food from third countries, often other developing nations, or from a different region of the receiving country and then transports that food to the intended recipients (Uvin 1992). This costly method of food distribution proves that food aid is more than just a political and economic tool.

Arguments against the political and economic focus of food aid raise important questions concerning the present context and use of food aid both by the U.S. and the international institutions. Has a change in the language and ideology of food aid led to a change in its practices? Who controls food aid in recipient countries: the recipient governments, the U.S., or international institutions? How have food-aid practices affected recipient countries? Does food aid serve the needs of the impoverished? If not, how can the practices be altered in order to reflect new goals? These questions are examined in this chapter through different ideological lenses that define food aid. Case studies of India and Central America follow that analyze food aid in practice. Finally, this chapter provides an examination and critique of the evolution of food aid in the modern context, concluding with some policy proposals.

MOTIVES OF FOOD AID

While it is easy to understand the background and overall goals of the food-aid regime on a large scale—aiding countries to better the welfare of human populations—it is worth questioning why such apparent generosity is a policy of self-interested governments and societies. Three main aspects help explain why some proponents of the food-aid regime see it as integral to a promising future. However, as the case studies show later in the chapter, food aid will only provide a promising future if nations prioritize the well-being of their citizens over international prestige. The three structured motives of the food-aid regime have consisted of humanitarian, economic, and ideological stances, all of which ideally work together toward ending starvation. Of course, several other motives exist to explain food assistance since the Second World Food Summit in 1966, but the three main purposes have produced the most prominent and recordable results in the last fifty years.

By definition, humanitarianism "is an active belief in the value of human life (humanism), whereby humans practice benevolent treatment and provide assistance to other humans, in order to better humanity for both moral and logical reasons" (Barrett and Maxwell 2005:4). The humanitarian motive has been the most promising catalyst in the evolution of food aid. From a liberal perspective, human nature makes people help others in need, and this allows the food-aid regime to thrive. Although legally implemented in 1966 with the inclusion of PL-480, the food-aid regime would not have had any success if it were not for the humanitarian efforts of people around the globe. Humanitarian methods are crucial for performance in situations where famine or natural disasters require emergency food aid. Food relief relies on volunteer work from individuals and organizations, demanding countless hours and sacrifice to develop the food-aid regime into a functioning reality.

Although the noble stance of the humanitarian food-aid regime allows for prosperity, heavy economic incentives also induce countries to participate for their self-interests. Beginning as a surplus-disposal method for developed countries, food aid has quickly shifted to accompany development programs to kick-start recipient economies and to bolster donor economies. Thus, some supporters believe that the food-aid regime has become a critical tool for economic aid and promotes market revival for agricultural economies. They argue that aid continuously works to rescue struggling nations from hunger, continuing a tradition that they believe has been successful in developing nations in South America, Africa, and Asia. Nonetheless, the ideals and successes of PL-480 have been much overhyped. Christopher B. Barrett and Daniel G. Maxwell (2005) relate the optimistic viewpoint that the food-aid regime does not always hurt the recipient country's producer incentives, nor does it create dependency from donor to beneficiary. The economic motive for the donor country's participation and inclusion lies in the fact that its results are beneficial to both the receiver and donor, be it a national front, developed or developing country, or a non-governmental organization (NGO).

When Food for Peace emerged in the 1960s, it caused food aid to gain more ideological perspective. The hope that such a program, to which the U.S. had committed itself by law, could promote peace was enough to motivate people to take action. This first program to institutionalize international food aid was followed by the Second World Food Summit in 1966, at which world leaders expressed a desire for an ideological future without drastic societal changes. The ideological and humanitarian stances go hand in hand, because they both follow the path of modernization to achieve desired socio-economic outcomes (Barrett and Maxwell 2005). Walt Rostow posits that economic growth goes through five stages of development from traditional society to age of mass consumption; the final stage identified by Rostow is characteristic of the First World development status, while the former is suspiciously similar to the economic realities of Third World development. Food for Peace is a Western construction that follows Rostow's model of development; it reinforces the ideology that developing nations must follow in the footsteps of First World development. Food aid thus functions as a catalyst for modernization in the Third World.

The humanitarian, economic, and ideological motives that have allowed the food-aid regime to grow in the last half-century also possess the potential to allow it to flourish within a more sustainable context if the aid regime's global managers utilize them responsibly. The ideological motive best encompasses its ideal form: the food-aid regime is established in order to modernize the world toward an alleviation of global inequalities, providing food security that helps less-fortunate societies and economies run more smoothly. These utopian motives, however, often fail to be realized. To explain it better, in the sections below, I contrast the food-aid regimes of the 1950s and 1960s and their modern forms in India and Central America and examine how and to what extent the aforementioned ideological motives have been realized.

What is apparent in the earlier discussion is that the food-aid regime profoundly increased the consumption of U.S. agricultural commodities in foreign countries and contributed to an advent of "underdevelopment and proletarianization" (Friedmann 1990:19). It generated an 'international food regime' that subsequently changed the dietary consumption patterns of the Third World population. This new revolution of capitalism was exemplified through the U.S. government's strategy of 'green power', which implemented aggressive agro-exporting to consolidate America's role as the 'breadbasket' of the world (McMichael 2008). International dietary consumption patterns shifted gradually, as many consumers moved up the food pyramid to consume more animal protein (such as beef, poultry, and pork). "American fast-food suppliers . . . mushroomed all over the world. Consumption of these new diets, resulting from the capitalist expansion, became identified with the 'American way of life', or 'modernization', that captured the imagination of millions of people, and went on unchallenged" (M. S. Islam 2005:4).

CASE STUDY: FOOD AID AND INDIA

To alleviate drought-induced famine, India received the bulk of its food aid in the 1950s and 1960s. Money from the U.S.-funded national-development programs increased agricultural production and gave the poor greater access to food resources. This focus on food production helped fuel the Green Revolution of the 1960s and helped drive India toward achieving self-sufficiency in food production (Shaw and Clay 1993). However, food aid did not resolve India's humanitarian problems. With India focused on increasing imports and advancing its technological and industrial sectors of food production, malnutrition persisted, and poverty remained rampant. New problems also arose. Agricultural advancements to increase food production contributed to environmental destruction, and India accumulated a large debt because it was unable to repay U.S. high-interest loans.

From 1956 to 1976, India received over 59 million tons of 'program' food aid, about 8.2 million tons each year, from the U.S. and Canada. Program food aid takes the form of bilateral government-to-government transfers. Food aid accounted for approximately 82 percent of net imports during the food shortages from 1964 to 1967. Food aid succeeded in "fill[ing] a food gap" during critical periods (Shaw and Clay 1993:58). This imported aid also helped stabilize supplies and consumer prices. For example, money earned by the Indian government from food sales and other commodities was used to fund public programs, "with priority given to investment in the infrastructure needed for the Green Revolution" (Shaw and Clay 1993:59). However, this focus on technology-based and industrial food production is one of the main negative implications of food aid. To spur growth, the U.S. lent India money in the form of Indian currency. Most of this funding was used for grants and loans to the Indian government to be used for economic development. The remaining money was "repayable over 40 years at 2 percent interest for the first 10 years and 3 percent for the subsequent 30 years of the repayment period" (Shaw and Clay 1993:59). This loan process shows that while India provided for its citizens, it also accumulated a large amount of national debt by the 1970s. India's increasing national debt would have significant future consequences.

Food aid began to evolve toward the end of the 1970s. The focus shifted in 1978 to 'project' food aid, which emphasized agricultural, rural, and human-resource development. Under the Agricultural and Rural Development Project, India received about $258 million in U.S. assistance. Project food aid largely aimed to improve forest management and conditions for the poor. To increase food production, a subproject focused on irrigation, rural infrastructure, expanded irrigation systems, and feeder roads. Other projects included livestock and dairy development and oil-seed production and processing. Human-resources development focused on providing programs for mothers and preschool children and providing primary-school education for youth (Shaw and Clay 1993).

Despite project food aid's goals to fight malnourishment and starvation, new problems emerged as a result of increased food production. Among countries receiving food aid, India received aid the longest, until 1971, and has suffered the most negative effects. First, environmental degradation became a problem. Second, with increased food production, more land fell fallow. As a result, less land could sustain given levels of food production, making it harder for India's poor to find livelihoods in agriculture. Third, despite increased food production, many Indians still suffered from malnutrition (Isenman and Singer 1977). In the early 1990s, there were still more than 200 million malnourished Indians, because food production had been biased toward particular areas. Fourth, a "lack of 'grainful' employment in rural areas is leading to an ever-increasing movement of resource-poor households to the towns, resulting in the emergence of mega-cities and the expansion of urban slums" (Isenman and Singer 1977:58). Malnourishment, migration to urban areas and increased poverty have led to low life expectancies for Indians; and the poor especially lack the training and education to participate in an expanding Indian and global economy.

Fifth, financial difficulties consumed India following the implementation of food aid. Increased debt servicing, a growing balance of payment deficits, and increased budget deficits emerged. In order to cope with these problems, the Indian government has relied on food aid and financial assistance from external global institutions, such as the International Monetary Fund (IMF) and the World Bank into the twenty-first century (Isenman and Singer 1977).

Sixth, food aid in India had an obvious First World bias. Drafted and implemented by First World countries, such as the U.S., food aid was geared toward increasing the import capacities of recipient countries. Feeding the hungry and advancing human rights was a secondary goal. For example, heavy industry received higher priority for development. The second and third Indian five-year plans focused on import-substitution industries. Food aid supported and aided in the implementation of the five-year plans, because it enabled the "Indian government to maintain large subsidized distribution programs while, in the eyes of many analysts, not adequately addressing some basic questions of food grain production and distribution" (Isenman and Singer 1977:9).

Many of the problems that plagued India in the twentieth century persist in the twenty-first century. India has the world's largest impoverished population; of over 1 billion inhabitants, about 260 million live below the poverty line. About 193 million of those reside in rural areas, while about 67 million live in urban areas (Azad India Foundation 2009). In 2007, India had higher rates of child malnourishment than Sub-Saharan Africa despite having received funding from UNICEF. Compared to Sub-Saharan Africa, where about 35 percent of children are malnourished, 46 percent of India's children under the age of three are malnourished. However, because India has critical resources that support modern development, such as a budget, an established transportation system, and other infrastructure, it is more likely to successfully resolve these problems. That said, although India possesses the characteristics necessary to improve the quality of life for its citizens, these problems may not be resolved in the near future, because the government fails to focus funding on improving humanitarian conditions. For example, the government spends less than 1 percent of the national budget on public health (Bhalla 2009).

These current issues provide insight into an unrealized implication of the food-aid regime: increased food production cannot solve all humanitarian problems. Food aid has revealed that in the 1950s and 1960s, the U.S. and major global institutions should have dealt with food production and distribution, with a greater focus on humanitarian goals. Because profit became a priority, malnutrition, environmental degradation, poverty, and financial problems persist at alarming rates. In the future, food aid should receive priority over industrial and technological development. A "neglect of agriculture is a recipe for slow growth" (Isenman and Singer 1977:10). If it cannot sufficiently produce and distribute such critical life-sustaining resources, how does a nation prosper without the strength of properly fed citizens? In order to resolve such problems still relevant in the twenty-first century, India must (re)prioritize its people over national profit.

CASE STUDY: FOOD AID AND CENTRAL AMERICA

The effects of food aid in Central America follow a path similar to that of India. In the context of food aid, the stated objectives of U.S. food-aid policy are "[to] develop and expand export markets for U.S. agricultural commodities; combat hunger and malnutrition; provide humanitarian relief to victims of disasters; encourage economic development in the developing countries, particularly those making efforts to expand agricultural production; and promote in other ways the foreign policy of the U.S." (Garst and Barry 1991:6). In spite of these goals, the story of the food-aid regime in Central America can be illusory. At first glance, the influx of food aid seems like a generous effort by the U.S. to help a region in crisis. After all, food aid has allowed Central American countries to maintain their food supplies and has consequently kept food prices down. However, a closer look at the history behind the situation demonstrates that food aid has done little to mitigate the crisis; instead, it has served as a political tool for the U.S. and other developed nations to expand their domination, control, and capital markets.

In the 1990s, Costa Rica, El Salvador, Guatemala, and Honduras received the majority of a large increase in food-aid supplies. However, this has not always been the case. Before the Nicaraguan Revolution in 1979, all of the countries in Central America, with the exception of Belize, received a minimal amount of food aid from the U.S., mostly for distributive programs to the poor. As a result of political turmoil there in the 1980s, Ronald Reagan's administration stopped all food aid to Nicaragua while increasing aid to the leftist regimes of surrounding countries, such as Honduras and Costa Rica. After a report in 1984 by the National Bipartisan Commission on Central America recommended increasing food assistance to "help stabilize and pacify the region," food aid to Guatemala, Honduras, El Salvador, and Costa Rica increased tenfold between 1979 and 1987 (Garst and Barry 1991:1). Specifically in 1986, these four countries received 10.7 percent of worldwide Title I concessional food aid, even though their combined population represented less than .003 percent of the global population. Honduras signed on in the early 1980s as a central U.S. ally in the Contra war against Nicaragua in exchange for massive amounts of food aid. The U.S. used Costa Rica as a base for fighting the contras but was also interested in quashing Costa Rican social unrest spawned by the financial crisis (Garst and Barry 1991).

Not only did food aid rise at this time, but so did military and economic aid. The majority of this increase in aid went to El Salvador, where the U.S.-backed government had been battling a guerrilla movement. Evidence that food aid was used as a political tool is even more evident in the willingness of the U.S. to contravene its own policy to ensure that El Salvador and Guatemala received aid. In spite of restrictions on PL-480 against aiding states that are clear human-rights violators, the U.S. continued to give food aid to both states, whose regimes have been documented as being among the worst for human-rights violations. In the case of Guatemala, American policy-makers rationalized aid as a 'reward for democracy' as well as a means of fighting poverty (Garst and Barry 1991).

Not only is the history of U.S. aid to Central America in the 1980s indicative of the use of food aid as a tool of foreign policy, but the logistics of the aid have also been implicated. Rachel Garst and Tom Barry (1991) argue that the food aid flowing into Central America had little to do with hunger and a great deal to do with satisfying global appetites. The majority of food aid consisted of government-to-government transfers, meaning the commodities were either sold at lowered rates or given to the recipient governments to resell domestically. Private processing companies often purchased these commodities, paying those governments directly. The recipient governments in effect received import savings and also collected the funds generated from the sale of the commodities to private companies. Essentially, this represented economic aid to the governments.

The problem then is twofold. First, the aid is not given directly to the poor, meaning they still cannot afford food despite the provision of aid. For example, much of the large influx of wheat and corn food aid in the 1990s ended up as animal feed for many agri-businesses. Second, even though food aid puts downward pressure on food prices, more well-off people consume the more affordable food. A Congressional Research Service Report notes that such foods as bread, milk, chicken, and vegetable-oil products have been advantaged with a decline in prices, yet these are the foods mainly consumed by the urban middle class (Garst and Barry 1991). The case of Central America demonstrates the versatility of the food-aid regime. Food aid can be thought of not only as a means of helping the poor but also as a foreign-policy tool. The degree to which food aid actually helps the needy proves somewhat doubtful in the cases of Central America and India. The next section provides a more general framework for why the food-aid regime has developed into a questionable tool of policy-makers and concludes by offering some policy propositions.

MODERN IMPLICATIONS OF FOOD AID

The evolution of the food-aid regime over the last fifty years highlights implications for the future of food-aid policies. In the first few decades, food aid mainly consisted of bilateral government to government transfers, or project food aid. After the Cold War in the 1990s, food aid shifted toward multilateralism. Currently, the effort is led by the World Food Program and NGOs for emergency relief. However, this shift caused "tension between private international capitalist accumulation and national political legitimacy" (McMichael 1992:360) that still exists today. Progress remains debatable, and many specialists and academics argue for more reform.

Multilateral Participation

While the food-aid regime began in the U.S., it expanded in 1961 with the creation of the World Food Program (WFP), an organization within the United Nations that is focused specifically on food aid. This organization began its operations by 1963 and today represents the "principal international channel of grant food aid for both development projects and emergency relief" (D. Shaw 2001:2). In its first few years, the WFP struggled with "instability and fluctuations of its resources" (D. Shaw 2001:67). It relied on the overproduction of resources and surplus crops from farmers of developed countries in North America and Europe. Years of poor performance in agricultural produce created shortages, leading to certain areas of the world receiving less assistance. In the 1970s, the International Grains Council noted the predominantly bilateral manner of food-aid distribution and declared that in the future, the UN should "draw the attention of member states to the advantages of channelling a greater proportion of food aid through multilateral channels" (D. Shaw 2001:77). Institutions began to see the value and credibility of multilaterally administered aid.

Following this, the 1974 World Food Conference proposed by Henry Kissinger was a landmark in the evolution of the food-aid regime. The global food crisis in the early 1970s amplified the need for food security. Leaders across the world convened in Rome to present proposals. While they reached no overarching consensus, the conference adopted twenty-three resolutions addressing the global food emergency. This conference further institutionalized the food-aid regime and solidified the identity of the WFP as a program focusing on project food aid. In the years following the conference, the WFP defined its six main objectives: improving nutrition, transferring income to workers on labor-intensive work projects, enabling participants to engage in activities on their own land, assisting farmers while their crops grow, offering budgetary support to recipient-country governments, and supporting positive policy changes by those recipient governments (D. Shaw 2001). Despite tightening institutional definitions of action, however, food aid nonetheless remained donor driven by the First World states concerned about their own interests and power.

Reforms of the 1990s

The end of the Cold War caused many changes within food-aid policy; it also led to an unprecedented era of instability and human-rights violations. With an upsurge in political turbulence and civil strife and the emergence of new states, refugees swelled in numbers, and the need for emergency aid increased. Many would have expected the end of Cold War hostilities to open the way for widespread economic growth that would improve food production and distribution. However, as D. John Shaw aptly observes, "economic growth does not usually trickle down, no one policy will trigger development everywhere, and people and their institutions really matter" (2001:226). Food-aid donors, particularly NGOs focused on relief, began to see the importance of putting people first. The European Union (EU) and the U.S. still comprise the two largest donors of food aid, and their policies since 1990 have shifted toward prioritizing more critical countries, increasing the proportion of locally sourced food aid, and placing greater emphasis on relief aid (Mousseau 2005). Three important events occurred in this decade that shaped the contemporary food-aid regime: the GATT

Uruguay Round, the 1995 U.S. Farm Bill, and the Food Aid Convention (FAC) of 1999.

Signed in 1994, the Marrakesh Decision of the Uruguay Round established the World Trade Organization (WTO). The WTO aimed to counter the adverse effects of increasing world food prices stemming from agricultural trade liberalization, but in practice "liberalization would further consolidate in the South a food system anchored in Western agriculture" (McMichael 1992:359). The WTO established a framework for global regulation, creating a "close relationship of food aid with food trade" (D. Shaw 2001:237). Critics of this decision noted its vagueness and wide possibilities of interpretation for developed countries as well as its consolidation of a corporate food-aid regime (Mousseau 2005).

The 1995 U.S. Farm Bill transferred decision-making powers of crop selection and stockpiling from the federal government to the farmers, undoing a policy passed by President Franklin D. Roosevelt under the New Deal to support farmers during the Great Depression (D. Shaw 2001). This policy further integrated American farmers into the world market, causing members of the developing world to worry about its effects on the stability of prices. This represents another case in which the U.S. has held its domestic interests above those of the developing world.

Each participant in the 1999 FAC promised to supply a minimum physical amount of food aid every year, regardless of fluctuating levels of production or prices. These amounts are usually somewhere in the millions of tons for each signatory. The 1999 FAC required a yearly commitment of 4.9 million tons of mostly cereals, with the priority recipients being the least developed and low-income states. The FAC sought "the alleviation of poverty and hunger of the most vulnerable population groups" (D. Shaw 2001:240).

These three events sparked debate about whether food aid should primarily focus on development or the alleviation of poverty. Furthermore, these policies led to the "internationalization of food production and markets" as well as "the substitution of global for national regulation" (McMichael 1992:345). Food aid for development dominated the discourse prior to the 1990s, but questions arose about its effectiveness. On the other hand, properly targeted food aid could directly address poverty, but First World bias has tended toward dismissiveness regarding that prospect.

The Fiftieth Anniversary of the Food-Aid Regime: Successes, Criticisms, and Future Prospects

The year 2005 marked the fiftieth anniversary of PL-480. Academics and policy-makers published substantial work in this milestone year critiquing the evolution and efficiency of food aid. World leaders and scholars in this subject area held conferences and forums around the world to assess the performance of the different agencies that provide food aid and the nature of their intentions. Despite vast integration of the developing countries into a liberal market economy, global managers maintain a developed world bias. Shifts over the last ten years point to minimal progress, yet the need for reform continues to be pressing, as the countries that need aid the most are still largely neglected.

While many countries remain neglected, some positive shifts have occurred. First, the increasing role of the WFP and NGOs at the national and international levels allows for multilateral food-aid distribution. Several institutions other than the U.S. government have become more involved in making decisions on aid allocation, including prominent NGOs in the field, such as CARE, Oxfam, CRS, and World Vision. Second, international relief agencies urged policy-makers to shift the focus of aid from development to emergency relief, thereby enabling short-term instant assistance. Collaboration with these policy-makers was necessary, because despite the best of intentions, these international organizations and NGOs cannot effectively alleviate poverty without understanding and engaging the important role of national governments. This represents the tension between national and international control of the world food order (McMichael 1992). Nonetheless, in India, Central America, and elsewhere, these organizations do strive to ensure that the poor receive the resources they need for survival.

Those skeptical of the current food-aid regime contend that it still causes problems for producers in recipient countries. Some say that food aid has come up "well short of its potential as a policy instrument to be used in support of a strategy to reduce poverty and acute food insecurity" (Barrett and Maxwell 2005:223). Many developing economies rely excessively on export monocultures, forcing them to import basic necessities. This weakens their foothold in the global integrated market. Small-scale farmers cannot compete with American and European farmers who receive subsidies. Commercial farming corporations dominate the market and have the support of multinational companies that rely on their production. While the shift to relief aid is a positive step, leaders of the developed world use it sparingly, and lags in implementation weaken its success. Emergency food aid remains under the discretion of donor countries, reinforcing the First World bias at the Third World's expense (Mousseau 2005). While the above only comprise a handful of criticisms, they further the widely accepted belief that the intentions of food aid need to be rethought and redirected to better combat global hunger.

CONCLUSION

In our globalized and technologically advanced world, global managers, NGOs, and individuals possess the ability to combat the striking poverty of the developing world through food aid. Many experts have offered their advice. Frederic Mousseau, a noted policy advisor for the NGO Oxfam, for instance, has proposed reforms for the aid system in a paper published for its fiftieth anniversary. He suggests that the WTO should stay out of food aid altogether, because it focuses too much on "trade interests and competition rather than genuine humanitarian and development concerns" (Mousseau 2005:29). By serving trade interests, the developed world that supplies the food aid benefits itself more than the poor and hungry it supposedly assists. Furthermore, Mousseau suggests that the WFP should focus on emergency relief. He calls for its specialization and a transformation into a 'World Relief Program', since the WFP already leads the world in relief aid. He argues for a focus on alleviating hunger—with the end goal being reducing the need for food aid altogether—and stresses that fighting hunger requires drastic and costly change.

Two other experts, Barrett and Maxwell (2005), offer variations of policy suggestions at various levels, including international policy, U.S. policy, recipient-government policy, and non-governmental policy. For example, at the international-policy level, they call for a 'Global Food Aid Compact' to replace the FAC by bringing recipient-government representatives to the table rather than restricting deliberation and decision making to donors only. In contrast to Mousseau, they believe the focus should rest on development rather than just relief, arguing that the latter leaves recipients mired in dependency. They highlight the importance of U.S. foreign-policy change, arguing that it is still driven by the objective of surplus disposal. As for recipient-government policy, Barrett and Maxwell recommend that it prioritize aid resources toward investment in domestic research to improve productivity and sustainability. Finally, they suggest improving food-aid targeting to make sure it reaches those with the least food security.

While the initial goal of the food-aid regime was to provide aid by disposing of domestic agricultural surpluses, its focus over time has shifted away from mainly political and economic motives toward providing humanitarian emergency relief to the most impoverished. Although the emergence of multilateral NGOs pushed the core purposes of food aid in a less self-interested direction and reforms have not been entirely negative, control of the aid still rests largely in the hands of First World governments serving their own economic and geopolitical interests. Inevitably, the system remains biased and inefficient. World leaders must take the initiative, advance discourse on effective food-aid policies, and implement positive changes in order to promote the food security of the majority of the world's population.

9   Climate Politics
Power and Development in Mortgaging the Planet

INTRODUCTION

Climate change is real, and human beings are responsible for a substantial part of it. It is putting our planet into peril, resulting in, among other far-reaching impacts, the loss of biodiversity, disaster vulnerabilities, and millions of climate refugees.[1] Currently there are about twenty million climate refugees, and this number will increase to fifty million within the next few decades (McMichael 2008). The world was expecting a conclusive and successful climate deal to be sealed during the Copenhagen talks in December 2009. However, a lack of consensus over issues including the character of differentiated responsibilities, financial support, technology transfer, trade subsidies, and trade sanctions hindered the progress of a successful deal. Drawing on the genealogies of climate politics from the Kyoto to Durban conferences, this chapter examines some key obstacles for a climate pact between developed and developing countries, delineating the role of power and development in mortgaging the planet in the age of disasters.

The history of national environmental movements and international cooperation related to climate change can be traced back to the first wave of environmentalism during the period of industrialization in the form of literary appreciation of nature (Guha 2000). This was followed by a second wave of environmentalism in 1970s, which was a result of different environmental cries (Gould and Lewis 2009). Since the 1970s, climate policies and politics have been evident in various talks and declarations, such as the Stockholm Declaration in 1972; followed by the Montreal Protocol in 1987; the United Nations Conference on Environment and Development in 1992; the Kyoto Protocol in 1997; the Gleneagles Dialogue in 2005; the Bali Road Map in 2007; the United Nations Climate Change Conference (UNCCC) in Copenhagen in 2009; the 16th Conference of Parties (COP) of the United Nations Framework Convention on Climate Change (UNFCCC) in Cancún, Mexico, in November 2010; and COP17 from November 28 to December 9, 2011, at Durban, South Africa. The 2012 UNCCC, COP18/CMP8 (the 18th COP to the UNFCCC, plus the 8th session of the COP serving as the meeting of the parties to the

Kyoto Protocol) took place in Qatar from November 26 to December 7, 2012. The Republic of Korea hosted a ministerial meeting to prepare for COP18/CMP8. Such ministerial meetings are a tradition in the UNFCCC negotiations and are instrumental in facilitating high-level discussions on central issues in the weeks before a COP.

The front page of the *New York Times* on July 8, 2009, reported that President Barack Obama placed "climate change front and center" on the agenda during a G8 meeting in July 2009 at Italy. The report noted that the meeting "demonstrated again the most vexing problem in reaching a consensus on climate change. . . . While the richest countries have produced the bulk of the pollution blamed for climate change, developing countries are producing increasing volumes of gases" (P. Baker 2009). The poorer countries feel that the demands placed on them to prioritize protecting the environment before pulling themselves out of poverty is nothing new: this script has played out at every major negotiation since the Stockholm Conference on Environment and Development in 1972. While the debate on climate treaties often addresses emissions-reduction targets, which is only half the problem, the most successful environmental treaties require built-in mechanisms to provide "financial and technological help for poorer nations" (P. Baker 2009). For the international community to work toward a meaningful global climate deal, the development of an effective framework in the form of a social-justice framework is necessary to address the complexity of the problems.

MIGHTY ECONOMY, VULNERABLE PLANET

More than a quarter-century ago, environmental sociologist Allan Schnaiberg introduced the concept of the 'treadmill of production'. According to Schnaiberg (1980), industrial capitalism is driven by higher rates of material throughput, which eventually creates so much waste (additions) and extracts so much of the Earth's natural resources (withdrawals) that it overwhelms the biosphere. Following the 'treadmill of production', James Gustave Speth (2008) concludes that capitalism is both the source of our success as a postindustrial economy and the obstacle to realizing environmental sustainability. He asserts that our capitalist economy, with its emphasis on continuous robust growth, is at loggerheads with the environment. He minces no words when he writes that to destroy life as we know it, all we have to do is "keep doing exactly what we are doing today" (2008:x). There is always a commitment to economic growth at any cost, and the wealth is concentrating in few to fewer hands. Economic growth is increasingly more costly than it is beneficial. It took all of history to build a US$7-trillion world economy in 1950; today, economic activity grows by that amount every decade (Speth 2008). The paradox is clear: the mightier the economy, the weaker the planet.

The current neoliberal economic pattern is one of the main drivers of the current climate change, contributing to an increasingly vulnerable planet. Germanwatch[2] released the 2012 edition of the Global Climate Risk Index at COP17 in Durban. Key messages of the report (Harmeling 2012:4) include the following:

- Bangladesh, Myanmar, and Honduras were the countries most affected by extreme weather events from 1991 to 2010.
- The ten most affected countries (1991–2010) were developing countries in the low-income or lower-middle-income country group.
- In total, more than 710,000 people died as a direct consequence of more than 14,000 extreme weather events, and losses of more than US$2.3 trillion (in purchasing power parity) occurred from 1991 to 2010 (US$1.5 trillion overall losses in original values).
- In 2010, the ranking of the most affected countries is led by Pakistan, Guatemala, Colombia, Russia, and Honduras.
- In the case of the Russian heat wave, some scientists see a high probability that without climate change, this event would not have occurred.
- Loss and damage from anthropogenic climate change is expected to further increase; therefore, the current lack of ambition in mitigating putting the world on a path of 4 to 5 degrees Celsius increase in average temperature would result in a large-scale experiment unprecedented in the history of mankind.
- Many developing countries are already taking action to prepare for climate-related disasters and to promote as well as to implement adaptation. However, adequate financial and institutional support provided by developed countries is required to further increase disaster preparedness and resilience of poor countries. Operationalizing the Green Climate Fund at COP17 in Durban could be one important step to build up long-term support.
- Through the adoption of the Cancún Adaptation Framework (CAF) at COP16, an important step was made by parties to the UNFCCC for a more ambitious and coherent approach to adaptation. The CAF also contained the decision on a work program on loss and damage from the adverse impacts of climate change. For COP17 in Durban, it is crucial to define concrete next steps, with a view to reaching a more comprehensive and ambitious decision at COP18.

Similar to Germanwatch, World Food Program (WFP; 2011) released a report on seven facts about climate change and hunger:

- Climate change is expected to add another 10 to 20 percent to the total number of hungry people by the year 2050.

- By 2050, we can expect twenty-four million more malnourished children as a result of climate change. Almost half of this increase, ten million children, will be in Sub-Saharan Africa.
- Between 1980 and 2006, the number of climate-related disasters quadrupled.
- The number of people affected by climate-related disasters is expected to reach 375 million per year by 2015.
- In 2010, climate-related extreme events and disasters affected some 300 million people, most often in countries that have little capacity to cope.
- With climate change, two-thirds of the arable land in Africa could be lost by 2025, according to the UN Food and Agriculture Organization.
- By 2030, climate change could push food prices up 50 to 90 percent more than they would otherwise be expected to rise, according to a recent report by Oxfam.

The world's poor, women and children in particular, will bear the brunt of the effects of climate change. As rainfall becomes increasingly unpredictable, smallholder farmers will find it harder than ever to grow the food they need. The poor, who have no support structures to protect themselves, will most likely suffer from the severe hunger resulting from a potential increase in the frequency of natural disasters. More often than not, the people who suffer first and worst during climate disasters are not the main contributors to the problem. An analysis of 4,040 climate-related disasters between 1980 and 2002 found that some poor nations had mortality and homelessness rates from climate disasters that were 200 to 300 times worse than in the U.S. (Roberts and Parks 2007). They have far less capacity to deal with and to recover from disasters. As the economy grows, and wealth increasingly concentrates from few to fewer hands, the woes of these marginalized masses are also constantly piling up.

CLIMATE POLITICS FROM KYOTO TO DURBAN

Kyoto Protocol

When the Intergovernmental Panel on Climate Change (IPCC), which includes thousands of scientists from around the world and whose reports are approved by nearly all governments around the world, published its second assessment report in 1996 confirming that climate change was occurring because of human actions, it became evident that the time had come for the international community to formulate a legally binding quantified emissions limitations program. This led to the COP3 in Kyoto, Japan, on December 10, 1997. The main objective of the Kyoto Protocol was the stabilization of greenhouse-gas concentrations in the atmosphere at a level that would prevent dangerous anthropogenic interference with the climate system. However, a major dilemma in the Kyoto Round arose over how to calculate who is polluting how much and how much they should be required to reduce their emissions. Many theories to resolve this issue were suggested at that time. One was to have a reasonable international level per-capita system in place. This would have allowed the developing countries to have some flexibility regarding their emissions, as they could increase them till they reached the internationally acceptable limits. Another one was of grandfathering emissions, which would reduce emissions by setting the 1990 levels as the baseline (Oberthür and Ott 1999; Roberts 2009).

The European Union (EU) emerged as a leader in the Kyoto Protocol. These countries wanted to have uniform policies and measures in any efforts to limit greenhouse-gas emissions. Some of them demanded 20 percent reductions in the 1990 levels by 2012. The U.S. and the JUSCANZ nations[3] appeared to be dragging their feet regarding the Protocol. The U.S. government wanted to put in place a system that would allow parties to be free to choose whatever policies and measures they wanted in meeting their obligations. It did not want to commit itself to a legally binding agreement regarding emission cuts. This led to the Kyoto Protocol's agreeing to the principle of 'common but differenti-ated responsibilities', which calls for the shared responsibility of humankind to address climate change while recognizing that member states have different historical responsibilities and capacities to address climate change.

The fifteen members of the EU had to collectively reduce their emis-sions by 8 percent of the 1990 levels by 2012. Under a scheme known as 'bubble' within the Protocol, the EU was allowed to redistribute the targets among its member nations (Roberts 2009; Victor 2001). Canada, Hungary, Japan, and Poland were required to reduce their emissions by 6 percent, and Croatia was required to reduce by 5 percent. New Zealand, the Rus-sian Federation, and Ukraine had to maintain the same levels as those in 1990. Norway was allowed a 1 percent, Australia 8 percent, and Iceland 10 percent increase in their 1990 emissions levels. The U.S. initially signed the treaty and agreed to a 7 percent cut in its 1990 emission levels by 2012. There were no emission restrictions placed on the developing countries (G77 + China). Then in 1997, the U.S. Senate passed the iconic Byrd-Hagel resolution with a 95–0 vote, which made it impossible for the U.S. govern-ment to enter into a treaty that did not include poor countries (Oberthür and Ott 1999; Victor 2001). Senator Robert C. Byrd declared on the senate floor: "I do not think the Senate should support a treaty that requires only . . . developed countries to endure the economic costs of reducing emis-sions, while developing countries are free to pollute the atmosphere, and, in so doing, siphon off American industries" (cited in Roberts 2001). Thus, Bill Clinton never submitted the treaty to the Senate, as he knew that he did not have the necessary votes to pass it. In 2001, President George W. Bush unsigned the treaty, thereby removing the nation entirely from the Protocol but keeping it in the UNFCCC (Roberts 2009). To date, 180 countries have ratified the Protocol. The key ratification was completed by Russia in 2004, which finally put the Protocol into effect on February 19, 2005.

Unfortunately, the Kyoto Protocol lacks global stature. The U.S., the world's largest emitter and the 'big brother', is not a part of it. It is an agreement between only thirty or so rich nations to reduce their emissions by approximately 5 percent from the 1990 levels by 2012. No restrictions have been placed on the developing countries whose emission rates are rapidly increasing. About five out of the six billion people in the world (80 percent of humanity) have not agreed to place any restrictions on their emissions in their search for a developed life (Roberts 2009). The Kyoto Protocol was unable to solve the North-South deadlock. The U.S. wanted the developing countries to take responsibility for reducing their emissions. The developing countries, on the other hand, were justifying their position to make the same mistakes that the industrial countries had made before. Developing nations, such as China and India, are seeking their 'rights' to industrialize— and therefore rights to pollute—which the developed nations have been enjoying for a long time. Shyam Saran, who heads India's international negotiating team on climate change, has argued that "greenhouse gases are taking up 'carbon space' in the atmosphere. Past emissions of carbon dioxide and other gases from rich countries have taken up much of that space. Now the poor countries are standing up for their right to a little bit of that space too" (*The Economist* 2009). The Kyoto Protocol reflects the power conflicts—between the developed and developing nations—plaguing the international negotiation climate. These conflicts have persisted through successive conferences till today, with planet Earth as the clear loser.

Copenhagen Accord

In December 2009, the entire world had its eyes on Copenhagen, where more than 45,000 people, including 120 heads of state, met at the Bella Centre to decide upon a human response to global climate change. According to the Bali Road Map,[4] a framework for climate-change mitigation beyond 2012 was to be discussed there. Despite having the world's expectations lying on its shoulders, the summit failed to produce any concrete results. The conference ended with a 'meaningful agreement', which was drafted by the U.S., China, India, Brazil, and South Africa, but it only provided suggestions on steps to tackle the climate problem and was non-binding. Just three months before the summit, following the EU leadership, Japan pledged to make highly ambitious 25 percent emission cuts below 1990 levels by 2020, and the U.S. offered 30 percent below 2005 by 2025 and 42 percent by 2030. Even developing countries for the first time came forward, with Brazil pledging 36 to 39 percent cuts by 2020, China 40 to 45 percent, and India agreeing to reduce its carbon intensity by 20 to 25 percent below the 2005 levels (Dimitrov 2010). The years leading up to the Copenhagen summit showed encouraging progress and increasing commitments from member states, but the actual summit disappointed many observers.

Several things went wrong at Copenhagen. First, it was marred with protests calling for a global agreement on climate. All the major governments did not want to commit themselves to any internationally binding agreement, which hinders any attempts at concluding a major deal. They were contented with informal agreements that were not legally binding. All the major players were only interested in protecting their own political and economic interests. There were many talkers but very few listeners (BBC 2009a). The Copenhagen Accord witnessed a change in the world order. The once strong and united Group of 77 + China started fragmenting. The EU's leadership in climate negotiations started weakening. China overtook the U.S. as the world's largest CO_2 emitter (Roberts 2011).

The delegations of the EU strategized for four possible outcomes: (1) a legal treaty, (2) a 'comprehensive core decision', (3) a political declaration, and (4) no output whatsoever. It became evident during the negotiations that option 4 was the most likely outcome (Dimitrov 2010). During the negotiations, the EU pushed for some major emission cuts. These countries led by example by promising to cut emissions by 20 percent from 1990 levels by 2010. They wanted the rich nations to commit to an 80 to 95 percent cut in emissions by 2050. They also proposed to have a US$150-billion fund to help developing countries tackle climate change. The block of the developing countries again reiterated the 'Polluter Pays Principle'. They wanted the developed countries to take responsibility and enforce cuts on their emissions. They also wanted the rich countries to pay 1 percent of their respective gross domestic products (GDPs) to help the developing countries adapt to climate change. India rejected any binding cuts to be placed on the developing countries but wanted the developed countries to be legally bound. The U.S., on the other hand, was against any Kyoto-style treaty that imposed legal obligations. It wanted the BASIC (Brazil, South Africa, India, and China) countries to commit to slowing down their emissions and was only prepared to work with other countries to raise US$100 billion each year by 2020 (BBC 2009b). Table 9.1 provides a brief overview of climate facts and diverse positionalities among different regions and countries. With a comprehensive deadlock at the negotiation tables and with none of the sides willing to budge, the talks and the construction of any meaningful deal collapsed. The Denmark government's dreams of having a 'Made in Denmark' pact that would solve climate change seemed impossible. In a last-ditch effort to save the international community's face, twenty-five prime ministers and presidents began crafting a declaration themselves. The U.S. and the BASIC countries negotiated the Accord behind closed doors. Despite being left out of the negotiations, but knowing that a weak deal would be better than none, the EU endorsed the Accord. If the EU had declined to endorse it, a number of developing countries would have followed suit, and the agreement would never have become international (BBC 2009a).

Table 9.1   Climate Facts and Diverse Positions

Country	What's on the Table	Climate Facts (2007)
China: "Developed countries should support developing countries in tackling climate change." *President Hu Jintao, September 22, 2009*	• Set a "binding goal" to cut CO2 per unit of GDP by 40 to 45% below 2005 levels by 2020 • Wants rich countries to reduce emissions to 40% below 1990 levels by 2020 • Says it should pay 1% of its GDP per year to help other countries adapt • Wants West to provide low-carbon technology	• The world's biggest GHG producer (20.7% of global emissions, 8,106 mt of CO2 equivalent) • Emissions per head: 30th in the world (6 tons of CO2 equivalent) • GDP (2008): $4.3 trillion • Amount of GHG emitted per $1 million of GDP: 1,152 tons • Kyoto: Signed as a developing country so not obliged to cut emissions
The U.S.: "This is not fiction, this is science. Unchecked, climate change will pose unacceptable risks to our security, our economies, and our planet." *President Barack Obama, December 18, 2009*	• Prepared to work "with other countries" to raise $100 billion a year by 2020 • Will cut emissions to 17% below 2005 levels by 2020 pending congressional approval; this is close to 4% below 1990 levels • Against Kyoto-style treaty imposing international legal obligations • Insists China, India, South Africa, and Brazil must commit to slow growth of emissions • Climate bill is currently bogged down in Senate	• The world's 2nd-biggest GHG producer (15.5% of global emissions, 6,087 mt of CO2 equivalent) • Emissions per head: 5th in the world (20 tons of CO2 equivalent) • GDP (2008): $14.2 trillion • Amount of GHG emitted per $1 million of GDP: 441 tons • Kyoto: Signed, but never ratified
EU*: "Things are fragile but I believe that common sense will prevail. We have to focus on the substance and we have to take political decisions." *Stavros Dimas, EU environment commissioner, December 18, 2009* *The EU is a grouping of 27 European states.	• Will cut emissions by 20% from 1990 levels by 2020, or 30% if other big emitters take tough action • Wants rich nations to make 80 to 95% cut by 2050 • Wants poorer nations to slow emissions growth • Says nations face costs of $150 billion per year by 2020, of which EU will pay $7 billion to $22 billion from public finances	• The world's 3rd-biggest GHG producer (11.8% of global emissions, 4,641 mt CO2 equivalent) • Emissions per head: 17th in the world (9 tons of CO2 equivalent) • GDP (2008): $18.3 trillion • Amount of GHG emitted per $1 million of GDP: 315 tons • Kyoto: Signed—has to get average emissions for 2008 to 2012 8% below 1990 levels

Japan: "Japan will, with this assistance, support a broad range of developing countries which are taking measures of mitigation, as well as those which are vulnerable." *Japan delegation, December 16, 2009*	• Will cut emissions to 25% below 1990 levels by 2020, if other countries show similar ambition • This amounts to a cut of 30% in 10 years, but is opposed by industry • "Hatoyama initiative" will increase financial and technical assistance to developing countries • Backs proposals in which each country would set its own commitments	• The world's 7th-biggest GHG producer (3.3% of global emissions, 1,293 mt of CO2 equivalent) • Emissions per head: 15th in the world (10 tons of CO2 equivalent) • GDP (2008): $4.9 trillion • Amount of GHG emitted per $1 million of GDP: 301 tons • Kyoto: Signed—has to get average emissions for 2008 to 2012 6% below 1990 levels
India: "The most vulnerable country in the world to climate change is India." *Jairam Ramesh, India's environment minister, December 3, 2009*	• Will cut CO2 emissions per unit of GDP by 20 to 25% from 2005 levels by 2020 • Rejects legally binding target, but wants rich countries legally bound • Says rich countries are to blame for climate change and points to big gap in per-capita emissions • Wants 40% cut in rich country emissions by 2020 • Opposes goal of halving world emissions by 2050	• The world's 6th-biggest GHG producer (5% of global emissions, 1,963 mt of CO2 equivalent) • Emissions per head: 66th in the world (2 tons of CO2 equivalent) • GDP (2008): $1.2 trillion • Amount of GHG emitted per $1 million of GDP: 655 tons • Kyoto: Signed as a developing country, so not obliged to cut emissions
African Union*: "My proposal scales back our expectation with respect to the level of funding, in return for more reliable funding." *Meles Zenawi of Ethiopia, December 16, 2009* *The African Union is a grouping of 52 African states.	• Wants climate funds to reach $100 billion a year by 2020 for rich countries to help poorer nations • Wants at least 50% for vulnerable and poor regions, such as African and small island states • Like China, wants rich countries legally bound to cut emissions to 40% below 1990 levels by 2020 • Describes 20 to 30% cuts as "unacceptable"	• The AU accounts for 8.1% of global emissions (3,164 mt of CO2 equivalent) • Emissions per head: 4 tons of CO2 equivalent • GDP (2008): $34 billion • Amount of GHG emitted per $1 million of GDP: 1,361 tons • Kyoto: African nations signed as developing countries, so not obliged to cut emissions

Continued

Table 9.1 Continued

Country	What's on the Table	Climate Facts (2007)
Gulf States*: "We are among the most economically vulnerable countries." *Mohammad S. Al Sabban, Saudi Arabia's lead negotiator, October 8, 2009* *Bahrain, Kuwait, Oman, Qatar, Saudi Arabia, UAE	• OPEC and Saudi Arabia seeking financial aid for oil producers if new agreement requires cuts of fossil fuels • Keen on a deal that would advance use of carbon capture and storage • In 2007 OPEC members pledged $750 million to fund climate-change research • Qatar and Abu Dhabi investing heavily in clean-energy technology	• Gulf States account for 2.3% of global emissions (894 mt of CO2 equivalent) • Emissions per head: 25 tons of CO2 equivalent • GDP (2008): $468 billion • Amount of GHG emitted per $1 million of GDP: 875 tons • Kyoto: Gulf States signed as developing countries, so not obliged to cut emissions
Small Islands: "The days of little money in the face of big problems are over." *Dessima Williams, head of the Alliance of Small Island States (AOSIS)*, October 9, 2009 *AOSIS is a bloc of 42 island and coastal states, mostly in the Pacific and Caribbean	• Regard rising sea level as threat to their existence • Seek to limit temperature rise to 1.5 degrees above preindustrial levels • Want concentration of CO2 in atmosphere lowered from 380 to 350 parts per million • Want global emissions to peak by 2015 and fall 85% below 1990 levels by 2050 • Want at least 1% of rich country GDP spent on "climate-inflicted damage"	• The Small Island states account for 0.6% of global GHG emissions (246 mt of CO2 equivalent) • Emissions per head: 4 tons of CO2 equivalent • GDP (2008): $46 billion • Amount of GHG emitted per $1 million of GDP: 551 tons • Kyoto: AOSIS members signed as developing countries, so not obliged to cut emissions

Source: BBC (2009b).

In the final plenary session of discussion, seven countries (Tuvalu, Nicaragua, Bolivia, Cuba, Venezuela, Sudan, and later Pakistan) vetoed the Accord, arguing that it was undemocratically elected. One of the Western delegates shouted at the delegates from Bolivia and Venezuela that they would never get any money again. The president of the Maldives pleaded with a Bolivian official, "Please Madam, this is our last chance. I have two daughters and wish to live with my grandchildren. Our nation is one and a half meters above sea level" (Dimitrov 2010:21). Despite the pleas, the countries did not drop their positions, and the Accord was not formally adopted. The final Copenhagen Accord was just another informal agreement among members of the international community: they wanted to limit the temperature rise to only 2 degrees Celsius, all the developed and developing countries could decide voluntarily what actions to take to limit climate change, and only the actions funded internationally were subject to legal monitoring. The only positive outcome of the Accord was the establishment of the Copenhagen Green Climate Fund, to the tune of US$100 billion by the year 2020 (Dimitrov 2010; Roberts 2011). The power conflicts and disagreements over development needs in Copenhagen unfortunately appeared to be an argument over who gets to plunder the planet; the rich countries wanted to retain their rights to continue plundering, while the poor countries exerted their rights to plunder in order to attain developed status. In short, economic growth for both rich and poor countries took priority over environmental (and existential) concerns.

Cancún Agreement

The 16th COP to the UNFCCC took place in November 2010 in Cancún and was hosted by the government of Mexico. About 12,000 participants, including 5,200 government officials, 5,400 representatives of UN bodies and agencies, intergovernmental organizations and non-governmental organizations (NGOs), and 1,270 accredited members of the media participated in this conference. The previous COP at Copenhagen had proven to be a complete disaster. The world began to question the ability of the UNFCCC to come to a concrete agreement regarding climate change. It was evident that Cancún had to produce an agreement to restore people's trust in the UN process (Cozier 2011). In the words of Christiana Figueres, an appointed UNFCCC executive secretary, "A concrete outcome in December [2010] is urgently needed to restore faith in the ability of Parties to take the negotiations forward" (UNEP 2010).

The anticipation for the Cancún conference was modest. A U.S. climate bill, which was introduced by Senators John Kerry and Joe Lieberman in May 2010, wanted a 17 percent reduction in U.S. greenhouse-gas emissions by 2020 compared to the 2005 levels. It was eventually scrapped by the Senate (Cozier 2011). In December 2010, WikiLeaks made public U.S. State Department secret cables that showed how several million dollars of funding to Bolivia and Ecuador were withdrawn in early 2010 due to their opposition to the Copenhagen Accord. It also showed how the U.S. government bribed and bullied smaller governments to gain support for the Copenhagen Accord (Bond 2011).

At Cancún, changes within the original negotiating blocks were reflected in power shifts and policy changes. The European leadership weakened because of its expansion; the initial seventeen wealthy nations had increased to twenty-four nations, which increased the EU's diversity. Even the G77 group broke up into smaller ones, each negotiating for its own interests. The EU wanted more ambitious reduction targets, whereas the JUSCANZ wanted to build upon the Copenhagen Accord. The G77 wanted to extend the Kyoto Protocol and wanted a decision to be made on the transfer of technology and the establishment of the adaptation and the mitigation fund. India, China, and the other larger developing nations were ready to agree to Nationally Appropriate Mitigation Actions (NAMAs), which provide nations with the freedom to design and to adopt mitigation measures in accordance with national circumstances. Mechanisms for measurement and reporting are to be built into the policies and actions, but they will only be subjected to verification if these measures involve foreign aid (Roberts 2011). The final Cancún agreement was far from being ideal. The decisions made at Cancún included the following (Vaughan 2010):

- The pledges made by the developed nations to reduce emissions at Copenhagen were finally incorporated into the official UN process. The developing countries agreed to take up nationally appropriate emission cuts, but no specific pledges were given. The world agreed to limit the temperature increase to 2 degrees Celsius, which could be brought down to 1.5 degrees Celsius in the near future.
- The countries agreed to set up a new climate green fund, which would raise US$100 billion each year by 2020 to help the developing countries handle the impacts of climate change. The World Bank was put in charge of this fund.
- Formal backing was given to the REDD (reducing emissions from deforestation and degradation) scheme, in which poor countries would be paid not to chop down the forests.
- The decision on the extension of the Kyoto Protocol was deferred to the next meeting, to be held in Durban.
- A new technology mechanism was proposed to facilitate enhanced action on technology development and transfer to support action on mitigation and adaptation.

These agreements were also criticized by many for not being substantial. The bottom-up voluntary approach effectively killed the Kyoto Protocol. The World Bank, under whose loans a lot of developing countries are debt ridden and which funds many polluting projects, was made the trustee of the green climate fund. There was no concrete decision regarding the intellectual-property rights. The controversial REDD program was given the green light, which practically rewards those responsible for deforestation in the past. Bolivian President Evo Morales had convened a People's Climate Summit in Cochabamba, Bolivia, in April 2010. About 35,000 activists had come from all over the world to formulate resolutions to be submitted at the COP16 in Cancún. This conference had massive support worldwide and was hosted by the indigenous people. In spite of such massive support, all of its proposals and recommendations were rejected at Cancún (Salleh 2011).

According to many scientists, even if the Cancún promises were kept, the world temperatures will rise by 4 to 5 degrees Celsius. The resulting melting of glaciers, sinking of islands, and flooding of coastal regions will cause massive damage (Bond 2011). Scientific estimates predict that to have a stable environment, the global CO_2 emissions in 2020 must be kept below forty-four billion tons. If the existing pledges are considered, the CO_2 emissions in 2020 will overshoot that amount by five to nine billion tons. Bolivia was the only country that refused to sign the agreement, because it did not agree with the outcomes. Delegation head Pablo Solon told the conference that current pledges to cut emissions "would mean more than 4°C" of warming. It would be "ecocide," he said (Pearce and Brahic 2010). Despite efforts made by Pablo Solon, the recommendations made by the People's Climate Summit were not taken up for the UNFCCC negotiating documents for Cancún. President Morales retorted, "It's easy for people in an air-conditioned room to continue with the policies of destruction of Mother Earth. We need instead to put ourselves in the shoes of families in Bolivia and worldwide that lack water and food and suffer misery and hunger. People here in Cancún have no idea what it is like to be a victim of climate change" (quoted in Bond 2011:5).

The Cancún agreement was in no way ideal, although it set up a platform upon which a comprehensive agreement could be built. It did indeed set the stage for progressive discussions at Durban and restored faith in the UN process. The Cancún outcome can be summarized in the words of UK Prime Minister David Cameron: "Now the world must deliver on its promises. There is more hard work to be done ahead of the climate change conference in South Africa next year" (BBC 2010).

A Deal in Durban

On December 11, 2011, after three days and nights of exhausting, often ill-tempered final negotiations, the UN's two-week-long climate-change summit in Durban ended with an agreement. Its terms—even assuming they are acted upon—are unlikely to prevent a global temperature rise of more than 2 degrees Celsius, which is the stated aim of the whole UN climate 'process'. Indeed, they might easily allow for a 4-degree rise. Yet with many governments distracted by pressing economic worries, the deal was as much as could have been expected, or perhaps a little more (*The Economist* 2011c).

The agreement—dubbed the 'Durban platform'—is different from the other partial deals that have been struck during the past two decades, with developing countries, including China, the world's biggest emitter, agreeing to be legally bound to curb their greenhouse gases. Previously, poorer nations have insisted that they should not bear any legal obligations for tackling climate change, whereas rich nations—which over more than a century have produced most of the carbon currently in the atmosphere—should (*The Guardian* 2011). The outcome of COP17 includes three major elements: some potentially important elaborations on various components of the Cancún Agreements, a second five-year commitment period for the Kyoto Protocol, and a non-binding agreement to reach an agreement by 2015 that will bring all countries under the same legal regime by 2020.

While the agreement puts more flesh on the bones of the Cancún agreements, it will obviously not solve the problem of climate change. As usual, the climate diplomats "fudged" or "punted" the important issues, says Bryan Walsh in *TIME* (2011). Sure, they managed to "stave off the total collapse of the U.N. climate process"; however, the truth is, our global league of nations will not be the hero that saves our planet. "If it's to be saved at all, the hard work will be done elsewhere: in national legislatures, in statehouses, in laboratories, and inside each person" (Walsh 2011). The question is, are we up to the task?

OBSESSION OVER POWER AND DEVELOPMENT CORRUPTS

The deadlock at the conferences from Kyoto in 1997 to Durban in 2011 as a result of climate politics is rooted in the seductive obsession with power and development, which (re)produced and maintained inequality across the planet. Timothy W. Luke reminds us that in the rise of the neoliberal quest for global dominance and power, "[a]ll natural resources now became strategic geo-power asset to be mobilized, not only for growth and wealth production, but also for market domination and power creation. To resist growth is not only to oppose economic prosperity; it is to subvert the political future, national interest and collective security for the nation state" (1999:125). In this context, both developed and developing nations are in a race to mobilize as much of Earth's material resources as possible while ignoring ecological considerations or, at best, giving only meaningless symbolic responses. "Having more material wealth or economic growth in one place, like a particular nation state, means not having it in another places—namely rival foreign nations. It also assumes that material scarcity is a continual constraint; hence, all resources, everywhere and at any time, must be subject to exploitation" (Luke 1999:125). This wild race for power and development has mortgaged our planet, possibly culminating in a 'tragedy of the commons', as the overexploitation of Earth by the powerful and wealthy few causes resource depletion and dire inequality for the global masses.

We cannot deal with environmental issues without addressing inequality. Inequality matters in addressing climate change for three reasons. First, there is an apparent *inequality in suffering*: the poor suffer more as a result of climate change. As indicated in Chapter 1 (this volume), the poor are less capable of dealing with disasters caused by climate change. While the effects and the ability to handle climate change are unequally distributed, *responsibility* for the problem is even more unequally distributed. For instance, with only 4 percent of the world's population, the U.S. is responsible for 24 percent of the global emissions (Roberts 2009, 2011).

Second, the poor have less bargaining power than the rich countries. The wealthy nations come to international meetings with lawyers, legal experts, scientists, economists, skilled diplomats, and observers, allowing them to read every document, to attend every committee meeting, and to painstakingly weigh the pros and cons of many proposals. It is difficult to overstate the importance of this impact of global inequality on climate-change negotiations. We need to understand that the debate about climate change occurs in a negotiating climate already poisoned by bad acts and unfulfilled promises from decades of other negotiations on trade and development. Poor nations feel they have repeatedly 'gotten the shaft' in such initiatives as the World Trade Organization (WTO), the Agreement on Trade Related Aspects of Intellectual Property Rights (TRIPS) treaty, the International Monetary Fund (IMF), the World Bank's 'conditions' on who gets loan and what they have to do to get them, and so on (Roberts 2009). Developing nations may continue to perceive the power inequalities evident in the climate change negotiations as an attempt by developed nations at neocolonialism, and perhaps rightly so.

Third, a painful lesson may be drawn from the failures of the Kyoto Protocol and the Copenhagen Accord: an effective climate deal cannot be reached at without addressing issues of inequality. Inequalities affect the willingness and ability of nations to address climate change, which was manifested in the Kyoto Protocol: (a) inequality within and between nations, of many sorts, drives desperation in the Global South (vulnerability); (b) it drives anger at the injustice of the unequal and unfair distribution of goods (wealth) and bads (emissions), since waste flows downhill; (c) it drives the inability and unwillingness of poor countries to participate effectively in international efforts to address climate change (participation in Kyoto Protocol and other environmental treaties); and (d) in some key nations, such as the U.S., Australia, and China, extreme wealth is an obstacle in any serious attempt to address the issue. Each of these impacts of inequality is complex and must be addressed to progress toward effective policies dealing with climate change (Roberts 2009).

To break the deadlock, the world should take a 'social-justice' framework that would contain both *procedural* (e.g., fairness principle, inclusion of poor nations effectively) and *compensatory* justice (losers will need to be compensated) (Roberts 2001, 2009). In *The Bridge at the Edge of the World* (2008), Speth presents bold solutions to problems that go deeper than simple environmental issues. As he asserts, the environment is tied to many other aspects of our existence, including our health, security, and community. With so much at stake, Speth proposes transforming the status quo by holding corporations accountable for their actions; refocusing our obsession with GDP growth to concentrate on ways to promote healthy, sustainable growth, such as universal access to quality health care and education; relying less on materialism as a measure of success and happiness; changing the market to one that works with the environment, not against it; and acknowledging that environmental policy should be connected to issues of humanity in order to be complete.

The IPCC should deal not only with the environment but with development and social justice. The newly industrializing countries should not just replicate what their First World counterparts did. What Chindia (China and India) is doing to the environment for its seductive development trajectory is costing not only themselves but also the entire planet. The First World, on the other hand, should immediately resolve its 'clash of interest' (between, for instance, the U.S. and the European Union) and have more genuine intentions and responsibilities for, for instance, a green climate fund, technology transfer, and administrative responsibility. Development status of a country needs to be redefined not just on GDP but on other indicators, such as contributions to CO_2, contributions to solutions for climate change, amount of responsibility taken, and so forth. There should be an international environmental judiciary system (such as 'Green Court') not just to punish the perpetrators but also to acknowledge certain nations that take more responsibility. The court should also deal with international environmental refugees. It requires a formation of a high-powered body comprising international civil-service professionals beyond the nation-state framework and interests. These professionals should have wider mandates from all nations and should be free of influence from the neoliberal global managers. Given the precarious state of the planet, delay is not an acceptable option.

10 Tipaimukh Dam

Triumph of Development over the Environment and Popular Voice

INTRODUCTION

Drawing insights from environmental philosophy and activism, existing literature on environmentalism has been dominated by studies of various movements emerging from the Global North, including the conservation movement, deep ecology, the environmental-justice paradigm, and the new environmental paradigm, among others. In recent times, some scholars have ventured to delve into environmentalism of the Global South. Ramachandra Guha and Joan Martinez-Alier (1997) refer to 'Southern environmentalism' as the 'environmentalism of the poor', because, among other reasons, environmental movements in the Global South have historically been initiated by poor people. The social construction of boundaries between Northern and Southern environmentalism often seems arbitrary. However, this distinction accurately reflects the lack of attention given to vibrant environmental movements of the Global South in current discourses of environmentalism. In this chapter, I elucidate environmental resistance against the Tipaimukh Dam (Tipaimukh Multipurpose Hydroelectric Project) in India as an example of the 'environmentalism of the poor'.

Bangladesh and India share fifty-four common rivers (Riaz 2011:106). The waters of these rivers play important economic, ecological, and social roles, particularly for agriculture, urban, and rural water supplies and navigation sectors. Until recently, the Ganges was the most debated shared rivers between the two countries because of withdrawals of its waters at the Farakka Barrage point and ninety other points above it within Indian territory. Thus far, Brahmaputra and the Meghna/Barak have remained virgin in terms of water impoundments and withdrawal/transfer. However, this will no longer be the case. India's recent decision to go ahead with plans to build a Dam at the Tipaimukh on the river Barak has ignited heated debates regarding its merit in India and Bangladesh (Mirza 2009). These debates have taken on transnational forms of environmental movements in various styles, such as protests and dialogues in Bangladesh, India, and many other countries.

After building the Farakka and Teesta barrages, India has started construction of the Tipaimukh Multipurpose Hydroelectric Dam Project (henceforth the Tipaimukh Dam) on the river Barak just one kilometer north of Zakiganj in Sylhet, Bangladesh. To be located five hundred meters downstream from the flowing rivers of the Barak and Tuivai rivers, the Tipaimukh Dam lies on the Southwestern corner of the Manipur state of India. The project, which was commissioned by India in 2006, involves three Northeast India states that make up the Manipur-Mizoram-Assam border. Its reservoir will have a water-storage capacity of 15,900 million cubic meters, with a maximum depth of 1,725.5 meters. The Barak River, which flows downstream to meet the Surma River system in Bangladesh, is considered to be the lifeline of the Sylhet region in Bangladesh. The Dam and barrage when completed are supposed to provide 1,500 megawatts of hydro-power to the Indian state of Assam, but in return, as estimated by experts, it is going to bring about a major environmental and social disaster for Bangladesh, practically contributing to the drying up of two rivers—the 350-kilometer Surma River and the 110-kilometer Kushiara River—which provide water for most of the Northeastern region of Bangladesh (Mirza 2009; Rahman 2009).

Over the last four decades, water has been a contentious issue plaguing bilateral relations between India and Bangladesh. Most of the rivers, which Bangladesh shares with India, are controlled and managed by India. The impact of climate change is one reason for India's plan to divert waters from the Northeast of the country to its drought-prone West and South from some fifty-four rivers that flow from India to Bangladesh (Kazmi 2009). Bangladesh has already been severely affected by both Farakka and Teesta barrages. India's plan to construct the third barrage has the effect of heightening bilateral tension between the neighboring countries. In addition, it has generated massive environmental protests. Since news of the project was released, there have been intense debates in Bangladesh among civil society, environmental groups, human-rights organizations, and media over the implications of the Tipaimukh Dam for the share of water coming from upper-riparian India. This debate continues to gather momentum, as the protest movement has taken a global form (Askari 2012; Rahman 2009).

A global ethnography based on a robust Internet search focusing on social media; correspondence with two dozen protesters in Canada, the U.S., the UK, and Bangladesh; and qualitative interviews with ten policy analysts comprising UN officials, academics, and government officers from India and Bangladesh shows a surge in strong environmental resistance movements to protest the construction of the Dam. The movement's aim is to protect Bangladesh and India from the risks and damage that may arise from the Dam's construction. The movement has taken different shapes, ranging from academic papers to seminar presentations to simple protests in various locations to the submission of petitions to the United Nations[1] and so forth. This chapter explores this movement to show how environmental resistance against the Tipaimukh Dam has transcended national borders and taken on a global and transnational form by examining such questions as who is protesting, why, in what ways, and with what effects. The chapter provides an important insight into Asian environmentalism, which has originated in Asia but formed a global alliance, and offers applied-policy recommendations seeking to encourage social change. It also demonstrates how power permeates environmental and social movements in their resistance against policies and decisions that can adversely affect vulnerable communities. The success and effectiveness of these movements depend in part on the solidarity of the participants and the depth of resources available to them.

ENVIRONMENTAL AND SOCIAL IMPACTS OF THE TIPAIMUKH DAM

The environmentalists at home and abroad have expressed deep concern that implementing the Tipaimukh Dam project could deprive Bangladesh of its share of the international river that supplies waters to hundreds of water bodies in the region. They fear that the Dam would ultimately dry up the Meghna River in the greater Sylhet region and nearby districts and the Surma and the Kushiara rivers in the winter season, which supply water to most of the Northeastern regions of Bangladesh. The Dam would seriously affect agricultural land and local flora and fauna, and it would generate a massive displacement of people and livestock. The Dam's construction would not only have serious consequences for the people of Bangladesh; the negative impact would also be felt by the people from the Indian states of Manipur and Nagaland. The Barak-Surma-Kushiara is an international river. Environmentalists, academics, members of civil society, and protesters argue that Bangladesh, being a lower-riparian country, has the right to an equitable share of the water from the river and also a right to examine the details of the construction of the Dam. Bangladesh has yet to be provided with detailed plans for the Dam, which it needs to appraise the project's full impact on Bangladesh. They also opine that India, being an upper-riparian country, has an obligation under international law to discuss the construction of such a massive infrastructure on the common river with lower-riparian Bangladesh.

Professor Mustafizur Rahman Tarafdar, a water-resources expert, in an article titled "Tipaimukh Dam: An Alarming Venture" (2009), discusses the ill effects of the Tipaimukh Dam. If this Dam is eventually constructed as intended, Bangladesh would suffer adverse effects that include hydrological drought and environmental degradation. The Dam would cause the Surma and Kushiara to run dry from November to May, which would eventually hamper agriculture, irrigation, and navigation and cause a shortage of drinking water, among other chain effects. This shortage of water in these few months would decrease the boost of groundwater, which would then lower the groundwater level over the years and, in turn, would affect all dugouts and shallow tube-wells. Agriculture, which is dependent on both surface as well as groundwater, would certainly be affected. In addition, any interference in the normal flow of water in the Barak would have an adverse effect on the Surma in Bangladesh, which feeds the mighty Meghna that flows through Bangladesh. This Dam would hamper the cultivation of an early variety of *boro* rice in the Northeast. Arable land would decrease and production of crops would fall, leading to an increase in poverty.

An estimated 7 to 8 percent of Bangladesh's water is obtained from the Barak. Millions of people are dependent on hundreds of water bodies fed by the Barak in the Sylhet region for fishing and agricultural activities. If the Dam were to collapse, it would impound billions of cubic meters of water and cause catastrophic floods because of its colossal structure. The Dam site is a hazardous zone that is at the highest risk seismically. Inhabitants of Manipur also believe that this Dam would prove to be a grave threat to the local biodiversity, including flora and fauna and endangered species, such as pythons, gibbons, and herbal and medicinal plants, and to tribal land rights. It would submerge as many as ninety villages within a 311-square-kilometer radius (Jahangir 2009). For Bangladesh, the potential impacts are even more severe. According to a group of water experts in Bangladesh, "if the Dam is constructed, 16 districts of greater Sylhet will be affected. The immense natural disaster that will take place would be irreversible. Even though the Indian government is saying once the Dam is constructed, electricity will be generated and Bangladesh will benefit by importing the electricity. It does not make sense to make a certain part of Bangladesh a desert area solely for the purpose of importing electricity" (Jahangir 2009:3).

The livelihoods of millions of people who rely on the Meghna for freshwater for their livelihoods and for the overall food security of the region are at stake. Bangladesh is already battling water shortages due to climate change. The Tipaimukh Dam would add to the environmental cataclysm already predicted by environmentalists. According to Ainun Nishat, the country director of the International Union for Conservation of Nature (IUCN), the Dam would increase the risk of floods, and the water bodies in Sylhet would be overflowing even during the winter season. More importantly, the average sea-water level would rise. Surface irrigation would be in danger, and cultivation and livelihoods in the area would be adversely affected. If India made a barrage at Fulertal (through which it would be able to manage water according to its needs) and procured water from river Barak, the rivers Surma and Kushiara would become virtually dry (Al-Mahmood 2009). Anticipating other long-term impacts of the Dam on Bangladesh, Tarafdar (2009) predicts:

> The rosy, prosperous and healthy scenario may soon turn into history causing despondency desperation and misery to the people inhabiting

the zone which is known for abundance of water, lush green field of crops and fish sanctuary. Massive environmental degradation will occur, drastically affecting weather and climate, turning a wet cooler habitat into a hot uncomfortable cauldron. The severity of micro-climate causing heat and dry conditions will gradually increase in intensity spreading over a large area over the years. It may be mentioned that rainfall that the area gets for 4 to 5 months and flood water that will be released from the Dam for a short period will not be enough to replenish the ground water. Climate and environmental change will force the farmers to reluctantly resort to planting low-yielding drought-resistant crops (unknown to them).

The controversial Tipaimukh Dam project has been contested by academics and environmentalists in India, too. Namdingpou Kamei (2006) lists the potential far-reaching environmental and social effects of the Dam on the local people:

- A land area totaling 286.20 square kilometers would be submerged forever.
- The Barak waterfalls and Zeilad Lake, which are connected with the history of the Zeliangrong people, would forever be underwater; all folklore and legends would have no verifying monuments and would become made-up stories for the next generation.
- More than 40,000 people would be rendered landless.
- Eight villages situated at the Barak Valley would be completely underwater.
- More than ninety villages, mostly in the Tamenglong district, would be adversely affected.
- About 27,242 hectares of cultivable land would be lost.
- The township of Nungba, subdivision headquarters, and the village along the NH-53 would be severely affected.
- The Dam would pose health hazards, including waterborne diseases, industrial pollution, and other environmental and ecological problems due to the increased water surface.
- Increased salinity of groundwater would make it unsafe for drinking and increase inconvenience to the people.
- Frequent occurrences of destructive earthquakes in the area would be possible.
- The decision was made without information from proper ecological studies, which thus overlooks the future challenges and problems that people will have to deal with.
- The construction would directly affect people's livelihoods. This natural product (water, plus its agriculture-related products), which the people rely upon for every aspect of their economy, would be totally cut off, which could result in economic and financial crises.

- Consequent displacement and destruction of the people by implementing the project would pose a grave threat to people's right to live in a vibrant democratic system.
- The project, once installed, would submerge the exotic flora and fauna and rich gene pools, as Manipur is located in one of the genetic hot spots of the world where rare biodiversity resources exist.
- There would be problems of displacement, resettlement, rehabilitation, repatriation, and development.
- The construction of the Dam would be a violation of democratic principles of governance, such as inclusiveness, which acknowledges and considers indigenous voices.
- The construction would show total disregard for the Zeliangrong ancient indigenous heritage, reflecting negatively on the partiality of the government.
- Not only would the Barak basin be affected, but the Dam's construction would also affect its tributaries.

Although the potential impacts of the Dam are largely estimated and sometimes exaggerated, the possible colossal environmental and social disasters cannot be denied. While the Indian government is continuously justifying the construction of this Dam by pointing to the benefits it would bring to people, such as the generation of electricity, the enormous costs of the project, such as the potential risk of environmental and social damages, are alarming. The Indian government has yet to reveal the full environmental-assessment report to the public. Nonetheless, experts' opinions on this issue have generated an enormous strain on the Dam's feasibility. People in India and Bangladesh have increasingly felt that the Indian government's decision is unjust, as they are convinced that the Dam would cause an irreparable environmental and social catastrophe. As a result of local protests against the Dam, construction was postponed in 2007. The Indian government subsequently employed various public-relations strategies, apparatuses, and resources to convince the local people and the government of Bangladesh of the benefits and feasibility of the project. Despite support and acceptance for the Dam project from the current ruling party of Bangladesh, Awami League (AL), which is historically pro-Indian, the local population has launched various types of movements and campaigns to contest their government's decision and support for the project. In light of the arguments and cost analysis made against the decision to construct the Dam, I now examine the subsequent backlash of resistance movements in Bangladesh and abroad.

ENVIRONMENTAL RESISTANCE AGAINST THE TIPAIMUKH DAM

As indicated earlier, there have been intense debates in Bangladesh among civil society, including environmental groups, human-rights organizations, and the media, over the implications of the Tipaimukh Dam on the share of water coming from upper-riparian India (Rahman 2009). The Dam issue continues to dominate the domain of political, media, intellectual, and civil society's discourse in Bangladesh, with a unilateral demand for revocation of India's decision to proceed with the project. Massive public protests in different forms—rallies, human chains, protest meetings, strikes, and so on—continue to gain momentum in Bangladesh. The movement has also taken different shapes—political and non-political, local and global—even though it is sometimes difficult to identify clear boundaries as the movement adapts to various conditions.

Environmental Resistance in Bangladesh

The ongoing Farakka dispute over the sharing of waters of the Ganges River, which is still under negotiation, is indicative of the political tensions and turbulent past shared by India and Bangladesh regarding issues of water sharing from transboundary rivers. This issue has been played to the hilt in the domestic political scene in Bangladesh in the past, and the lines between the government and opposition are clearly drawn now, with the opposition, led by Begum Khaleda Zia, actively supporting the anti–Tipaimukh Dam civil-society groups in Bangladesh. The political opposition has been vociferously attacking the Sheikh Hasina–led government, which was voted to power in Bangladesh in late 2008 and is seen as pro-India. The four-party alliance led by the Bangladesh Nationalist Party (BNP) has vowed to take the Tipaimukh Dam issue to international forums if the government fails to stop it (Rahman 2009).

Feeling the heat from the opposition parties and the civil-society movement, a parliamentary delegation formed from the Bangladesh Parliamentary Standing Committee on Water Resources led by Bangladeshi Water Resources Minister Abdur Razzaq visited New Delhi en route to the Tipaimukh Dam site in Manipur in early August 2009. Under pressure from growing domestic criticism at home in Bangladesh, the delegation members stressed to their Indian counterparts the need for negotiations regarding the concerns and issues raised between both countries. Bangladesh has urged India to conduct a joint study to examine the implications of the Tipaimukh Dam project on the region and the future flow of water in the concerned river system, which directly affects Bangladesh due to its position as a lower-riparian country. In addition, Prime Minister Hasina brought up Bangladesh's concerns relating to the Tipaimukh Dam Project with Prime Minister Manmohan Singh during their meeting on the sidelines of the Non-Aligned Movement Summit in Egypt (Rahman 2009).

Environmentalists and other civil-society groups in Bangladesh have formed the National Tipaimukh Dam Resistance Committee (TDRC). A 'long march' organized by various Bangladeshi civil-society organizations, which included TDRC and Sylhet Division Unnayan Sangram Samiti (a

committee that fights for development in Sylhet Division) and was supported by leaders of BNP and the hardliner Bangladesh Jamaat-e-Islami
(BJI), marched toward the Tipaimukh Dam site on August 10, 2009, but
were stopped at the international border by the Bangladesh Rifles (BDR).[2]
The support from BJI on this issue could become a serious source of concern for India (Rahman 2009). Before the 'long march', BJI tried to organize massive protests to mobilize people's support against the Dam, but the
government managed to foil these protest movements. The top leaders of
the party were arrested by the government in 2010. While the current government is committed to banning or foiling any popular political-resistance
movement surrounding the Tipaimukh Dam in Bangladesh, massive environmental resistance abroad and online continues.

In August 2009, leaders of TDRC at a discussion stressed the need for
spontaneous participation of the people in the movement against the construction of the Dam by India. They called upon the people to remain alert
on the issue so that the Indian government could not construct the Dam
on Barak River. If India constructed the Dam, the Northeastern region of
the country would turn into a desert, they said. The discussion was held
at Dhaka Reporters Unity (DRU) in the city as a part of the observance of
the 'Global Solidarity Sit-in the Tipaimukh Dam Program'. The program
was also observed in different district headquarters around the country and
in cities around the world, including Shilchar, Calcutta, and Patna, India;
Canberra, Australia; Tokyo, Japan; and New York, U.S. Referring to fifty
large dams in the world, an engineer named Hilal, a discussion participant,
said that a "water syndicate" is now active to build more dams on big rivers
to serve their own interests. "Such immoral activities of the syndicate have
also contributed to global climate change," he continued. Renowned Indian
journalist Shankar Roy and Indian engineer Dinesh Mitra, who is also a
veteran leader of the Tipaimukh Dam issue, both expressed solidarity with
the participants of the program (The *New Nation* 2009d).

Visiting British parliamentarian George Galloway showed his solidarity
with this movement and called for an international inquiry into the prob-
able environmental impact of India's proposed Tipaimukh Dam. He stated
that the inquiry would need to examine the impact on both the Bangladesh
and Indian population and noted that the project is an international issue
due to its implications for the climate and the environment. Arguing that
the Tipaimukh Dam is not an issue concerning only Bangladesh and India,
Galloway answered a query by stating that building this Dam would be "a
criminal offense" by India. He affirmed his support by saying, "I will fight
to prevent making this Dam. Not only Bangladeshi people, a section of
Indian people will also be affected. Even the Indian expatriates in London
protested . . . against the proposed Dam." Galloway led a UK delegation
and a huge Bangladeshi crowd on a march on November 29, 2009, from
Sylhet city to the border with India where the river Barak divides into the
Shurma and Kushiara. The march was arranged to draw global attention to

the potentially devastating impact of the proposed Dam on Sylhet and the entire Northeastern region of Bangladesh (Reuters UK 2009).

The *New Nation* (2009c) reported that a conference of Surma Kushi-ara Meghna Bachao Andolan (a movement to save Surma, Kushiara, and Meghna) in Dhaka on August 20, 2009, was organized to drum up sup-port from the people for the movement against the construction of the Tipaimukh Dam. The conference was held at the Dr. Ma Hadi Auditorium in the city and was attended by delegates from eighteen districts from the basin of the rivers Surma, Kushiara, and Meghna. Speakers unanimously agreed that the Bangladeshi government should discuss the issue with the Indian government, and if the latter did not stop the construction of the Dam, the Bangladeshi government should raise the issue in the Interna-tional Court of Justice.

In August 2009, leaders of Islami Andolan Bangladesh (IAB) submitted a memorandum to UN Secretary General Ban Ki Mun through a UNDP repre-sentative of Bangladesh, requesting help to stop the construction of the Dam. The memorandum contended that the plan to construct the Tipaimukh Dam was a complete violation of the 1996 Bangladesh-India Joint River Commis-sion (JRC), the International Helsinki Convention, and International River Law. It also pointed out that if India constructed the Dam, it would bring about negative ecological and environmental changes in vast areas of Bangla-desh and various states of India. IAB leaders urged the UN secretary general to intervene to stop the construction of the Dam to save vast areas of Bangla-desh from desertification (The *New Nation* 2009b). On September 18, 2009, the supporters of IAB again marched on to the Indian High Commission to protest against the Dam (Demotix 2009).

Observers claim that only Bangladesh's Awami League (AL), which is the leading party of the ruling coalition, did not openly oppose the construc-tion of the Dam. They attributed this to the perceived strategic friendly relations AL has with the Indian government. A few other parties of the ruling coalition have launched protests against the Dam. It was reported that Bangladesh's Juba Union, a front body of the Communist Party of Bangladesh (CPB), which is a part of the ruling coalition, held a two-day Dhaka-Sylhet road-march program to demand an immediate halt to the construction of the Dam. Despite AL's claim that the protest against the Dam was a strategy by the opposition parties to harvest political gains, many political analysts have argued that the government has failed to understand the people's demands (Nazrul 2010). As the protests against the Dam continue in various forms, the government has also taken hard lines to crush the movement. Nevertheless, the issue of the Dam continues to dominate the media in Bangladesh, and the resistance movement extends beyond the Bangladeshi border.

The movement has been strongest and most spontaneous in Bangla-desh, because the local population is the most vulnerable to the project's potential risks to the water supply. The movement has unified diverse elements from society, drawing members from all walks of life, occupations, and statuses. These protesters feel a strong sense of injustice for what is deemed a unilateral decision by the Indian government and the betrayal of AL, the only party that supported the project, and a lack of effective government action to protect the local population's interests. Their spontaneity has subsequently spread beyond Bangladesh's borders, where sympathizers rally behind the resistance movement in a show of solidarity against perceived injustice.

Movement in India

Hundreds of people representing Bengali, Manipuri, Naga, Khasi, Reang, Dimasa, and other communities in the Southern part of Assam district in India staged a demonstration in front of the District Commissioner's office at Silchar in the first week of April 2009. The demonstrators condemned the government's decision and demanded the immediate termination of the Dam project. Pijus Kanti Das, secretary general of the Committee on Peoples and Environment (COPE), and a number of leaders from different organizations and groups joined the demonstration held at the office of the District Commissioner (DC). The demonstrators subsequently sent memoranda separately to President Pratibha Devi Singh Patil; Prime Minister Singh; Union Minister for Forest and Environment Jairam Ramesh; Assam Chief Minister Tarun Gogoi; and Manipur Chief Minister O Ibobi Singh through DC Cachar. In these memoranda, they expressed their concern for the people living upstream of Barak River and the potential environmental impact of the Dam's construction. Protests were also seen in Manipur, Mizoram, and Barak Valley of Assam. Protestors demanded an extensive downstream environmental-impact study from the proposed Dam site up to the sea-mouth. The protestors insisted that the study should be a joint initiative by the government of India and Bangladesh and include experts from NGOs, particularly environmental NGOs, the Indian Institute of Technology, and other universities. Without a downstream-impact study, the project would put both the environment and the poor rural people of India and Bangladesh at enormous risk (Merinews 2010).

The proposed Dam is situated at the convergence of three biodiversity hot spots—namely, the Indo-Burma, Indo-Malayan, and Indo-Chinese regions. These areas are characterized by the presence of a large number of plant and animal species unique to their regions. A large number of these species have been categorized as endangered by the IUCN Red Data Book and the Wildlife (Protection) Act of 1972. The construction of the Dam would threaten the natural habitats and likely cause the extinction of these endangered species. Moreover, a number of tribal people, including Hmar, Zeliangrong, Kuki, Mizo, and others who have been living in the Dam's area for generations, would be displaced and forced to relocate, giving up their indigenous ways of life. In short, the construction of the Dam would seriously derail efforts at biodiversity conservation and threaten the livelihood of indigenous communities (Merinews 2010).

COPE observed that the Dam would be constructed at the earthquake zone-V. Should there be any cracks in the Dam's wall, the constant pressure of water may cause a full-blown collapse of the entire structure. In such an event, the flood that followed would swallow up any downstream settlement; the age-old Barak-Surma culture may perish. In short, protesters have highlighted the serious consequences of the project on the existing vulnerable ecosystems (both human and non-human) within and around the proposed site of the Dam.

The people of Cachar in the Indian state of Assam initially favored the Dam's construction. However, they joined the movement against the proposed Dam when it became apparent they had been misled. A joint meeting between various environmental organizations of Cachar and the Monipur groups opposing the construction of the Dam was held in August 2009. The group alleged that the Indian government had been misleading the downstream people regarding the benefits of the Dam for a long time. The leader of the Anti-Tipai Dam Project, Ramananda, had this expectation: "Downstream communities of different races and environmental organizations . . . decided to join anti-Dam movement. People of Barak's upper region in Manipur have been waging movement for a long time. Anti-Dam movement has begun in Bangladesh. Now the people of downstream Cachar region have joined this movement. As a result, the anti-Dam movement will gain momentum and pressure will be exerted on the government to abandon this project" (News from Bangladesh 2009).

The Hmar People's Convention (Democratic) of Monipur issued a press release on July 18, 2009. It stated that the proposed Tipaimukh Multipurpose Hydroelectric Project is a war imposed on the indigenous Hmar people and various other communities located upstream and downstream. The power-hungry governments and Dam builders in India, who are driven by short-term interests in their blind pursuit of profits, are putting indigenous communities at risk. The consent and opinions of these indigenous communities were not sought. A statement from the press release stressed that "[t]he Rivers that nursed and fed our honored generations before shall continue to flow for all the generations to come. We cannot allow the rivers to be disturbed and are obligated to see that no outsiders, their forces and might will dam, destroy or disturb the natural flow of the rivers of life" (quoted in Nesar 2009). It also appealed to the visiting Bangladeshi parliamentary delegates to steadfastly share their concern to save the rivers Tuiruong and Tuivai for all purposes, to work together for the collective good, and to save the rivers from irreparable damage.

In early March 2010, hundreds of people held a rally in an interior town of Manipur's Tamenglong district to protest the proposed construction of the Dam. The participants marched through Nungba town, which they said would be affected by the proposed Dam, and submitted a memorandum to the state's chief minister through the subdivisional officer of Nungba subdivision on March 9, 2010. The memorandum claimed that the Dam would have serious effects on the ecology, environment, biodiversity, and identity of the indigenous people living in Tipaimukh and surrounding areas. Official responses stated that India and Bangladesh held discussions over the construction of the Dam and concluded that it would solve the flood problem caused by the Barak River in the Cachar district of Assam and parts of Bangladesh (ZeeNews 2010); however, no clear-cut plans have been released to the public.

Protest in the U.S.

Human Rights and Development for Bangladesh (HRDB) held a massive demonstration on July 17 in front of the United Nations to protest the construction of the Tipaimukh Dam. More than 600 people from New York participated. Among others, the demonstration was addressed by community activists Badrunnahar Mita, Mahtab Uddin Ahmed, Mir Masum Ali, Abdul Hasib Chowdhury, Abu Samiha Md Sirajul Islam, Professor Nurul Islam, Abdul Kadir Khan, Barrister Golam Mostafa, Mahmudur Rahman, and Moulana Delwar Hossen. A memorandum was also handed over to the United Nations afterward on behalf of the demonstrators. Meanwhile, another activist, Khondaker Abu Sufiyan, organized a seminar in association with the International Centre for Advancement of Bangladesh (ICAB) and in collaboration with a section of Bangladeshi engineers living in the U.S. on July 16, 2009, at the Jewish Community Center in Jackson Heights, New York (Nesar 2009). On May 19, 2009, an organization named Long Live Bangladesh (LLB) organized a seminar called Environmental and Political Crises Looming in Bangladesh[3] at the Marriott Hotel in Washington, D.C., to discuss the pros and cons of the Tipaimukh Dam. Several engineers and some environmentalists presented their papers and opined that the benefits of the Dam would not outweigh the costs for both India and Bangladesh. LLB subsequently issued press releases to various local and global media.

A radio channel called the Bangladesh News Network (BNN) was established by some Bangladeshi expatriates in Los Angeles to protest against the Dam and Indian hegemony in Bangladesh, and then the station organized a seminar against the Dam in Los Angeles. Both the president and the general secretary of the International Farakka Committee (IFC) participated in this seminar and pledged their commitment and support. BNN Radio broadcast interviews with several professors on the issue of the Tipaimukh Dam. Members of South Asian communities living in other parts of the U.S. also expressed their concern about the Dam and showed support for the anti-Dam movement.

Resistance in Canada

Several media portals, including the *New Nation* (2009a), reported that members of the Bangladeshi community in Montreal, led by Save Bangladesh International, Global Environmental Concern, and the Canadian chapter of IFC, initiated a long march to Ottawa in a protest against the Dam. The march was accompanied by slogan chants of "Cholo Cholo Ottawa Cholo" ["Let's march toward Ottawa"]. The group marched from Montréal on foot for a while before taking transportation to arrive at the Parliament building. Addressing the rally near the flame in front of the Parliament building, conference organizer Mamunur Rashid of Save Bangladesh International said, "India being known globally as a peace-loving country should practice what it preaches. Building Dams over the Ganges, Tista and now Tipaimukh is not helping to promote peace in the region" (Rashid 2009:1). The speakers urged the Indian government to be more responsible and to reconsider the plight of human communities and biodiversity conservation efforts that would be adversely affected by the Dam's construction (New Nation 2009a).

The meeting concluded that India is ignoring the concerns from Bangladesh and the international environmental groups. Participants also agreed that Bangladeshis in Bangladesh and abroad should continue to fight and should keep up their pressure through demonstrations and protests against India's unilateral decision. The demonstration in Ottawa also included non-Bangladeshis—mainly other South Asians and Canadian members of Friends of Bangladeshi. The demonstrators also informed a representative of the Canadian prime minister's office that India is adamantly going ahead with the plan despite expert claims that there would be an increased risk of the Tipaimukh Dam's failure due to its location in a high-risk earthquake zone. In the case of such a failure, the projected Dam would cause a tsunami-like disaster for Bangladesh's Eastern region. The demonstrators sought help from the Canadian government to mediate this serious international issue that concerns the lives of millions (The *New Nation* 2009a). Save Bangladesh International reported that it also organized several meetings and seminars to discuss the Dam project in some major cities of Canada, including Toronto.

Resistance through the Internet

The issue of the Tipaimukh Dam has been stormily debated in blogs, newspapers, and rallies. More than one hundred Facebook groups have been created, including Protest Tipaimukh Dam, Stop Tipaimukh Dam, Protest against Tipaimukh Dam, Tipaimukh Dam & Fulertal Barrage—Let's Stop India, Save Our Bangladesh, Tipaimukh Dissemination, Tipaimukh Barrage, and so forth. Dedicated blog sites have been launched to organize and to disseminate Tipaimukh Dam–related news. *Protest Tipaimukh Dam,* for instance, posted 208 articles and pieces of news analysis related to the Dam in 2009. Various other virtual forums have been formed to resist the Dam's construction.

There have been over a dozen online petitions sent to the prime minister of India that collected signatures in order to stop the construction. One example is the "Cancel the Tipaimukh Dam, Let the Ahu (Barak River) Run Free" petition, which was submitted by the Action Committee against Tipaimukh Project (ACTIP) with support from Zeliangrong Union (ZU), Nungba Area Village Authority Chairmen's Association (NAVACA), Zeliangrong Students' Union Manipur Nungba Zone (ZSUM Nungba Zone) and Tipaimukh Dam Affected Villages Committee (TIDAVCOM) and presented over two thousand signatures. The last paragraph of the petition stated, "As our elders say, 'We cannot eat electricity.' How long must we wait, while our fundamental and basic rights are denied? When will we see you come to us to ask us what we really want for our future, for our land, and not just to tell us what we must sacrifice and what is good for us? Cancel the Tipaimukh Dam, let the Ahu run free and be with us to make the right choices for ourselves, for our future generations and for our natural heritage" (Amader Bangladesh 2009).

Apart from Bangladesh, India, the U.S., and Canada, South Asian people living in other parts of the world, including the UK, Australia, Japan, and Malaysia, have expressed their serious concerns about the construction of the Dam. Through protests, petitions, and other forms of resistance, their efforts have been targeted at increasing pressure on the Indian government to reconsider and to abandon the Dam project.

LOCAL ISSUE, GLOBAL MOVEMENT: POWER THROUGH SOLIDARITY

The protests and initiatives against the Dam project demonstrate how environmental movements transcend national boundaries when participants rally behind a common goal. The participants share a common understanding of the risks involved in proceeding with the Dam project. Environmental movements, such as this resistance against the decision to build the Dam, gather momentum when participants come from diverse nationalities. With Indians joining the movement, the decision-makers are under more pressure regarding the collective interests expressed by the different stakeholders. Power is generated from this collective voice that is expressing a common interest in protecting the livelihood of vulnerable communities and biodiversity. The power of this environmental movement to effect change is manifest in the early, although temporary, success of forcing a delay in the project. With diverse talents among the participants, the movement has also been able to tap on its resources to mobilize both soft power (seminars, petitions) and hard power (physical protests, long marches).

As the environmental movement becomes increasingly transnational, a local and regional issue is now framed as a global one. The movement spread to the U.S. and Canada, while overseas, Bangladeshis rallied behind the environmental cause and were joined by sympathizers from their host countries and international environmental groups. The increase in scale and number of participants in this increasingly globalized environmental movement united against the construction of the Dam has further empowered the movement and the legitimacy of its demands. These demands were made to international government bodies, such as the United Nations, to put pressure on the Indian government to reconsider its decision and to abandon the project. The movement has also harnessed the power of online social media, relying on the platforms for instant communication to make the organizing of protests and other events more efficient and effective. Through the solidarity garnered and with such resources as technical skills, organizational skills, expert opinions and reports, and international NGO support at its disposal, the movement is increasingly empowered to advance toward its aim of stopping the Dam project.

SEMI-PERIPHERY DEVELOPMENT, PERIPHERY BURDEN

Scholars of world-systems theory argue that the nation-state as a unit of analysis is no longer reflective of the current global economic system; instead, they divide the world into three geo-ecological regions that constitute the existing global division of labor—namely, the core, the periphery, and the semi-periphery (see J. Smith 2004; Wallerstein 2004). Core regions are characterized by highly industrialized economies, with wealth generation from financial and trade dominance in the division of labor. Periphery regions, in contrast, are resource-rich and offer raw materials and cheap labor to the other regions. Periphery regions are exploited for their resources and labor; they are attractive regions for outsourcing production activities, leaving the core regions to concentrate on highly skilled financial and trading services. Semi-periphery regions lie somewhere in the middle; suffice to say that countries that are classified in this category are striving to attain core status, often imitating 'Western' models of development and their industrialization programs.

According to Immanuel M. Wallerstein (1976), India qualifies as a semi-periphery state. Energy security is crucial for any aspiring state in its development project. Ensuring a steady supply of energy would require looking for alternatives to rapidly depleting traditional sources of energy, such as coal and oil. Hydro-power is one such alternative that would generate the high levels of electricity needed to drive economic development. India's insistence on building the Tipaimukh Dam can be understood in the context of its wider development agenda. Moreover, hydro-power development is a venture that can attract huge amounts of foreign investment and investment into the infrastructure by the energy corporations. However, the development benefits of one country would necessitate transferring the burden of risks to another country—in this case, to the periphery state of Bangladesh. Ultimately, the burden would be borne by the local communities that are most vulnerable to exploitation from the semi-periphery states and their profit-driven energy companies. Karen Bakker aptly sums up the politics of hydro-development:

> Due in part to its scale of construction and impact, hydrodevelopment is a far more public process than other types of resource exploitation. Simultaneously, however, it is a far less transparent process for local communities and individual countries, due to the degree of expertise involved, the complexity of the bureaucracies funding, assessing, and building dams, and the tendency to employ foreign consultants from a handful of OECD countries. The 'public transcript' of hydrodevelopment is thus heavily weighted towards international discourses of development. (1999:211)

Clearly, while India—or, more specifically, the corporations and individuals behind the Dam construction project—would get to enjoy the benefits of additional profits, the burden of risks would be transferred over to the vulnerable communities that live downstream in Bangladesh and to periphery regions within India itself.

CONCLUSION

Environmental resistance against the Tipaimukh Dam has been largely initiated by the poor; however, the magnitude and scope of the movement is undoubtedly diverse and widespread. Whether and to what extent these movements are successful is still up for debate. Despite massive resistance and protest at home and abroad, both the governments of Bangladesh and India are ironically in favor of constructing the Dam. The resistance movement was temporarily successful when the construction work was stalled in March 2007 in the face of protests from within and outside India. Once the Indian government decided to continue with the project, environmental resistance continued to gain momentum. People in India and Bangladesh feel that the construction in the name of development and helping the local population through the provision of free electricity will ultimately lead to environmental and social injustice. Tipaimukh has become a source of strain for the people of Bangladesh. One of their common slogans is that 'Tipaimukh Dam is death to Sylhet and Bangladesh—it must be stopped'. We have also observed that the movement has taken different shapes—from simple protests to expressing discontent in various forums and meetings to launching protests through Facebook, blogs, and other Internet portals to generating different environmental and social-justice organizations to creating alliances among different groups to submitting petitions to the United Nations. This chapter has examined how and why this single environmental resistance movement against the Tipaimukh Dam transcended national borders and took a global and transnational form.

In general, India has been using its upper-riparian position and its economic and financial strength to take unilateral steps with regard to the flow of these international rivers. Most of these unilateral steps have been of diversionary character, involving the diversion of water flow to destinations inside India and thus reducing the flow of water into the rivers of Bangladesh. These diversionary projects of India go against the international norms regarding the sharing of international rivers. In particular, they violate Bangladesh's right to prior and customary use of river water. These unilateral projects are also deteriorating Bangladesh-India bilateral relations. After a long hiatus, Bangladesh and India signed the Ganges Water Treaty in 1996, specifying the sharing of the Ganges water at Farakka. Article IX of this treaty enjoins India not to undertake unilateral projects involving rivers shared with Bangladesh. In practice, India has not respected this provision of the treaty and has moved ahead with many unilateral projects. India's disregard for its initial commitments is manifest in its action of floating international tender to invite bids for the construction of Tipaimukh Dam without even sharing the detailed project report with Bangladesh. Only recently, when the news of the construction of Tipaimukh Dam generated considerable protests in Bangladesh and abroad, the government of India reportedly sent some information about the project to the Bangladesh foreign ministry. However, the government of Bangladesh has yet to make this information public. Bangladesh does not yet have the necessary facts to assess the changes in the Barak flow that may be caused by the Tipaimukh Dam construction (M. N. Islam 2009).

Historical and global experience shows that large-scale interventions in rivers are generally not beneficial in the long run. It remains an open question whether Tipaimukh Dam will be beneficial in the long run and in net terms, even for India. This study has shown that many in India are opposed to the Dam, including indigenous people, the state governments of Manipur and Mizoram, environmentalists, river activists, human-rights advocates, and even economists and social scientists, among others. The North East Electricity Production Company (NEEPCO), the current Tipaimukh implementing agency, has been able to pacify the state governments through offering monetary benefits and free electricity (Md Nazrul Islam 2009). Nonetheless, opposition to Tipaimukh continues in India, albeit at a lesser scale.

River-intervention structures have generally been the outcome of the commercial approach to rivers, which suggests that any flow of river water to the sea is a waste and that all of it should be used up. Such an approach contributes to the degradation of rivers and increased conflict and animosity among countries of the river basin. It appears that the development imperative of semi-periphery countries, such as India, is placing vulnerable communities in periphery regions, such as Bangladesh, at great risk, transferring the burden of the damage likely to be brought about by the Dam's construction.

In view of this experience, there is now a move toward the ecological approach, which recommends preservation of the natural volume and direction of river flow. Instead of being a source of discord, as is the case with the commercial approach, under the ecological approach rivers represent a bond of friendship and good neighborliness. Globally, there is also a move away from the unilateral approach toward a multilateral, basin-wide approach that includes all the countries of a river basin in decision-making processes regarding the use of the river. Taking insights from the environmental and social-justice movements surrounding the Tipaimukh Dam, I can offer some applied public-policy recommendations:

(a) India should stop proceeding any further with Tipaimukh and engage in serious and sincere discussions with Bangladesh about the fate of this and all other projects of intervention in the shared international rivers.

(b) India should abandon its current unilateral approach; adopt a multilateral, basin-wide, integrated resource-management approach to the rivers of the region; and invite Bangladesh, Nepal, Bhutan, and China to join this effort.

(c) India should not undertake a water-diversionary project (such as at Fulertal or at other points) on the Barak River under any circumstances.

(d) India should refrain from water-diversionary projects on other rivers shared with Bangladesh.

(e) Bangladesh, India, and the other countries of the subcontinent should abandon their current commercial approach to rivers and adopt the ecological approach.

(f) The government of Bangladesh should immediately make public the information that it has received from the government of India regarding Tipaimukh so that all interested parties and scholars can use this information for the necessary analysis.

(g) The government of Bangladesh should sponsor independent research by Bangladeshi experts on the possible impact of Tipaimukh on Bangladesh's economy and ecology.

(h) All Bangladeshi political parties should adopt a nonpartisan approach to the Tipaimukh issue and issues of water sharing with India in general and cooperate to develop a united national position.

(i) All political parties should cooperate with the government of Bangladesh to the extent that it sincerely tries to find a solution with India regarding Tipaimukh, defending Bangladesh's national interests and legitimate rights.

(j) All political parties represented in Parliament should join the proposed all-party delegation of Bangladesh's Parliament to visit Tipaimukh to find out the facts and to submit a report.

(k) Citizens of Bangladesh should join en masse the developing civic movement to save the rivers of the country.

(l) All the concerned stakeholders in Bangladesh, including political parties, civil-society organizations, NGOs, think tanks, media, mass organizations, local people's organizations, nonresident Bangladeshis, and so forth, should come together, leaving behind narrow partisan and sectarian interests. They should develop and rally behind a united national position regarding Tipaimukh Dam and other river-sharing issues, as Bangladesh needs national unity in order to defend its rivers.

The effectiveness of an environmental movement depends, in part, on the solidarity of the movement and the strength in numbers and diversity of participants' backgrounds. The policy recommendations discussed here are aimed at promoting greater solidarity among all stakeholders in environmental resistance movements against projects that would adversely affect vulnerable communities and the environment.

11 Labeling Tribal
State Power in Forming and Transforming Identities

INTRODUCTION

This chapter examines how 'tribals' are defined through public-policy practices and discusses the impact of such labeling for the people involved. Under neoliberalism, hegemonic power does not simply manipulate given differences between individuals and social groups but actively produces and reproduces differences as a key strategy to create and to maintain modes of social and special division that are advantageous to its continued empowerment (Soja and Hooper 1993). Dominating groups in neoliberal developmentalism actively use 'labeling' as a key strategy to perpetuate their domination over the dominated. Induced by a neoliberal vision of accumulation and power creation, some developmental states in the global periphery demonstrate a kind of 'soft power' in forming and transforming identities of their 'subalterns' that subsequently justify certain 'hard' interventions. The highlanders (people living in the forests and/or hills) in Thailand and Indonesia are marginalized; they are made 'foreign' in their own land as a result of state policies delineating and legitimizing differences in identities. Taking 'labels' as a conceptual metaphor and using empirical data collected from existing literature on the upland people of Thailand and Indonesia, this chapter explores how and with what consequences people become labeled as 'tribals'. How is an identity formed, transformed, and manipulated within the context of public policy? How are highlanders' basic rights compromised by and through bureaucratic practices?

In the past few years a number of writers have begun to explore the intersection between racial/ethnic identities, community-based resource management, and access to resources in Southeast Asia (see for example Brosius, Tsing, and Zerner 1998; Li 2000a, 2000b; McDermott 2000). These contributions are in part framed as a commentary on an advocacy agenda (see Lynch and Talbott 1995) that appeals to indigenous or tribal identities as a way of arguing for the resource rights of the inhabitants of forested zones. In other words, activists often argue that people identified as indigenous or tribal should be accorded community-based resource rights because of their dependence on these resources and capabilities in managing them. Writers in the field of political ecology have expressed considerable ambivalence about this strategy (see Brosius, Tsing, and Zerner 1998; Li 1999a, 1999b). Tania Li's argument is that a group's self-identification as tribal or indigenous is not natural or inevitable, but neither is it simply invented, adopted, or imposed. Instead, it is "a *positioning* [emphasis in original], which draws upon historically sedimented practices, landscapes, and repertoires of meaning, and emerges through particular patterns of engagement and struggle" (Li 2000b:151). She elaborates that the conjectures at which some people come to identify themselves as indigenous while realigning the ways they connect to the nation, the government, and their own unique tribal place are the contingent products of agency and the cultural and political work of *articulation*. Central to her analysis are the concepts of *articulation* and *positioning*, which she draws from Stuart Hall (1991, 1996). In contrast, Peter Vandergeest (2003) uses the idea of 'racialization' to understand the link between identity and resource politics. He argues that the production of space through cadastral mapping, forest reservation, and community forests has been racialized to the point that the production of these spaces is also associated with the production of naturalized forms of ethnic identity. Here I use 'labeling' as an alternative approach in understanding the formation and transformation of identity of the highlanders in the official discourse in Thailand and Indonesia.

LABELING

'Tribals' are subjected to labels constructed through social- and development-policy discourses. Labeling is a way of referring to the process by which policy agendas are established. It particularly refers to the way in which people, conceived as *objects of policy*, are defined in convenient images (G. Wood 1985). This conceptualization is predicated on a series of propositions (Schaffer 1985; G. Wood 1985). Propositions relevant to this chapter are briefly summarized below.

First, the *processes* of labeling are as significant as the labels themselves for my purpose of exploring how labeling works for people and with what effects. Second, labeling is a process of *stereotyping* that involves disaggregation, standardization, and the formulation of clear-cut categories (G. Wood 1985). In the institutional setting, these characteristics assume considerable power in allowing labeling to simultaneously define a client group and to prescribe an assumed set of needs (food, shelter, and protection, for example), complete with appropriate distributional apparatus. With the symmetry of defining a client group and prescribing a set of needs, institutional action acquires its own legitimacy and is often viewed as 'apparent benevolence'. It is precisely through this prescriptive process that an institutional identity is being formed:

What is being exchanged . . . is the way in which people can present themselves as applicants and present their wants and needs for the items and privileges of institutional services. That is . . . a disaggregation into programme terms. . . . It reduces the whole man and family into formal sets of compartmentalized data . . . a sort of individuation and alienation of a man from a large part of his being. (Schaffer 1977:32)

Third, in this separation of an individual's needs from their context and the process of reconstruction into a *programmatic identity*, the important distinction between 'case' and 'story' is created (G. Wood 1985:13). Delinkage takes place whereby an individual identity is replaced by a stereotyped identity with a categorical prescription of assumed needs. These categories are usually absolute and not relative or comparative. Labels replicate the professional, bureaucratic, and political values that create them; a story is reformed into a case, a category. I examine in some detail, in the next part of this chapter, how the formation of a tribal stereotype in this way takes place in Thailand and Indonesia.

The counterpart to stereotyping is *control*, since a considerable degree of client loyalty and conformity with the stereotype is required (Hirschman 1970). Such control, although not always physically enforced in Thailand and Indonesia in many tribal situations, has been nonetheless instrumental in determining the meaning of the label 'tribals'. These processes of categorization and differentiation have been significant factors in forming a stereotyped identity for the 'tribals' that I show in Thailand and Indonesia. I argue that the need to conform to an institutionally imposed stereotype can both reinforce control and transform an identity.

Fourth, labeling is a process of *designation*, for it involves making judgments and distinction, and it is mostly if not always *non-participatory*. The process of labeling, by its very commonality in bureaucratic activity, may almost go unnoticed or unquestioned. It suggests neutrality; the very conformity it produces conveys "a substantive objectivity" (G. Wood 1985:7). But bureaucratic producers, resource distribution, and the underlying political interests they represent suggest that the labeling of target groups and their needs is not neutral or precise (Rosenblat 1984). Due to their self-evident humanitarian derivation, tribal rehabilitation programs are particularly prone to the neutralizing conformity. Labels reveal "the political in the apparently non-political" (G. Wood 1985:6) and the power displayed through administrative procedure and practice.

Finally, and by extension, labels are not only political but also *dynamic*. A program's goods and services acquire a status; a client group, such as the 'tribals', does not necessarily remain acquiescent and 'loyal'. Accordingly, the label may be not only the consequence of but also the cause of further policy development, institutional activity, and demands made by the labeled group (Schaffer 1985; Wood 1985). These may be factors in restructuring the political interests. The case studies below analyze these.

HIGHLANDERS IN THAILAND AND INDONESIA

One prominent world terrain of racial oppression stretches between the lowlanders and the highlanders of Southeast Asia, where valley-based states have regularly attempted to sedentarize and control the hill-dwelling ethnic minorities. Racist patterns and processes in the region have been sustained and strengthened through the activities of international environmentalists and development activists. In a scheme that would affect sixty million people in China, Laos, Burma, Thailand, Indonesia, Cambodia, and Vietnam, the Asian Development bank has proposed to "reduce the population of people in mountainous areas and bring them to normal life" (Lohmann 1999:70).

In Thailand, more than a half-million hill dwellers, who were made scapegoats for deforestation, have faced official resettlement threats for decades. International agencies, such as Food and Agricultural Organization (FAO), support theories about the destructiveness of the swidden agriculture, which are often used to legitimize the threats against hill dwellers (Laungaramsri 1998). The potential for racial violence in the region is exemplified by the conflict over water and forests in Chom Thong, a district of 1,736 square kilometers in Chiang Mai province of Northern Thailand, encompassing some 106 villagers and a terrain that is half lowland, half highland. Here, over the past decades, elite conservationists, state bureaucracies, and politicians have helped each other exploit the legacy of highland-lowland ethnic tensions. They have pressurized mountain communities on 'environmental' grounds to legitimize greater elite and state control over mountain resources (Lohmann 1999).

Indonesia is an archipelagic state, whose frontiers are the hilly and forested interiors of the larger islands and the smaller islands of Eastern Indonesia. The populations who occupy these spaces are classified by the state according to two rather distinct frames of meaning and action and classified by the social and environmental activists according to a third, competing frame. Each of these frames narrows or simplifies the field of vision in its own particular way, highlighting some aspects of the landscapes and its inhabitants and overlooking others. The 'tribal' slot, like the 'savage' slot described by Michel-Rolph Trouillot (1991), is a simplified frame of this sort (Li 2000b). There are thousands of people living in the hills. The Lauje, for example, currently numbering about thirty thousand, occupy the hilly interior and the narrow coastal strip of the peninsula to the north of Tomini Bay.

FORMING AND TRANSFORMING IDENTITY IN THAILAND

The 'Thai' ethnicity or 'Thai-ness' in construction of identity is evident in the historical discourse of Thailand. Before 1939, Thailand was known as Siam, but subsequently it was transformed into 'Thai-land', the land for the Thai ethnic group. The people in the hills living within the national borders of Thailand are termed as 'non-Thai'; their identity is constructed by the state based on exclusion or otherness. In the official documents, the mountain minorities are called *Chao-khao*, which means 'hill-tribes' or 'them-people', whereas the people of the lowlands are termed *Chao-rao*, or 'us-people' (Lohmann 1999). The binary opposition is built into the official discourse, which constructs the identity of the highlanders despite the knowledge that the highlanders do not necessarily identify themselves as *Chao-khao*. Apart from this binary opposition in constructing the identity of the highlanders, the labeling process involves attaching several negative stereotypes, including dirtiness, primitiveness, and 'free-sex', a portmanteau category of immorality that includes promiscuity and prostitution in addition to the perceived sexual license accorded to young courted couples among some highland groups (Jonsson 1996; Lohmann 1999).

Highlanders, often conceived of as the 'object of policies', are labeled or defined in convenient images. After official authorization for opium commerce was withdrawn in 1958 under international pressure, blame for the new 'opium problem' was often placed on the highlanders, whose newfound innate 'cultural affinity' for the crop became a focus of solemn analysis, which was ironically conducted by officials and non-minorities profiting directly from the drug trade (Tapp 1989). Many highland minority communities, particularly the Hmong, joined or were driven by government persecution into the ill-fated movement of the Communist Party of Thailand (CPT) in the 1960s and 1970s, which helped the state further reaffirm official stereotypes of mountain dwellers as outlaws. At the same time, a number of Hmong communities that had supported the government side and been persuaded to act as bulwarks against the CPT by settling and farming alongside new strategic roads constructed in the forest were accused of forest encroachment and dispossessed as soon as the Communist movement collapsed in 1982 (R. Cooper 1979; Lohmann 1999).

Evidence suggests that state-sanctioned commercial deforestation is partly, if not mainly, responsible for the resource conflicts. The Royal Forest Department leased approximately half Thailand's land area to commercial logging concessionaries between 1969 and 1979 alone. The responsibility was, however, placed on the 'hill tribes'—the group least able to defend itself against the change. Here, the Thai state drew strength from long-standing official international biases against swidden cultivation, mobile populations, and highlanders' forestry practices. During the 1980s, although mountain minorities' activities were the cause of perhaps 5 percent of annual deforestation and were restricted to the Northern and Western parts of the country, they were regularly named by officials and technocrats as the primary cause of the entire country's deforestation problem (Lohmann 1993).

The counterpart of stereotyping is control, and the state's legalistic invasion on the highlanders is a form of control. In line with the narrative of National Park Ideology, the land in Thailand was dichotomized into permanent agricultural fields and forest in which no agriculture was supposed to be practiced. All types of swidden agricultural systems practiced by the highlanders were lumped together, stigmatized as irrational and destructive, and claimed to be the invention and property of an abstract group called 'hill tribes' (Laungaramsri 1998; Lohmann 1993).

The state amplified its control over the forest space by making minority-defined agriculture outlaw. Consequently, minority-defined forests as community spaces were legislated into eclipse; the landscape itself was redefined in a way that made it possible to join up both sides of the classic racist double bind. Exclusion from the forests, which were to be regarded as empty, non-human spaces, became one with assimilation in the form of adaptation of permanent agriculture (Lohmann 1999). In this way, the state managed to expand its territorial control in addition to criminalizing the cultivation in the forestland.

In addition to violating the new 'non-human' space of the forest, swidden systems have also been seen as disorderly, un-Thai pursuits. The highlanders are subjected to moral and legal structures that reflect double standards. Other, often more invasive activities practiced by lowlanders, such as mining or construction of dams, roads, tourist resorts, and plantations, have all been regarded as disciplined 'development' activities and are often exempted from the strict moral and legal structures imposed on highlanders and their practices. Forests transformed by state officials, middle-class conservationists, tourists, plantation workers, scientific researchers, road builders, royal-palace personnel, and so forth are frequently characterized as 'undisturbed' or 'restored'. Contrarily, forests transformed under the agricultural stewardship of highland farmers, which often involves setting fire to clear land for swidden practices, are defined as 'degraded' or 'endangered' (Laungaramsri 1998; Lohmann 1999).

The stereotyped identities and meanings attached to the highlanders are constantly caricatured and castigated in the state's mainstream media. They are portrayed on the radio, on television, and in newspapers as 'wicked' and a 'threat to the country' (Lohmann 1999). The media violence inflicted on them is often unquestioned. Sometimes, the labeling, and thereby control, becomes intense and violent. As the commander of the Third Army sternly put it, "[T]hose who destroy the nation are not the ones who illegally cut down 20 to 30 trees, but the hill tribes." The deputy director general of the Royal Forestry Department opined that the solution to the "hill-tribe problem" was to "sterilize them by force so that they cannot increase their number any further" (*Siam Rath*, February 27, 1987, quoted in Lohmann 1999).

Labeling is not only political but also dynamic; the tactics of the government are constantly changing. The officials sense that highlanders' ethnicity can be marketed as a tourist commodity; as a result, they pressure some highlanders to preserve the cultural distinctiveness that makes them become more subject and subservient to the state policies (Smalley 1994). However, the state officials present it as evidence that the state honors these cultural differences and promotes the preservation of highlanders' culture, showing an 'apparent benevolence' of the former toward the latter. Preserved 'cultural distinctiveness' as a cultural commodity to be enjoyed by tourists temporarily occludes and camouflages the state's symbolic violence on the highlanders.

The above discussion of the terrain of Thailand reveals the formation and transformation of the highlanders' identity: (a) how they are labeled as 'tribals', associated with several negative stereotyped identities; (b) and how bureaucratic practices and national discourse actively construct stereotyped identities and reconstruct them in convenient images so as to amplify control over highlanders. We see that labeling is a process of designation, since it involves making judgments and distinctions; and in the bureaucratic activities of Thailand, these practices are quite common. However, constructing discursive differences or binary opposition becomes a problem when any element of racism and control is involved. It creates a set of winners at the expense of the other. In the official discourse and practices of Thailand, labels unfortunately become ways of manipulating the highlanders, making them 'foreigners' or subjugated subalterns in their own land.

FORMING AND TRANSFORMING IDENTITY IN INDONESIA

Similar labeling processes and bureaucratic practices are found in Indonesia, too. In Indonesia, the state power sometimes imposes an identity on highlanders, sometimes ignores their identity, and sometimes renders their identity ambiguous. The construction of highlanders' identity justifies the state's policies of rehabilitation and reservation of forestland for development purposes. As with the highlander groups in Thailand, the highlanders in Indonesia also become subjected to manipulations through deliberate state policies.

The Western imaginations of highlander groups are greatly influenced by popular media programs shown on such channels as National Geographic. Such programs shape both the public's and activists' images of tribes as naturally bounded, culturally distinct groups occupying spatially continuous and usually remote terrain. Tribes that fit these imagined characteristics are hard to find in Indonesia. An analysis of history and social structures reflects the political nature of the formation process. The precolonial coastal kingdoms were not much interested in details of cultural variation and ethnic affiliation in the uplands and interiors of their domains. The primary goal was to monopolize trade and, in some cases, to control labor through direct enslavement or debt bondage. Coastal powers were often thwarted in both these endeavors by the capacity of the interior peoples to subsist on swidden fields, to avoid trade engagements, and to retreat to inaccessible areas when faced with violence or unreasonable demands. James C. Scott (2009) has argued that these strategies are deliberate decisions made by people of hill tribes to avoid being absorbed into organized states. Muslim coastal powers have relegated most of the inhabitants of the interior to a tribal slot and stereotyped them as associated with animism, backwardness, and savagery (Kahn 1999; Li 1999a, 1999b). Following Scott (2009), the state constructs a negative image of these hill-tribe people to justify its repressive policies as attempts to 'civilize' these groups of people.

Interior peoples meanwhile developed positive identities stressing independence, autonomy, and their capacity to carve a livelihood out of their hilly, forested terrain. Domination and difference emerged within a single political and cultural system, as distinctive identities began to be attributed to, imposed upon, and forged by interior populations through a complex and resistance-permeated process, which Gerald Sider (1987:17) terms "create and incorporate." When confronted with state-defined identities, tribal-like social units were found in the interior, and their emergence could often be traced to conditions of warfare and conflict. In the absence of such encounters and confrontations, loosely structured, decentered, often scattered populations did not view themselves as distinct ethnic groups or tribes, and their identities remained only vaguely specified (Li 2000a, 2000b).

The Dutch colonial authorities played an important role in ethnicizing or traditionalizing the Indonesian interior. In frontier areas where the indigenous political structures were amorphous, they set about consolidating people into tribe-like groups under centralized and hierarchical leadership. They used the notion of tradition deliberately to legitimate colonial policies of indirect rule and to help consolidate the authority of the Dutch-appointed 'traditional' leaders through whom this rule would be exercised (Kahn 1993; Ruiter 1999).

The New Order Government unilaterally classified about one million rural people as 'estranged and isolated' (*masyarakat terasing, masyarakat terpencil*). The official programs designed to 'civilize' such people view them as generic primitives, occupants of a tribal slot that is negatively constructed. Their ethnic or tribal identities, cultural distinctiveness, livelihood practices, and ancient ties to the places they inhabit are presented in the program documents as 'problems', evidence of closed minds and a developmental deficit that a well-meaning government must help overcome. This is to be accomplished via a resettlement program, a successor to Dutch efforts, that attempts to narrow the distance (in time, space, and social mores) between *masyarakat terasing* and the 'normal average Indonesian citizen' (Li 1999a). The cultural distinctiveness they are encouraged to retain is of the song-and-dance variety, mainly for commercial purposes of the state.

Resettlement program guidelines specify that *masyarakat terasing* can be recognized by their tendency to move from one place to another as well as by their lack of a world religion, strong commitment to local customs and beliefs, and deficient housings, clothing, education, diet, health, and transportation facilities (Department of Social Affairs 1994). But there is a problem with this list: elements of the description could apply to almost all the rural population outside Java, especially to the tens of millions engaged in swidden agriculture or living in or near forests (Li 1999b). Identifying suitable subjects to be classified as *masyarakat terasing* is, therefore, a matter of interpretation and negotiation. This is how the highlanders who are so-called *masyarakat terasing* are subjected to policy and how their programmatic identities are formed.

In contrast to the few classified as *masyarakat terasing* whose ethnic distinctiveness is acknowledged and whose unique cultural characteristics are officially marked (albeit negatively), the majority of people occupying forested, mountainous, or other types of frontier land are classified simply as village folk, *orang kampong*. The development programs designed for such people ignore ethnic differences and assume, at the same time as they seek to create, homogenous forms of family and village life and a common administrative structure throughout the archipelago. Many of these programs encourage or enforce mobility across the rural landscape. In the past few decades, Indonesians have moved from one place to another as migrants, transmigrants, or workers attracted to, or ejected from, bottom/burst industries (Bookfield and Byron 1995). They have been forced to move when the state, which claims control over most of Indonesia's land (approximately 75 percent of it under the Ministry of Forestry), allocates their lands to other users or for other uses (Evers 1995; Zerner 1990).

As Hall (1996) observes, the most important articulations go beyond the 'cut', through which localized groups position themselves, to connect with broader social forces. For social movements to take off and to be effective, they need to focus on specific issues from a broader canvas to position themselves and to build alliances. From this point of view, images of environmentally friendly tribes in exemplary places may be necessary, at least as a starting point. But there are limitations to a social movement built around such images. To the extent that they highlight primordial otherness, separating us from them, traditional from modern, and victim from aggressor or protector, they reinforce differences and channel alliances along binary pathways. Moreover, ideal candidates for the tribal slot are difficult to find in Indonesia, and their identification is a contingent matter. Taking advantage of such ambiguities, the government could set out new rules to identify and to accommodate a few 'primitives' or traditional/indigenous people, and even acknowledge their rights to special treatment, without fundamentally shifting its ground on the fundamental issue that affects tens of millions: recognition of their rights to land and forests on which they depend. Some people would gain official recognition as 'indigenous peoples', but such differential treatment might heighten tensions between and within neighboring or intermingled populations.

In sum, the formation and transformation of identity is quite complex in Indonesia. The nature of labeling is dynamic; identities are not only formed by bureaucratic action but also transformed by it. Compartmentalizing the highlanders into different categories or different convenient images is a bureaucratic way of fulfilling a set of managerial objectives. For the highlanders in Indonesia, their designation is instrumental in gaining access to important resources. However, it is disturbing that schemes offered to the highlanders are mechanisms for control. The perceived advantages of settlement schemes are often illusory. Schemes create a category of 'tribal', with an identity largely based on development and integration as priorities. The reality, however, is a somewhat contrasting model of problem containment and management. In this alternative configuration, schemes become a vehicle for transforming an identity where highlanders are marginalized into a segregated and permanently transient and dependent status. These outcomes suggest that a labeled identity is being formed and transformed in ways often unacceptable and detrimental to the highlanders.

CONCLUSION

Labeling is an inescapable part of public-policy formulation. The language of labeling reflects its pervasiveness in everyday life. A theory of labeling enables us to observe the way bureaucratic procedures and practices create tribal identity. This chapter has explored the instrumentality of these procedures in creating an official status and in establishing the asymmetrical relationship between power and powerlessness. Through reinforcing actions of designations, labeling means conditionality and differentiation, inclusion and exclusion, stereotyping and control.

Through exploring case studies in Thailand and Indonesia with regards to the identity of highlanders, the point is not that one model of identity is necessarily superior to another. Rather, three things are crucial: (1) how identities are defined and adopted; (2) who controls them; (3) and how the different categories complement or conflict with each other. This chapter has explored the extreme vulnerability of 'tribals' to imposed labels, the importance of symbolic meanings, the dynamic nature of identity, and, fundamentally, the non-participatory nature and powerlessness of the 'tribals' in these processes. Although many of these discursive categorizations can be traced back to a colonial past, current neoliberal states have reinvented these for the accumulation of resources and the creation of power. This is an apparent paradox of neoliberal governance.

12 A Neoliberal Knowledge/Power/ Security Regime after 9/11

The Case of the 'Muslim Patient'

INTRODUCTION

Since the horrific events of September 11, 2001, scholars and policy-makers in the North have been preoccupied with issues like security and emerging relations between 'Muslims'[1] and the U.S. The relations have focused on various issues, such as international terrorism, change of regimes, economic and political development, and the promotion of Western democracy and human rights. To suggest that these issues exhaust the content of the relations, however, obscures the *productivity* of the governing practices that have been important aspects of these relations. In other words, the various issues that have been central to the relations between Muslims and the U.S. have been characterized by practices that have been implicated in the production of meanings and identities. These meanings and identities cannot be separated from the relations that have developed between Muslims and the U.S. In contrast to traditional orientations, I suggest that the relations have been more than these issues; rather, the relations fundamentally revolve around the practices of *representation* of Muslims by the neoliberal wing of the U.S. and its close allies. By representation, I mean the ways in which policy-makers, scholars, journalists, and others have discursively represented Muslims. This does not refer to the 'truth' and 'knowledge' that the neoliberal project has discovered and accumulated about Muslims (and Arabs), but rather to the ways in which regimes of 'truth' and 'knowledge' have been produced and constructed in order to justify and to normalize governance and certain interventions. The representational practices contain a homogenizing tendency that equates Arabs with Islam and vice versa. This negates the heterogeneity present within Islam (the religion) and its followers (the Muslims).

Drawing on a conceptual framework of development discourse and representation, this chapter argues that the neoliberal wing of the U.S. and its Western allies propagate a particular Orientalist/racist 'development discourse' that designates 'Muslims' as 'patients' to be diagnosed, studied, problematized, and surveilled, primarily for the purpose of normalizing an imperialistic neoliberal order and justifying both economic and military interventions. I show how the new post-9/11 development discourse that has amalgamated and blended with the discourses of national/global security as well as with a nationalism hostile to Muslims and Arabs contains a powerful knowledge/power regime that has produced normalizing principles, differences, and subjectivities.

DEVELOPMENT DISCOURSE AND REPRESENTATIONS

As the earlier chapters have shown, development is perhaps the most fundamental concept shaping human destiny. Critical literature on development in the last four decades shows that development is both empowering and disempowering, operating and functioning in very complex, interwoven types of power relations.[2] Scholars have identified that development discourse has historically become a 'governing tool' for the dominating groups over the dominated (e.g., Burns 1980; Goldman 2005; Hoogvelt 2001; Scott 1998). One of the methods of governance is discursive categorization and production of meanings in order to justify certain interventions. Development discourse thus efficiently creates categories of knowledge through use of representational practices that collude with colonialism, Orientalism, imperialism, and forms of capitalism. Regimes of representation can be analyzed as, to quote Arturo Escobar, "places of encounter where identities are constructed and also where violence is organized, symbolized, and managed" (1995:10). After a careful look at development discourse, I discern at least three different in terms of time and place yet characteristically similar knowledge/power regimes: colonialism; developmentalism, or the creation of the Third World; and the post-9/11 neoliberal security regime, also known as the 'war on terror'.

The notion of 'development' was introduced and popularized during the time of colonization as colonial empires were seeking legitimacy for governance (McMichael 2008). As British Colonial Secretary Malcolm MacDonald observed in 1940, "If we are not going to do something fairly good for the Colonial Empire, and something which helps them to get proper social services, we shall deserve to lose the colonies and it will only be a matter of time before we get what we deserve" (F. Cooper 1997:66–67). While the introduction of 'development' during the time of colonization promised abundance, the discourse and strategy produced the opposite: untold exploitation and oppression, massive underdevelopment, and impoverishment. The deployment of this discourse, which Chandra Mohanty (1991) calls "the colonialist move," entails specific construction of the colonial subjects in ways that allow the exercise of power over it. It produced an efficient apparatus, that, according to Homi Bhabha,

> turns on the recognition and disavowal of racial/cultural/historical differences. Its predominant strategic function is the creation of a space

for "subject peoples" through the production of knowledge in terms of which surveillance is exercised and a complex form of pleasure/unpleasure is incited. . . . The objective of colonial discourse is to construe the colonized as a population of a degenerate type on the basis of racial origin, in order to justify conquest and to establish a system of administration and instruction. (1990:75)

After the end of the Second World War, the notion of development embraced numerous transformations and meanings; however, discursive categorizations and representational practices have remained largely inherent in the discourse of development, albeit in different forms. The new postwar knowledge/power regime in the discourse of development, largely governed by the same principles of "the colonialist move," emerged when the chapter of colonization was almost over: "This apparatus came into existence roughly in the period 1945 to 1955 and has not since ceased to produce new arrangements of knowledge and power, new practices, theories, strategies, and so on. In sum, it has successfully deployed a regime of government over the Third World, a "space for 'subject peoples'" that ensures certain control over it" (Escobar 1995:9).

Development discourse has inevitably contained what Edward Said (1979) calls "a series of imaginative geographies" that has shaped the meaning of development for more than four decades. "It is implicit in expressions such as First and Third World, North and South, centre and periphery. The social production of space implicit in these terms is bound with the production of differences, subjectivities and social orders . . . [and these categories] continue to function imaginatively in powerful ways" (Escobar 1995:9–10). Thinking of North-South relations, for example, in terms of *representation*, as elaborated by Roxanne Lynn Doty (1996), reorients and complicates the way we understand this particular aspect of global politics. North-South relations become more than an area of theory and practice in which various policies have been enacted and theories formulated: "They become a realm of politics wherein the very identities of peoples, states, and regions are constructed through representational practices" (Doty 1996:2). Thinking in terms of representational practices calls our attention to an economy of abstract binary oppositions that we routinely draw upon and that frame our thinking. Doty reminds us:

Developed/under-developed, "first world"/"third world," core/periphery, metropolis/satellite, advanced industrialized/less-developed, modern/traditional, and real states/quasi states are just a few that readily come to mind. While there is nothing natural, inevitable, or arguably even useful about these divisions, they remain widely circulated and accepted as legitimate ways to categorize regions and peoples of the world. Thinking in terms of representational practices highlights the arbitrary, constructed, and political nature of these and many other oppositions through which we have come to "know" the world and its inhabitants and that have enabled and justified certain practices and policies. (1996:2–3)

By constructing the discourse of 'sustainable development' and problematizing 'global survival', the knowledge/power regime in postwar development discourse conquered 'nature', thereby legitimizing its exploitation (Brosius 1999; Escobar 1995; Scott 1998). If we delve deeply into these constructions and discursive practices, we find an inherent power relation where the Third World is constructed by *distancing* it from the 'civilized' and developed 'West'. Because of this construction of the Third World, the power relation between the agency that constructs and the subjects who are constructed becomes "father-child" or "doctor-patient" (Escobar 1995:159). This is akin to what Said sees in 'Orientalism':

[Orientalism] can be discussed and analyzed as the corporate institution for dealing with the Orient—dealing with it by making statements about it, authorizing views of it, describing it, by teaching it, setting it, ruling over it: in short, Orientalism as a western style for dominating, restructuring, and having authority over the Orient. . . . My contention is that without examining Orientalism as a discourse we cannot possibly understand the enormously systematic discipline by which European culture was able to manage—and even produce—the Orient politically, sociologically, ideologically, scientifically, and imaginatively during the post-Enlightenment period. (1979:3)

One of the apparent implications of such discursive practices is that they empower certain actors, spaces, and species, while disempowering others. "All development projects involve reorganizing the meaning and control of space" and have "the potential of causing displacement" (Vandergeest 2003:47), not only for human beings but also for other species. With powerful vocabularies and various discursive practices, development creates categories, makes different spaces, and disempowers those who appear inimical to, or compete with, development projects. Thus, in the process of reorganizing nature—by both empowering and disempowering—"[p]lants that are valued become 'crops', the species that compete with them are stigmatized as 'pests'. Thus, trees that are valued become 'timber', while species that compete with them become 'trash' trees or 'underbrush'. The same logic applies to fauna. Highly valued animals become 'game' or 'livestock', while those animals that compete with or prey upon them become 'predators' or 'varmints'" (Scott 1998:13).

These knowledge/power regimes follow a conspicuous process: *problematization*, creating knowledge in a very efficient way to represent that domain; *institutionalization*, bureaucratization and managerialism to create or to deny agency; and finally, *normalization of power*, rationalization of the effects of power, a rationalization by which power remains uncontested and subjectivity is subsequently created. This is what Michel Foucault (1979, 1986) discovers and explicates: the relation and exercise of power in modern society. "The ensemble of forms found along these axes constitutes development as a discursive formation, giving rise to an efficient apparatus that systematically relates forms of knowledge and techniques of power" (Escobar 1995:10). One of the apparent implications of the development discourse is that it "privilege[s] certain actors, and marginalize[s] others" (Brosius 1999:38). As Doty puts it, in the case of North-South relations, "[O]ne entity has been able to construct 'realities' that were taken seriously and acted upon and the other entity has been denied equal degrees or kinds of agency" (1996:3). The process is going on largely unchallenged. The central character of these regimes of discourse and representation is not merely an economic one but rather a whole package of power, production, governance, and social relations.

Historically, the development discourse changes its contents from time to time and sometimes colludes with other discourses, but the central characteristics remain the same. While development discourse has created two efficient apparatuses of knowledge and regimes of representation during colonization and the Cold War, we find a third knowledge/power regime after the end of Cold War, a regime that was largely built up on, and justified by, the terrorist attacks on September 11, 2001. David Campbell's (1998) notion of 'threats' in order to justify U.S. national-security projects is an example of how development, security, and capitalism come together to form an unholy trinity. While this unholy trinity largely shaped the Western body politic during the Cold War, a new knowledge/power regime surrounding 'Muslims' has emerged in post-9/11 development discourse.

MAKING A NEW KNOWLEDGE/POWER REGIME

Since 9/11, development discourse has largely been located within a particular national-security discourse within the governments of the U.S. and its close allies, and this discourse has replaced communism with 'Muslims' as the main threat to the march of progress, evolution of civilization, and survival of the global order. Although the construction and representation of Muslims in the discourse of development started long before, it became quite apparent after the Cold War and more intense after September 11, 2001. M. S. Islam (2005) elaborates that after the end of the Cold War, the center of capitalist power did not have any common enemy to fight against, and hence a new 'adversary' was necessary to construct. Different intellectuals emerged in the U.S. to construct this 'new enemy'. Samuel Huntington (1996), for example, in his theory 'the clash of civilizations', constructs a future clash between civilizations and suggests that the U.S. dismantle and emasculate any kind of military as well as economic buildup in other countries, especially in the East. He vehemently advocates that the U.S. redesign its foreign policy in the 'unipolar world' in order to limit the expansion of the military strength of, and to exploit differences and conflicts among, Confucian and Islamic states. His book also immediately reminds us of issues raised in different theoretical fashions by Campbell (*Writing Security*, 1998) and Ken Booth ("Cold Wars of the Mind," 1998) about the discursive and ideational perpetuation of dangers that are said to threaten the Western body politic in order to imbue notions of security, politics, and the state itself with purposes and meanings that make particular types of policy possible. While the formation and construction of 'security threats' largely shaped Cold War and post–Cold War politics, the 9/11 terrorist attack on America provided a 'solid reality' of the threats in people's imaginations.

The immediate shock of 9/11, however, resulted in serious disorientation and an urgent popular demand that the authorities make sense of what had happened. As Said Amir Arjomand elaborates:

> Beyond the universities and schools, the media and organized groups watching them engaged in the enterprise of the construction of reality in a great crisis, and in the framing of a discourse around September 11 which would henceforth constitute the objective facts of terrorism. The contest for the control of reality and constitution of objectivity through the forging and appropriation of the emerging dominant discourse was highly uneven. The well-organized [groups] . . . were drawn into the business of defining reality and shaping public discourse, as we shall see presently. The minimally organized Arab and Muslim Americans, by contrast, found themselves totally on the defensive against guilt by association and the general moral outrage of the American society. (n.d.)

In this context, Muslims became almost overnight a 'new object of analysis' and labeled as 'patients' to be treated and diagnosed through a new body of knowledge and interventions. Different prominent figures then pioneered in constructing Muslims as 'others' and as 'adversaries' to America's neoliberal order. Notable among them are Bernard Lewis and Fouad Azmi. Lewis, who came to the U.S. from the UK some thirty years ago to teach at Princeton, became a prominent figure in the neoconservative lobby because of his fervent anti-communism, disapproval of everything about contemporary Arabs and Islam, and portrayal of Arab backwardness as a viable route to truth. In Lewis's words, "In the course of the twentieth century it became abundantly clear that things had gone badly wrong in the Middle East—and, indeed, in all the lands of Islam. Compared with Christendom, its rival for more than a millennium, the world of Islam had become poor, weak, and ignorant" (2002a:1).

While some of these conditions (being poor, weak, ignorant) are prevalent in 'the world of Islam', as they are prevalent in almost every society in the world, his construction of a binary opposition between 'the world of Islam' and 'Christendom' is discursive, arbitrary, and problematic. Huntington derives his lucrative concept from one of Lewis's essays about the "Return of Islam" in his book *Islam and the West* (1993). According to Said (2003), what makes Lewis's work so damaging is its appeal—in the absence of any counter-argument—to American policy-makers. That, together with the superciliousness of his manner, turned him into an 'authority' even though he had not entered, much less lived in, the Arab world in decades. His book *What Went Wrong?* (2002b) became a post-9/11 best seller and required reading for the U.S. military despite its unsupported and often factually incorrect statements about the history of Arabs over the past five hundred years. Reading the book, one gets the idea that 'Arabs' are a primitive tribe, easier to attack and destroy than ever before.

Speaking on *What Went Wrong*, Juan Cole asserts, "How a profoundly learned and highly respected historian, whose career spans some sixty years, could produce such a hodgepodge of muddled thinking, inaccurate assertions and one-sided punditry is a profound mystery" (2003:1). What is important to look at is that, despite various wrong and overgeneralized assertions, Lewis's discursive construction of 'Muslims' or 'the world of Islam', to use his phrase, finds a fertile ground in and entrenched with 'the unholy trinity' (comprising development, security, and capitalism) that has significantly contributed to generating a new knowledge/power regime in post-9/11 development discourse. The legacy of this new regime may date back even further. Many members of Bill Clinton's administration (including Clinton himself), for example, acknowledged reading Robert Kaplan's book on the former Yugoslavia (*Balkan Ghosts*, 1993), which argues that the ethnic violence was long-standing, inevitable, and impossible to stop. These discursive assumptions and constructions were unfortunately the main basis for U.S. intervention in the region. A similar situation with Lewis and Huntington made the Bush Doctrine's Middle East policy possible. Lewis, Kaplan, and others have contributed greatly to creating *a priori* 'truth' about people in the developing world—that such people are 'always already' destined to being involved in violence.

Fouad Ajami, a Lebanese Shia educated in the U.S., also has made a remarkable contribution in generating this new knowledge/power regime. He made his name as a pro-Palestinian commentator, but by the time he began teaching at Johns Hopkins in the mid-1980s, he had become a fervent anti-Arab ideologue and had been taken up by the neoconservative lobby. He now works for Martin Peretz, Mort Zuckerman, and the Council on Foreign Relations. In Said's analysis:

> [Ajami] is fond of describing himself as a non-fiction Naipaul and quotes Conrad while sounding as hokey as Khalil Gibran. He also has a penchant for catchy one-liners, ideally suited to television. The author of two or three books, he has become influential as a 'native

informant'—the Arab 'expert' is a rare species on American networks. Ten years ago, he started deploying 'we' as an imperial collectivity which, along with Israel, never does anything wrong. Arabs are to blame for everything and therefore deserve 'our' contempt and hostility. (2003:2)

Like Lewis, Ajami has resided outside the Arab world for years, although he is rumored to be close to the Saudis, whom he has recently described as models for the Arab world's future governance (Said 2003). What is interesting and yet ironic is that despite various problematic and factually incorrect assertions, Ajami's discursive concoction of Muslims and Arabs has been well taken and given a wider market currency by the neoliberal lobby in the U.S. By constructing 'Muslims' as a new adversary to, or a 'new patient' for, the neoliberal capitalist order, some critics think, these intellectuals have committed "homicidal blunder" and "intellectual atrocities" (M. S. Islam 2005:5).

Intellectual grounds, such as the above, have provided a solid foundation for a new knowledge/power regime surrounding Muslims in the discourse of development. The discursive constructions sometimes shift between Muslims, Arabs, and Islam itself. Many of these constructions equate Islam with evil through portrayals of Muslims as irrational, uncivilized, threatening, and uniquely fundamentalist 'others'. For example, Franklin Graham—who, like his father, Reverend Billy Graham, is one of America's most powerful evangelical leaders—stated, "Islam has attacked us" in North Carolina shortly after the 9/11 attacks (*NBC Nightly News* 2001). He delivered the benediction at George W. Bush's inauguration and is heir to his father's extensive ministry. Americans of all faiths were asked to embrace one another and to unite against terrorism. Graham's words, however, dismissed any interfaith dialogue: "The God of Islam is not the same God," he alleged. "Islam," Graham concluded, "is a very evil and wicked religion" (quoted in Muscati 2003).

Graham's perception of Islam as an 'evil' religion strikes a familiar tone in the U.S. Here, hostilities with elements within the Muslim world are commonly constructed and presented as conflicts between good and evil (Md Saidul Islam 2005; Muscati 2003). President Bush responded to the 9/11 attacks by launching a "crusade" against terrorism.[3] He promised to "rid the world of evil"[4] and to "fight the evil ones,"[5] and he inventoried an "axis of evil"[6] constituting primarily Muslim nations. His rhetoric fits a pattern. His father, George H. W. Bush, in the crisis leading up to the 1991 Gulf War, implored Americans to "confront evil for the sake of good."[7] Their predecessor, President Ronald Reagan, in 1986 referred to Libya's Colonel Moammar Gadhafi as an "evil man" (Slevin 2002) before bombing his country.

The discursive construction of Muslims in the neoliberal development discourse is very painful, yet interesting. Muslims have been constructed

with negativity, as opposed to the positivity of the West. "America was targeted for attack," said President Bush, "because we're the brightest beacon
for freedom and opportunity in the world."[8] "This conflict," he continued,
"is a fight to save the civilized world," because the terrorists hate freedom and democracy.[9] He was joined by other politicians. Newt Gingrich,
speaker of the House of Representatives, insisted that "civilization must
win" in this conflict.[10] U.S. Secretary of State Colin Powell added that the
terrorists hate "civilization."[11] From the outset, the war was justified as one
in defense of freedom, democracy, and civilization itself, even before it was
established who the terrorists were or what had motivated them to act. The
rhetoric was vague and obscure, with the exception that the threat posed
had something to do with Islam and the Middle East.

President Bush's declaration that "you are with us or you are with the
terrorists"[12] implies a binary construction of spaces. By applying Escobar's
conceptual lens to such rhetoric, we can see that "the social production
of space implicit in these terms is bound with the production of difference, subjectivities, and social order" (1995:9). This distance is not a simple
marker of cultural diversity but is branded with inferiority and negativity, such as terrorist, evil, militant, backward, underdeveloped, poor, lacking, traditional, and so forth. As stated elsewhere, "When these kinds of
negative images are constructed on a group of people, they automatically
become preamble to certain treatments and interventions, and thus, the
former justifies the latter" (M. S. Islam 2005:6).

The discursive construction does not stop there; rather, it permeates the
arena of social consciousness. One example of a negative construction of
Muslim comes from Ann Coulter, a best-selling author, prominent political
analyst, and columnist. One of her articles (2002a) recounts an incident
where a 'Muslim' passenger en route from Germany to Kosovo attacked
a stewardess on the flight. In it, Coulter bitterly complains about how
few newspapers reported the story and how "not one mentioned that the
attacker was a Muslim." Sina Ali Muscati explains:

> At first glance, the basis for her complaint is confusing. It seems non-
> sensical that we should strive to identify the religion of any given crim-
> inal when reporting stories about their criminal acts. How is Islam
> relevant to this story? The relevance, sadly, is found in the minds of
> people like Ms. Coulter who seem to believe that only Islam can serve
> as the motive for a Muslim's actions. For this reason, they find it neces-
> sary to condemn newspapers that do not identify this erroneous con-
> nection between Islam and violence, and that do not thereby further
> isolate Muslim communities and further instil dangerous anti-Muslim
> stereotypes among their readership. (2003:251)

Coulter's views resurface in a subsequent article (2002b) she wrote following the revelation that one of the suspects in the 2002 Washington, D.C.,

area sniper shootings was a Muslim convert. She ridicules attempts that were made to find psychological or other non-Islamic causes for the sniper's violent behavior and instead implores, "He's a Muslim, that's his condition and his diagnosis." In this way, Coulter presents Islam as a 'disease' responsible for the alleged sniper's violence and the violence of countless other 'Muslim' criminals. There is no attempt at entertaining other possible causes or of ascribing blame to other plausible issues—not the U.S. Army, where the sniper developed his marksmanship, nor his chronic unemployment, nor any mental delusions he might have been suffering from. It was Coulter who remarked two days after 9/11, "We should invade [Muslim] countries, kill their leaders and convert them to Christianity."[13]

Furthermore, even where the motives of such criminals have religious elements, there is a tendency to automatically attribute their actions to Islam as a whole rather than to distortions of it. Other popular figures have joined in the attacks. Oriana Fallaci, one of Italy's most renowned journalists, who lectured at such respected institutions as Harvard, Columbia, and Yale, published a book shortly after September 11 entitled *Rage and Pride* (2002). It quickly became a best seller in Italy and elsewhere in Europe. In it, Fallaci refers to Muslims as the peculiar "sons of Allah." She describes them as "vile creatures" that like to "urinate on baptisteries" and "multiply like rats." Freedom-of-expression arguments aside, one is left to question whether the publication of such hateful words about Jewish or other vulnerable religious minorities would today be tolerated in the West, let alone render an author a best seller (Muscati 2003). Yet these kinds of derogatory comments have gained a huge market currency and provided a solid foundation for the neoliberal development discourse. Although Pope Benedict XVI may not be a partner in the neoliberal order, he however contributed, if perhaps unwittingly, to the construction of Islam as dangerous when he quoted the words of the fourteenth-century Byzantine emperor Manuel II: "Show me just what Muhammad brought that was new, and there you will find things only evil and inhuman, such as his command to spread by the sword the faith he preached" (Benedict 2006).

Because of information technology, the new knowledge/power regime became both powerful and efficient in creating 'alien' subjectivities. The media's continuous castigation of the horrible images of the destruction of the Twin Towers, excessive obsession with 9/11 (e.g., politics, talk shows, community works, election campaigns, foreign relations, trade and business, and so on), and continuous display of the turbaned and bearded images of Osama bin Laden provided powerful thrusts for both nationalist (anti-Muslim) and security discourses. Thus the new neoliberal development discourse was fused with other powerful normalizing discourses: nationalism and security. President Bush extended these nationalist discourses beyond American borders when he addressed the leaders of other countries by saying, "[Y]ou are with us or with the terrorists," leaving no alternative in between. With powerful yet fragile nationalist and security discourses, media, and other information technology, the new knowledge/power regime almost overnight turned into a very efficient and powerful apparatus for the neoliberal capitalist order. In this context, the new institution of the U.S. Department of Homeland Security was launched, an anti-terrorism act was enacted, and the regime provided not only a justification but also a significant push for the Afghan war, although the preparations for this war started long before 9/11 (Mamdani 2004).

The 'alien' subjectivities who are arbitrarily composed of Arabs, people with Arabic names, Muslims, and even some Hispanics who look like Arabs face enormous backlash at home and abroad. A massive national campaign was launched for national security by constructing 'Al-Qaeda'—comprising Muslims—as the greatest threat to humanity. The campaign was predominantly guided by not only a disapproval and extreme rebuff of but also extreme hatred toward the 'alien' creatures. The extreme hatred and backlash faced by the 'alien' creatures was evident in different national polls. For example, some polls conducted in the U.S. suggested that while 38 percent of Americans hold very negative views about Islam and Muslims, only 2 percent have anything good to say about them (CAIR 2006), and over 44 percent of Americans are willing to deprive Muslims of freedoms and rights available to other Americans (*Cornell News* 2004). Muslims in America have become 'alien' creatures, ostracized species that do not deserve freedom, liberty, and human dignity but rather get subjected to others' contempt, hatred, and exclusions. The images of Muslims/Arabs constructed in the new knowledge/power regime ironically become a valid way and a yardstick by which to look at, to judge, and to treat the 'alien' communities at home and abroad, particularly in the Middle East. The far-reaching implication of this knowledge/power regime is quite apparent:

> [The regime] has undermined the quality of life of Western Muslims. Many face discrimination in the work place, are victims of racial and religious profiling, businesses are failing, international travel has become difficult and risky and Islamic institutions, and particularly mosques and Islamic charities face harassment and unnecessary scrutiny. . . . [T]he fear of Islam and the now embedded antipathy towards Muslims, frequently surfaces in the western media, in popular discourse, in casual conversation, in parliamentary discussions and in new legislations. . . . [The Muslims] remain second-class citizens, constantly watched, regularly demonized, systematically marginalized, feared, despised and portrayed as a potential fifth column. (Khan and Esposito 2008:27)

The regime signals a significant shift in power relations between the center of neoliberal power and 'Muslims'—the relations of domination and subordination. Muslims then feel themselves like alien creatures in their own homeland. This is akin to what marginalized visible minorities feel: "We cannot be successfully ingested, or assimilated, or made to vanish from where we are not wanted. We remain an ambiguous presence, our existence a question mark in the side of the nation" (Bannerji 1996:105). To understand this power relation, one must look not at the elements themselves but at the system of relations established among them, to quote Escobar again: "It is a system that allows the systematic creation of objects, concepts, and strategies . . . the system of relations establishes discursive practices that set the rule of the game: who can speak, from what point of view, with what authority, and according to what criteria of expertise. It sets the rules that must be followed for this or that problem, theory, or object to emerge and be named, analyzed, and eventually transformed into a policy plan" (1995:40–41).

Not all, however, have authority to do that. Some clear principles of authority are in operation concerning the roles of experts, from whom certain criteria of knowledge and competence are asked; of institutions, such as different think tanks, the FBI, the CIA, and Homeland Security, which have the moral, professional, and legal authority to name subjects and to define strategies; and of the U.S. administration, the White House, which carries the symbols of capital and power. It is hegemonic, because it blocks all other forms of knowledge and other models of knowing. It erodes in a deeper manner the Muslims' ability to define themselves and to take care of their own lives (M. S. Islam 2005:7). A regime of truth and norms about Muslims has been produced by passing judgment on the whole social group and forecasting its future. It leads the Muslim subjects to react in various forms, ranging from discontent through submission and internalization of inferiority, to a variety of resistances—from everyday forms through sporadic uprisings to mass political mobilization. The fanatics, on the other hand, resort to more violence.

Although the discursive construction of Muslims found its fertile ground during the Bush era, it did not stop with the change of American administration. If World War I was to be "the war to end all wars," President Bush's so-called war on terror was conceived as a war without end. Just days after Al-Qaeda's suicide airliner attacks on September 11, 2001, Bush declared that he would "rid the world of evildoers," and Vice President Dick Cheney warned that the U.S. would fight indefinitely: "There's not going to be an end date when we're going to say, 'There, it's all over with'" (*Los Angeles Times* 2009). Like Bush, President Barack Obama—despite his repeated promise to end the war—has eventually become a "Commander in Chief for an endless cluster of global wars" (Bom 2008:1). The so-called Bush Doctrine was articulated in a 2002 National Security Strategy, which stated that the U.S. would act against threats before they were fully formed: "We will not hesitate to act alone, if necessary, to exercise our right of self-defense by acting preemptively against such terrorists. . . . In fact, the doctrine conflated two very different concepts: preemptive war and preventive war" (*Los Angeles Times* 2009). Obama wants to withdraw U.S. troops from Iraq and send them to Afghanistan, which he calls 'the real front on the war on terror.' He also has repeated threats to attack Pakistan 'if necessary', and he did so. Like Bush, President Obama has emerged as a 'war president' (Bom 2008; Kain 2009; Margolis 2008; North 2009). Eric Margolis writes, "Obama has long called the U.S.-led occupation of Afghanistan a 'good war', a view most Americans and Canadians share. They see Afghanistan—and now Pakistan—as hotbeds of al-Qaida and Taliban terrorists that must be eradicated. It is distressing to see Obama succumb to the blitz of war propaganda over Afghanistan and adopt George Bush's faux terminology of terrorism" (2008:1). Although President Obama has been working to establish a 'good relationship' with Arabs and Muslims, his legacy as a 'War President' will not cease and challenge but rather sustain the new knowledge/power/security regime. It's worth mentioning that Osama bin Laden was killed on Obama's watch.

DECONSTRUCTING THE DISCOURSE

After problematizing discursive constructions in different knowledge/power regimes, what we see is that contents of discourse differ and change from time to time, but the internal dynamics remain the same. Hegemony has three goals: economic, political, and cultural. However, economic and political goals almost always remain occluded, and the cultural construction largely serves as a 'legitimate tool' for the former two. In development discourse, Escobar (1995) asserts that behind all discursive constructions, wars, and destruction lie the economic interests of capitalist corporations.

The new knowledge/power/security regime's discursive construction of Muslims has provided an efficient apparatus that justifies and normalizes not only the neoliberal order and intervention abroad (particularly in Afghanistan and Iraq) but also a series of actions and interventions at home for its continuous empowerment. The regime at home has created a huge job market, as 'terrorism and security' have become a very profitable sector of investments. Society now requires new experts in terrorism, new laws and lawyers, and new policies, rules, regulations, and interventions in order to save American citizens from further attack. This remarkable interest has led different universities to open a new discipline called 'terrorism and security studies' to diagnose and to examine 'Muslim patients'. Such institutions as Homeland Security have emerged to justify actions and interventions. The regime has created a series of new modes of productions and sectors of investments for the neoliberal capitalists: fingerprinting, numerous new technologies to detect terrorism, terrorism law firms, training and deployment of additional security personnel during emergencies, reshaping of airport security, production and massive sale of masks and other equipment and medicine in case of bioterrorism, and a huge investment in military industry. The period has become a heyday for the print and electronic media, as Muslim subjects have become a 'new commodity' for news consumers. Different categories and levels of terrorist alerts have been introduced. For every national terrorist alert, people, out of fear, buy additional products for consumption during emergencies, a situation that has eventually stimulated the national economy. Creating fear now has become a new but efficient marketing strategy to sell products in a quick and sophisticated manner. Both at home and abroad, the ultimate remittances go to the corporate neoliberal capitalists, to the detriment of Muslim subjects and the civil rights of other citizens. The most significant aspect of these series of actions and interventions is, to quote Escobar, "the setting into place of apparatuses of knowledge and power that took upon themselves to optimize life by producing it under modern, 'scientific' conditions" (1995:23).

What is apparent is that the new knowledge/power/security regime in development discourse became consolidated and was justified largely with the horrendous events of 9/11. It is interesting, yet ironic, to see how various problems were gradually (before 9/11) and suddenly (after 9/11) discovered in Muslim societies, how Muslims were problematized and constructed with various negative images in the discourse of development, and how one-fifth of the world population was put under the regime of control and intervention by discursive practices, as occurred with the so-called Third World population after the Second World War. It is remarkable to see how Muslims have been constructed and treated as a homogeneous mass or a monolithic entity despite their political, religious, and cultural diversity. The reality is that the majority of the world's Muslims live in Asia and Africa, not in Arab countries. The largest communities are in Nigeria, Indonesia, Bangladesh, Pakistan, and India. Therefore, the new development regime's discursive construction that Islam is a religion solely of the Arabs is erroneous. Like Christians and Jews, Muslims vary widely in their lifestyles and degrees of piety. Muslims around the world are as diverse as the countries they represent in their cultures, adherence to Muslim traditions, languages, ways of life, and more. Sunnis and Shia alike may be observant or nonobservant, conservative, fundamentalist, reformist, secular, mainstream, or extremist (Esposito and Mogahed 2007). "Muslims" as constructed and treated by the development discourse as a homogeneous mass may not be "strictly" Muslims, and their identities could be fluid and hybrid and not fit into the constructed category. The same goes to the discursive categorization of the 'West'. As Ashis Nandy writes, "[T]he 'west' is now everywhere, within the West and outside: in structures and minds" (1983:xii).

It is deeply regrettable that the horrific actions of a handful of fundamentalists—a tiny deviated fraction of the whole Muslim spectrum—are treated as representative of the whole community. In the new knowledge/power/security regime, Muslims have often been judged *en masse* by the standards of their worst representatives, while Gallup's extensive survey[14] on Muslims around the world found that most Muslims strongly denounced terrorism and condemned the attacks of September 11 (Gallup 2008).[15] Terrorists erroneously use Islam as justification for their actions. Ironically, the new knowledge/power/security regime's discursive construction conforms to what the terrorists propagate rather than to what most Muslims believe. The beginning of war in Afghanistan and Iraq has contributed to bin Laden's project of provoking war between the Islamic world and the U.S.

Huntington's *Clash of Civilizations* is a lucrative and powerful tool for framing the neoliberal order. However, based on Gallup's surveys, a 'clash of civilizations' between the West and Muslims is not inevitable. Islam's image problem now stems from a monolithic stereotype of the religion: the West, particularly the U.S., judges Muslims and Islam on the actions of an extremist minority not necessarily representative of pious, practicing Muslims. Instead, terrorists act from a militant theology borne of the political radicalization of religion (Esposito and Mogahed 2007; Mamdani 2004). Mahmood Mamdani (2004) elaborates that on the one hand, there are 'good Muslims', who are described as secular and Westernized; on the other hand, we have 'bad Muslims', who are described as premodern and fanatical. In reality, though, the 'bad Muslims' are whichever Muslims happen to be fighting America, regardless of their actual religious beliefs.[16] Thus the distinction between the two groups is really political rather than religious. Mamdani argues that all (or most) 'bad Muslims' were actually once 'good Muslims'.[17] Their ideology and religion did not change, causing them to be recategorized; rather, the Cold War ended, and instead of opposing the Soviet Union, they began to oppose American hegemony.

The regime's discursive constructions have converged with and then further reinforced the already-existing Islamophobia. Pope Benedict's remark regarding a link between Islam and force, as mentioned earlier, came at a time when the West was grappling with a fear of and paranoia about Muslims in the post-9/11 world, and the remark has added fuel to the rocky relationship between the West and the world of Islam. "We cannot afford to maintain these ancient prejudices against Islam. The Pope's remarks were dangerous, and will convince many more Muslims that the West is incurably Islamophobic," remarks noted scholar Karen Armstrong, the author of the book *Islam: A Short History* (2000). With regard to the spreading of Islam by the use of sword, noted historian De Lacy O'Leary says, "History makes it clear, however, that the legend of fanatical Muslims sweeping through the world and forcing Islam at the point of the sword upon conquered races is one of the most fantastically absurd myths that historians have ever repeated" (quoted in AbuRabi 2003:8).

Even then, why does the West indulge in, and more apparently create discursively and intentionally, hatred against Islam and its followers, constructing a fabricated tale linking Islam with force or terrorism, in which the West *per se* is risking a huge blunder and the stigma of doing the same for the last few centuries, especially during the time of colonization? Armstrong (2006) reminds us:

Our Islamophobia dates back to the time of the Crusades, and is entwined with our chronic anti-semitism. Some of the first Crusaders began their journey to the Holy Land by massacring the Jewish communities along the Rhine valley; the Crusaders ended their campaign in 1099 by slaughtering some 30,000 Muslims and Jews in Jerusalem. It is always difficult to forgive people we know we have wronged. Thenceforth Jews and Muslims became the shadow-self of Christendom, the mirror image of everything that we hoped we were not—or feared that we were.

Debasing the holy Qur'an at Guantanamo Bay as well as in the Abu Ghraib prison, lampooning Islam's prophet Muhammad through caricatured images in the Danish newspaper and their reappearance in other European papers, hearing the pope's remark on Islam and its prophet, burning the Qur'an in public, and finally releasing the anti-Islamic video *Innocence of Muslims* (written and produced by Nakoula Basseley Nakoula, using the pseudonym 'Sam Bacile') show the same genealogy of discursive construction on and hatred against Muslims. Armstrong adds, "Hatred of Islam is so ubiquitous and so deeply rooted in Western culture that it brings together people who are usually at daggers drawn. Neither the Danish cartoonists, who published the offensive caricatures of the Prophet Muhammad . . . nor the Christian fundamentalists who have called him a paedophile and a terrorist, would ordinarily make common cause with the Pope; yet on the subject of Islam they are in full agreement" (2006).

The pope's remark does not contribute to, but rather disrupts, interfaith dialogue at a juncture when the peace-loving world is grappling with finding a common platform for Abrahamic faiths—Islam, Christianity, and Judaism. The cultural crusades on Islam and Muslims in the name of 'the clash of civilization' or a 'holy war against the terrorists' are leaving ongoing catastrophic legacies in Iraq, Afghanistan, and the Israeli-occupied territories. Discursive concoction of Muslims and their prophet and history with negative images is little more than an attempt to justify Bush's brutal 'war on terror' that has already claimed about a million lives but serves the interests of a powerful neoliberal capitalist few. Gary Leupp (2002) reminds us, "Islamic fundamentalism (or what some, including CNN *Moneyline*'s Lou Dobbs calls 'Islamism', meaning a specifically political Islam) has NOT, historically, posed a great threat to Western interests (by which I mean corporate, oil, and geopolitical interests) but rather been exploited to SERVE those interests."

CONCLUSION

This chapter argues that development discourse has historically produced at least three efficient and powerful knowledge/power regimes: colonialism, in the name of spreading superior civilization or the 'white man's burden' during the time of European colonization; developmentalism, in the name of 'development projects' during the Cold War; and post-9/11 neoliberalism, in the name of the 'war on terror'. This chapter shows that the development discourse propagated by the U.S. and its Western allies after 9/11 has generated a unique knowledge/power regime that is inherently Orientalist and racist. The regime's designation of 'Muslims' as patients to be diagnosed, studied, problematized, surveilled, and intervened is primarily geared toward normalizing an imperialistic neoliberal order and justifying both economic and military interventions at home and abroad. The discursive construction of Muslims in the post-9/11 development discourse elucidates how Muslims have been put under severe surveillance and control by different discursive practices and interventions, with an apparent intention to serve a capitalist few at the expense of others. As Muslims—taken as a homogeneous mass—are branded with negative images (such as patients, aliens, terrorists, and militants), they will need a form of 'treatment'. Similar to the way a patient needs treatment from a doctor, the U.S., self-proclaimed as 'Good' and 'Civilized', has an automatic role in intervening with these 'Muslim patients'.

This chapter critically uncovers a very powerful segment of development discourse: the segment that has infused itself into the greater discourse of development on which foreign policy in particular is based. The discourse has been contested for its reckless attempts to discursively create and re-create domains of thought that justify certain interventions. I argue that the new knowledge/power/security regime in the development discourse after 9/11 has created a 'new body of knowledge' and 'truths' on Muslim subjects in order to employ a regime of governance. The forms of understanding and representing the Muslim subjects are still dictated by the same basic tenets found in colonialism and developmentalism: "The forms of power that have appeared act not so much by repression but by normalization; not by ignorance but by controlled knowledge; not by humanitarian concern but by bureaucratization of social action" (Escobar 1995:53).

Terrorism—the use of terror by organized groups to achieve given ends—is not only the actions of isolated groups; states also act in a terrorist manner when they resort to the indiscriminate use of violence. Daniele Archibugi (2001) reminds us:

> A war waged against civilians is thus an act of terrorism. . . . [T]hroughout the 1990s, democratic states—the U.S. in particular—were active in international terrorism: Panama, the Persian Gulf, the Balkans are some of the examples. In all these cases, military force was used, mowing down civilian victims, people who had nothing whatsoever to do with the acts America was attempting to combat. The 'indirect' component—the establishing of the predominance of the West, meaning the U.S.—played a more important role than the direct one. The entire

Third World has metabolized the tough lesson: namely, that anyone who enters into conflict with the U.S. risks being bombed.

The chapter does not suggest that the terrorist threat from Al-Qaeda should be downplayed or ignored. What is crucial is that rather than addressing the root cause of terrorism, the creation and deployment of the knowledge/power/security regime elucidated in this chapter will only limit human freedom and complicate the prospects for a peaceful coexistence. Louay M. Safi (2001) suggests that terrorism cannot be fought through military war but by bringing justice and eliminating the roots of depression. History, both old and new, is rampant with examples of great powers that wasted their resources, and hence lost their privileged positions in the world, by improving war apparatuses and overlooking the system of justice. The neoliberal violence to eliminate violence is paradoxical and always counterproductive. Arjomand, an American author, reminds us, "Those who see our weapons used to destroy Palestinian civilian targets on the television screens throughout the Middle East are more likely to hate our destructive power than to consider us champions of freedom and democracy" (n.d.).

The current development discourse and its knowledge/power regime serve as a mechanism of control that is as pervasive and effective as its colonial counterparts. It has generated categories powerful enough to shape and to influence the thinking even of its occasional critics, while fear and terror have become widespread. The regime should therefore be treated not as a commonsense attempt to solve the global problem of terrorism but as a historically and culturally specific project whose emergence and governing practices must be denaturalized, problematized, and resisted. In the name of combating terror, the regime in effect creates more terror and horror. The Iraq war is an abhorrent legacy of this regime. Discursive constructions are always self-defeating: their aim is to justify and to normalize an imperial order, but when we look at them more closely, the same discursive constructions pose enough justification for delegitimizing the order.

Part III

Sustainable Earth amid Vulnerabilities

13 Third World Vulnerabilities
Towards a Double-Risk Society

INTRODUCTION

> "[T]he history of risk distribution shows that, like wealth, risks adhere to the class pattern, only inversely: wealth accumulates at the top, risks at the bottom."
> —Ulrich Beck (1992:35, cited in Frey 2001b:106).

The founding fathers of sociology—namely, Karl Marx, Emile Durkheim, and Max Weber—were concerned with the conditions of modernity: its characteristics, causes, and consequences on social life. Their contributions toward our understanding of modernity and its link to capitalism, industrialization, and an explanation of the changing conditions of life in modern societies have been built upon or critiqued by contemporary thinkers. Ulrich Beck, a German sociologist, is one contemporary thinker who has argued that we have moved into another phase of modernity. In a radical break from the past, with new conditions of living in contemporary societies, we have moved from '*first modernity*' into '*second modernity*'. His initial thesis on the risk society (see Beck 1992) is further developed in his next work, *World Risk Society* (1999) and has been followed by his latest book, *World at Risk* ([2007] 2009). In these works, among other things, Beck argues for a new understanding of modernity organized around the concept of risk: "Modern society has become a risk society in the sense that it is increasingly occupied with debating, preventing and managing risks that it itself has produced" (2006:332).

This chapter first examines Beck's ideas on risk and the (world) risk society, explaining what exactly it means to live in a (world) risk society. It then explores the idea of a *double-risk society*.[1] A distinction is made between the experience of risk and practice of risk management between First World and Third World societies, mirroring the distinction between risk society and double-risk society. The chapter ends with a discussion on the practice of Third World reflexivity and reflexive modernity.

RISK-SOCIETY THESIS AND MODERNITY

Beck and Anthony Giddens are two prominent sociologists interested in examining the transformations in social life as industrial societies have evolved into contemporary modern societies. In their sociological studies of risk, Beck and Giddens develop the concept of the 'risk society', which "offers not only an analytical tool and an interpretation of the society in which they live—they also outline new methods of social management they would like to see implemented in order to help counteract both the weakening of so-called 'traditional' management methods (trade unions, class struggle, political parties with clearly defined proposals) and the danger of modernity to the whole of humanity" (Boudia and Jas 2007:327). For Beck, contemporary modern society is characterized by and organized around risk. The concept of risk and its relationship to catastrophe, disaster, danger, and threat may be understood as follows.

Risk does not mean catastrophe; risk means the *anticipation* of catastrophe. Risks exist in a permanent state of virtuality and become 'topical' only to the extent that they are anticipated. Risks "are not real in themselves" (Loon 2000:166) but are "becoming real" (p. 177). According to this explanation, risks arise from the anticipation of threatening events, such as environmental catastrophes, nuclear disasters, terrorist attacks, and global financial meltdowns. In anticipation of such threats, society is compelled to act—to assess, to manage, and to alleviate risk. I now turn to Beck's theoretical argument, which consists of two interrelated theses: the risk thesis and the argument for 'reflexive modernization'. In his discussion of risk, Beck observes that industrial society is primarily concerned with the distribution of goods, while contemporary modern society is increasingly concerned by the distribution of 'bads' (danger in its all forms). He calls this 'the risk society'.

Beck argues that, in the past, society was organized based on class positions. In contemporary modern society, he observes that there is a restructuring process that has led to society's becoming organized based on risk positions instead. Beck further posits that in industrial society, *"being determines consciousness,* but in contemporary society, it is the reverse; *consciousness (knowledge) determines being"* (1992:53; emphasis added). This represents a fundamental change from industrial society to contemporary society, and it "results in a decline in the importance of structures, like class, and the individualization of social agents (actors) who, forced to make risk decisions, reflect on the social institutions responsible for those decisions" (Dietz, Frey, and Rosa 2001:285–286).

Beck argues that risk is egalitarian in that it does not discriminate between the rich and the poor, be they individuals or countries. In short, risk is global and universal. As he writes, "Being at risk is the way of being and ruling in the world of modernity; being at global risk is the human condition at the beginning of the twenty-first century" (2006:330). Global risks affect everyone, regardless of their class, ethnicity, nationality, and other identity markers. But as I discuss later, the distribution of risks and their impact are still shaped by some of these traditional markers. The global nature of risk, demonstrated by such threats as terrorism, climate change, and financial crises, transcends and crosses national boundaries; Beck coins the term "world risk society" as an extension of his risk-society thesis to account for its global nature. Living in the world risk society forces an awakening of a world consciousness and an awareness of the political and economic interdependence of the contemporary world we live in. The Indian Ocean tsunami in 2004, the SARS outbreak in 2003, and the recent global financial crisis of 2008 are reminders of the power of such international disasters to 'enlighten' and to remind us of the global nature of risk. The development of such a consciousness leads to a recognition of the need for increased cross-border cooperation to better manage the global risks threatening human lives. Political, religious, and ethnic differences are necessarily cast aside amid intensified intercultural and international dialogue and assistance toward collective responses and action in the face of risks. In sum, the global nature of risk means that in the world risk society, no nation can attempt to cope or to manage with risk alone.

Beck's second thesis argues that scientific and technological progress has brought about the centrality of risk in contemporary modern society. This is akin to the proverbial situation of the creator creating a monster that goes out of control. Scientific and technological rationality and products are relied upon to assess, to manage, and to prevent the risks produced, in part, by other advances in science and technology. Scientific knowledge is also relied upon in managing and assessing risk, as is manifest in the insurance industry. But Beck notes that "because risks are difficult to define and ambiguous, [they are] subject to competing interpretations and conflicting claims" (Dietz, Frey, and Rosa 2001:286). Alternatively, Socrates' aphorism "I know that I know nothing" (cited in Beck 2006:329) aptly describes this perspective of science and technology. Science allows us to know that there is much more we do not know and that in these undiscovered mysteries lie dangers that could threaten humanity. Yet 'knowing that we know nothing' also means that we understand the limitations of scientific rationalism and its ability to provide solutions to everything.

As modernity gives way to postmodernity, the certainties of science and faith in scientific knowledge lose their grip in influencing the perception and assessment of risk. Global risks posed by environmental threats and terrorism are more difficult to perceive, to assess, and to control through scientific knowledge and claims. Subsequently, it has become more difficult for these risks to be insured against. Beck is concerned with how risk societies understand and cope with the knowledge claims of increased risk, given that science has lost its privileged position. His answer is found in 'reflexive modernity', which refers to the "negotiation of knowledge claims between science, political interests and laypersons—in effect, negotiation between different epistemologies" (Dietz, Frey, and Rosa 2001:286). The new social movements, for instance, such as those related to environmental and feminist causes, are considered expressions of 'reflexive modernization'.

Beck explains 'reflexive modernization' as the radicalization of modernity and the increasing pervasiveness of scientific rationality in every aspect of everyday life in contemporary society: "Radicalization of modernity produces this fundamental irony of risk: science, the state and the military are becoming part of the problem they are supposed to solve. This is what 'reflexive modernization' means: we are not living in a post-modern world, but in a more-modern world. It is not the crisis, but the victory of modernity, which, through the logics of unintended and unknown side-effects, undermines basic institutions of first modernity" (2006:338).

Beck's critics have alleged that he presumes the (world) risk society experience is a homogenous one across various communities around the globe. Indeed, they and other scholars point out that societies are not becoming more egalitarian because of the 'democratic nature of risk'; the experience of risk and the management of risk are structured by prevailing social and global inequalities. In vulnerable communities, class stratification continues to shape the nature and extent of risk. As Peter Taylor-Gooby and Andreas Cebulla observe, various "studies indicate that risk is neither a simple, nor a universal category in the understanding of lived experience; there are 'important differences between countries and between geographical regions in the same city or region' in how risk is understood" (2010:733). Perhaps in response to critics of his earlier works, Beck has made a point of emphasizing his recognition of the inequalities of risk experienced by various communities; he lays down as the first law of world risk society the idea that *"catastrophic risk follows the poor"* (2006:339; emphasis original).

In modern society, there is a belief that risk can be assessed and controlled with science and technology. Ironically, however, it is precisely the limitations of scientific and technological rationality and quantitative analysis that create more uncertainty. Insofar that risk can be quantified, it can be insured. In industrial society during early modernity, risks were insurable (e.g., health insurance, unemployment insurance, industrial injury insurance, etc.). Risk in late modernity is more difficult to identify, to predict, and to quantify. Going forward, risk will be even less easy to control and to prevent, and consequently will be less insurable. The world risk society is a clash between reality and ideas. In principle, risk is quantifiable, but in reality, especially so in late modernity as a historical stage, risk is increasingly incalculable. Living in the risk society, the precautionary principle replaces the compensation principle (Beck [2007] 2009:118). The latter principle is characteristic of early and premodernity when risk was quantifiable; in the past, the quantifiability of risk through the science of probability allowed for compensation. The precautionary principle dictates that in contemporary times, catastrophes of the worst possible consequences can hardly be knowable or even imagined and have to be prevented.

However, the assumption that one historical stage (industrial society) where risks were more quantifiable is distinct from another stage (world risk society) that is less insurable because risks are less quantifiable is flawed. Such an assumption does not take into account how certain communities across the world vary in their level of industrialization as a result of structural global inequality. These communities could be still stuck in the early industrialization stages; but the nature of the world risk society is such that the increasing incalculability of risk and its dangerous consequences affect Third World societies, even though these societies are not the main contributors to the emergence of these risks. As I discuss later in the conception of a double-risk society, the more vulnerable communities of the Third World suffer even more risk than those in First World societies due to systemic distributional inequities.

MULTIPLE MODERNITIES, MULTIPLE RISK SOCIETIES?

The extant literature favors the argument for 'multiple modernities', as opposed to the idea that 'modernity' is a single homogenous experience or a model of convergence for all societies, the latter idea usually being referred to as 'modernization theory' (see Chapter 3, this volume). The concept of multiple modernities emerged in the 1990s as a response to modernization theory, which was commonly criticized as an oversimplified understanding of a homogenizing process for countries go through. Critics of modernization theory point to its central assumption that all societies go through a homogenizing process of modernization leading to convergence, often with the 'Western' model as a historical yardstick. Volker H. Schmidt aptly observes the cultural and institutional diversity across all societies: "Not only are there, according to these critics (of modernization theory), several paths to modernity, but different historical trajectories and socio-cultural backgrounds also give rise to highly distinct forms of modernity in different parts of the world. In fact, even Europe, where it all began, exhibits a great deal of cultural and institutional diversity" (2006:78). Critics of modernization theory disagree that modernization processes will lead to societies' becoming more similar over time in cultural and institutional models. Instead, they emphasize that cultural and institutional differences will prevail. In short, it appears that there are as many modernities as there are societies, or perhaps even communities, in part a result of their cultural, social, and institutional differences.

The preceding discussion on different pathways of modernization alludes to the possibilities for a multiplicity of varieties of risk society and its lived experience across societies and communities. At the broadest generalization, Third World societies would experience risk society differently from First World societies. The former lack the institutions and resources (a) to decide on the distribution of risk that is shaped by global economic and political inequalities and (b) to develop effective risk-management procedures and systems to deal with the dangers and threats that such challenges as the environmental crisis and terrorism pose in the twenty-first century. Let us now turn to the concept of the 'double-risk society' to describe the experience of Third World societies and their characteristics of vulnerabilities.

A DOUBLE-RISK SOCIETY

A central aim of introducing the notion of a double-risk society is to distinguish the experience of risk between First World and Third World societies and to more adequately describe the type and extent of risks facing Third World societies. This allows us to better understand the lived experience of risk in Third World societies based on their existing political conditions and the availability of resources and capabilities to manage risk. In terms of resource and capacity, political infrastructure, and nature of risk, Table 13.1 shows how First World societies experience 'risk society', while Third World societies endure a double-risk society.

Wealthier communities usually found in First World societies have more resources, financial and otherwise, to engage in research to improve risk-management programs. In addition, scientific knowledge and technological competency are closely associated with the availability of economic resources. Better risk-management programs developed through research initiatives require substantial financial resources, which allow the community to improve or to reduce its vulnerability to risks and to recover faster when faced with the dangers of an actual catastrophe.

Table 13.1 Risk Society and Double-Risk Society

	Increasing Vulnerabilities ⟶	
	First World Societies	**Third World Societies**
Resource and Capability	High: Usually wealthy and with technical expertise, knowledge in risk assessment and management	Low: Lacking in financial resources, knowledge, and expertise in risk-management systems
Political Infrastructure	Democracy; rule of law Strong civil society: More public debates and contestation on policy decisions that will incur risk; more checks and balances Rule of law protects public interest More accountability	Inclination toward pervasive corruption; non-democratic or less democratic forms of political systems and government Overall activities do not fall within the framework of but largely subvert the institutions of democracy and the rule of law
Type of Risk Experienced	Risk society Experience risks associated with science and technology—scientific and technological rationality dominate industrial and economic decisions; scientific and technological progress	Double-risk society Experience more risk than First World societies due to the global distribution of risks and lack the institutional framework and resources to resolve, improve, and manage those risks

The political systems of First World societies generally follow some form of democracy. For this discussion, I shall broadly use 'democracy' to refer to "rule of the people or citizens" (Scott and Marshall 2005:143), where the rights of the citizens to have a voice in the decision-making processes are upheld. There are variants of democracy that have been discussed at length elsewhere (see Crick 2002), but it is sufficient for my purposes here to note that most First World societies that adopt democratic forms of political systems and government have some central commonalities, including, for example, free and fair elections, some extent of freedom of speech and political association, space for civil society to flourish, and the rule of law, in which the law is a representation of the will of the people, usually sanctioned by elected representatives (e.g., parliamentary members). Third World societies, on the contrary, adopt political systems that are much less democratic, sometimes to the extreme of being dictatorial (e.g., as with the case of rule by military dictatorships), in which the rule of law is not representative of the people's will and is usually inconsistently applied in order to serve the interests of the powerful.

A framework of democracy and the rule of law in First World societies increase the likelihood of better risk management. There are more checks and balances, with power spread across different institutions. Neoliberal economic policies have an affinity with political frameworks of democracy and rely on the rule of law to ensure predictability and the belief that businessmen and investors can trust that their individual property rights will be protected. Wealthy nations are usually characterized by successful neoliberal economic policies. The world economic system favors the wealthy nation-states, translating economic power into political power on the international stage as well. As Beck observes:

> Risk exposure is replacing class as the principal inequality of modern society, because of how risk is reflexively defined by actors: 'In risk society *relations of definition* are to be conceived analogous to Marx's relations of production'. The inequalities of definition enable powerful actors to maximize risks for 'others' and minimize risks for 'themselves'. Risk definition, essentially, is a power game. This is especially true for world risk society where Western governments or powerful economic actors define risks for others. (2006:333; emphasis original)

In short, political power generated from the position of powerful nation-states in the global economic order allows them much leverage in minimizing risk for themselves and in redistributing risk to the less developed and more vulnerable communities around the world.

Perhaps the most important advantage that frameworks of democracy and rule of law bring to First World societies is that civil society is allowed to grow and to flourish. "There is widespread belief that in a democracy, the media plays an important role in providing the public both with information and a forum for debate about new technologies" (Fitzgerald and Rubin 2010:393). Democratic political systems ensure, at least in principle, the integrity of independent media in society to educate the masses of the risks inherent in the adoption of any particular technology. Such independent media institutions allow a more educated public to debate the use of new technology and to take an active role in developing risk-management systems to better cope with the potential dangers of scientific and technological progress. For example, Beck (1992) implies, as explained by Scott T. Fitzgerald and Beth A. Rubin (2010:393), that "the less the public is involved in the development of science (generated risks), the greater the risks that science will create."

Civil society is especially important in filling in gaps left by weak or unwilling governments in providing disaster relief and postdisaster recovery work. Cassidy Johnson's (2011) case-study analysis shows the importance of civil society in providing disaster recovery and risk reduction following the 1999 earthquakes in Turkey. This was especially so for the immediate period following the earthquakes, when government programs failed to reach the citizens in desperate need of food, shelter, medical aid, and so forth. Johnson's work also demonstrates that strong governance structures are still important in the long term to complement an active civil society for more effective disaster recovery and risk management. The above-mentioned case study points to the affinity between strong democratic governance structures, a strong civil society, and effective risk management. Civil society very usefully provides much needed intermediate-level social programs to promote strong community support. Civil society also complements government efforts and focus in large-scale infrastructure projects.

In Third World societies, the weakness or lack of democratic systems of governance leads to heightened vulnerabilities to the risks generated by scientific and technological applications in industrial projects. A weak or non-existent civil society also leads to a lack of contestation against extremes of mechanistic scientific and technological rationality, which may be detrimental to public interests. There will be a distinct lack of accountability in decision-makers' actions. Third World societies also lack public participation in important decision-making processes related to the management of risk or decisions on adopting risky ventures and technology. As Thomas Dietz, R. Scott Frey, and Eugene Rosa aptly sum up: "Less developed nations, on the other hand, have a limited ability to access and manage technological risks. . . . The legislative basis for risk protection is often weak or nonexistent. In turn, existing legislation and regulations are not adequately enforced. The problem is exacerbated by the fact that less developed nations do not have enough trained operators and managers with skills necessary for managing risky technologies effectively" (2001:280).

In sum, the risk society is more applicable in describing the lived experience of First World societies, while the more vulnerable Third World societies experience the 'double-risk society', as discussed below. Third World societies experience more risk; they lack the resources and political institutions to assess the risk associated with scientific and technological progress. In times of catastrophe, they also lack the resources, expertise, and strong civil societies or governments to provide support to meet the immediate needs that would allow their citizens to recover swiftly.

GLOBAL INEQUALITIES AND THE DOUBLE-RISK SOCIETY

Why do Third World societies and vulnerable communities experience more risk? This unequal distribution of risk is found both within and between First World societies and Third World societies. Risk distribution is closely associated with the existing system of inequalities. In other words, poor and more vulnerable communities are likely to experience more risk due to their position in the stratified economy and the political hierarchy, both nationally and internationally. In such democracies as the U.S., the impact of Hurricane Katrina in 2005 has shown that poorer and black communities are at greater risk than the wealthier and middle-class groups. As Robert D. Bullard argues, "Communities are not all created equal. In the U.S., for example, some communities are routinely poisoned while the government looks the other way" (2001:97). Bullard's observation encapsulates the concern with environmental justice and environmental racism that extends beyond the example of the U.S. and is equally applicable for communities across different countries and continents.

The prevalence of environmental racism in the U.S. has been well documented (see Hannigan 2006:49). Not only are the marginalized minorities' communities at the receiving end of large corporations' toxic waste, but they are also victims of systemic social and economic inequality that renders them powerless and voiceless in decision-making processes, even as resistance against these decisions also places their freedom and well-being at high risk. Research in the 1980s by such academics as Bullard helped bring forth the realities of environmental racism into the public discourse and forced the government to take action to tackle the problem.

The environmental justice and racism paradigms, initially an analysis of inequities occurring in the U.S., have been extended to an analysis of the global inequities, particularly those between the Global North and South. Such analysis could also be extended to understanding the inequities related to the global distribution of risk and differences in capabilities for risk management between the Global North and South. In particular, the vulnerable communities of the Global South are faced with more environmental risk as the developed nations of the Global North redistribute 'environmental bads' through such actions as relocating toxic and hazardous waste sites to the vulnerable communities' locations. Bullard observes that "[t]he practice of targeting poor communities of colour in the Third

World for waste disposal and the introduction of risky technologies from industrialized countries are forms of 'toxic colonialism', what some activists have dubbed the 'subjugation of people to an ecologically destructive economic order entities over which people have no control'" (2001:100).

Just as with environmental racism, the inequalities of risk distribution are enforced by government, legal, economic, political, and military institutions, both at national and international levels. The inequities inherent in the world economic system as a result of globalization processes ensure that Third World societies and vulnerable communities will continue to be victims of the double-risk society. Frey (2001b), using the world-systems analysis (see Wallerstein 2004), examines how hazardous waste and the risks that come with it are redistributed through flows from the core regions to the periphery regions. He shows how such flows have been institutionalized through the inequalities of an emerging world economic system where wealth accumulates at the top and risk accumulates at the bottom.

REFLEXIVITY IN DOUBLE-RISK SOCIETY: THE THIRD WORLD'S 'REFLEXIVE MODERNIZATION'

'Reflexive modernization' represents a particular stage of modernization characterized by a radicalization process involving transformations of key institutions and principles foundational to modern society. As Beck would have us believe, we are now living in the Second Modernity; he observes a transformation from the *First Modernity*, which is largely synonymous with the nation-state, to the *Second Modernity*, which is still taking shape and is rendering questionable the continued relevance of the nation-state as a unit of analysis in understanding the organization of society and social change. Beck, Wolfgang Bonss, and Christoph Lau argue, "Modernity has not vanished, but it is becoming increasingly problematic. While crises, transformation and radical social change have always been part of modernity, the transition to a reflexive second modernity not only changes social structures but revolutionizes the very coordinates, categories and conceptions of change itself" (2003:2).

Giddens's conception of reflexivity in reflexive modernization rests on the assumption that as societies experience modernization processes, there is increasing consciousness of the conditions of modern society at both individual and institutional levels. Individuals are liberated from ignorance and prejudice, and decisions for social change are made under this new context. Contrary to Giddens's understanding of reflexivity as being associated with knowledge, Beck conceives of reflexivity as *non-knowledge,* of not knowing (see Beck's discussion of this distinction in [2007] 2009:119). 'Reflexive' signifies not an 'increase of mastery and consciousness, but a heightened awareness that mastery is impossible' (Latour 2003, cited in Beck, Bonss, and Lau 2003:3). For Beck, reflexivity is a characteristic of second modernity; in first modernity, there is reflection (knowledge), while in second modernity, there is reflexivity (both knowledge and non-knowledge). Klaus Rasborg suggests, "In the risk society, modernity becomes reflexive insofar as it is increasingly confronted with its own results. The detraditionalization of late modern society leads to an increasing individualization in as much as individuals are liberated from traditional communities and forms of life such as the church, social classes, the family, membership of political parties, etc." (2012:4).

Empirical investigations into specific experience of risk abound, one of which is an empirical study of the risk society and use of pesticides. In a case study of risk arising from the development and use of pesticides (see Jensen and Blok 2008), the impact of those pesticides on human health and environmental risks is examined, with a particular focus on pesticides' effects on food production. Reflexivity is practiced through social criticisms that arise from the knowledge and awareness of these risks, followed by actions to resist and to reform the existing arrangements and to produce positive social change.

In the risk society, there is an increasing awareness of the risk produced by techno-social developments, the scientific and technological progress in nuclear energy, nanotechnology, genetic engineering, and so forth. People are more conscious of the limitations of scientific rationality in assessing, evaluating, predicting, and preventing risks, even as threats posed by climate change, environmental risks, nuclear technology, and genetic engineering are intensified. Ironically, the critical scrutiny of scientific rationality is carried out using scientific reasoning and knowledge. Reflexivity in this sense is limited in its reliance on scientific rationality to reflect upon the validity of existing knowledge and to arrive at a realization of non-knowledge.

However, as Mette Jensen and Anders Blok point out, a lack of emphasis has been given to the equal importance of 'lay knowledge' in contributing to this reflexivity. Lay knowledge is equally important in formulating responses to risk and initiating resistance. Using the example of pesticides, societies also rely on 'lay epistemology'; they recognize indicators of risk, such as the changing color of well water or the mysterious 'poisoning' of fishes, affecting their livelihood and food sources. Jensen and Blok observe:

> [V]isual clues and day-to-day observations of the local states of nature also strongly influence risk perceptions, through forms of 'lay ecology'. Hence, when water in the private well turns brown, or when tree branches visibly wither from pesticide exposure, it serves to prove that these are 'very toxic' substances (Peder). On a somewhat larger scale, fish lying dead 'with their belly upside down' in the local stream come to serve as tangible evidence of some chemical pollution leak (Lise). (2008:770)

The role of 'lay knowledge making' for 'knowing' and 'acting upon' risk is usually evident in Third World societies and vulnerable communities, which are less developed in their scientific and technological rationality or institutions—hence their reliance on expert authorities in knowledge making. But even in First World societies, there is also an interweaving of scientific and lay knowledge in contributing to the reflexivity within contemporary risk society. As Beck himself explains, risk is reflexively defined (2006:333). He acknowledges that not all actors will benefit equally from the definition of risk; it depends on who has the ability and power to define their own risk. Risk definition in this sense becomes a power game. Inequalities in the distribution of risk are evident in the "world risk society where Western governments or powerful economic actors define risks for others" (Beck 2006:333). In short, Third World and First World societies do not have equal or similar reflexivity in defining risk.

Third World societies and vulnerable communities are equally capable of being reflexive in that they can be aware of the risk produced by science and technological progress, on the one hand, and on the other, the intensification of that risk through global systems of inequalities, such as the unequal power relations they are subjected to by the wealthier and more developed First World societies, which have greater voice in decision making over issues of risk distribution. They can also be aware of their lack of resources to cope with and to manage risk brought about by climate change, industrial pollution, and so forth.

One of the key differences in the reflexivity of Third World societies and that of First World societies is that for the former, the communities are constrained in their ability and resources to effect changes at the institutional level. Their reflexivity is limited to the communal or individual level in responding to and coping with risk. They are powerless to stop the transfer of risk (e.g., generated from dumping chemical and toxic waste) from First World societies to their backyards. Such Third World vulnerability and reflexivity is in part explained by the lack of democratic political framework and the weak or lack of civil society; citizens are generally not empowered to effect changes in their national policies or to resist against the international order that favors the politically empowered First World societies. In this way, First World societies' decisions affect the risk experienced by Third World societies.

Another difference is that Third World societies are not as connected to the global neoliberal economy (see Chapter 5, this volume) as First World societies are. They may not experience the risks associated with scientific and technological progress that First World societies are burdened with, constraining their reflexivity in defining risk. For First World societies, the risks associated with scientific and technological progress are evident in their lifestyle dependence on technology, such as computers, electricity, automobiles, and cell phones. This reliance exposes people from First World societies to the possibility of major disruptions to their taken-for-granted lifestyles, or even their very survival, when faced with threats ranging from lifestyle-gadget failures and electricity-supply disruptions to natural disasters, such as floods and hurricanes, or human-induced disasters of war and nuclear accidents. Third World societies and vulnerable communities, on the contrary, are less affected by these threats, as they are not overly reliant on technology. Electricity-supply disruptions, for instance, are not uncommon in Third World societies due to the inefficient infrastructural support in rural regions and suburban slum areas. Local communities develop lay knowledge of nature and their surroundings and systems of coping. In this instance, Third World societies are sometimes more empowered through their 'lay reflexivity' than First World societies are in coping with risk.

In short, to compare Third World and First World societies, the former are not as connected to the global economic order, and they are not as reliant on the use of technology in everyday life. When these technologies fail, such as during power failures or Internet server crashes, the lives of Third World societies and vulnerable communities are not severely disrupted. This is perhaps due in part to their ability to cope with the frequent breakdowns or failures they experience. In addition, their own national governments may have neglected and isolated them, leaving many of these communities to develop strong communal support systems reliant on trust and neighborly relations to look out for one another. As such, the reflexivity of Third World societies in this regard should not be discounted on the basis of their lack of scientific and technological progress. Instead, their condition of being less reliant on science and technology for survival and the routines of their everyday lives make them somewhat less susceptible to major disruptions and dangers from technologically related failures and disasters.

In addition, while Third World societies may not have the political or economic resources to change the present unfair system of international risk distribution, their vulnerability has led to the emergence of international non-governmental organizations (NGOs) dedicated to representing their voice at international negotiation tables. Third World reflexivity is in part reliant on the broader reflexivity of the world as a global society. Globalization has intensified the interdependence of societies around the world and produced greater awareness of worldwide poverty, powerlessness, and inequality, especially in First World societies; this has spurred the growth of NGOs in taking up the role of being a voice for the voiceless. For example, environmental NGOs have consistently reminded the international community and transnational corporations (TNCs) of the unequal power relations between the more developed and developing world and their impact on the livelihood of disempowered communities. We can thus speak of a distinction between a double-risk society that is experienced by Third World societies and vulnerable communities around the world and the risk society that is experienced by First World societies and wealthier (somewhat less vulnerable) communities.

CONCLUSION

In sum, the risk-society thesis as posited by Beck and his contemporaries does not adequately account for the lived experience of risk and vulnerability in Third World societies. In contributing to the risk-society thesis and the sociological understanding of risk in modern societies, this chapter proposes the concept of a double-risk society to account for the lived experience of Third World societies. The lived experience of risk is shaped by the political infrastructure of a society and the availability of resources at its disposal, which affects its ability to assess, to manage, to predict, and to prevent risk. Third World vulnerabilities arise from these communities' lack of democratic political systems, weak civil societies, and lack of scientific, technological, material, and financial resources. Such vulnerabilities and disempowerment place them at a disadvantage in the global distribution of risk. Third World societies suffer a 'double risk' in that they do not have the capabilities to effectively cope with their own naturally occurring risks and are furthermore likely to be powerless in resisting imported risks amid the inequitable system of global risk distribution. However, Third World societies' agency and reflexivity should not be entirely discounted; given their unique circumstances, they may be stronger and more effective in coping with risk through their possession of 'lay knowledge' of risk and communal solidarity in times of trouble.

14 Toward a Sustainable Earth?

INTRODUCTION

This book starts with the aim of exploring the relationship between power, development, and the environment in the context of the vulnerable planet under neoliberal governance. While chapters throughout the book are presented to contribute to existing scholarship looking at this relationship, this closing chapter reviews those discussions thus far and assesses the possibilities or alternatives for a sustainable future. Uncovering key environmental problems, such as climate change and global warming, loss of biodiversity, deforestation, and water pollution, I find that most environmental and social problems and issues are deeply connected to, and contingent upon, the global processes. The 'collective irresponsibility' of current economic and political structure generates the 'tragedy of the commons', putting the powerless human and other non-human communities in deeper vulnerabilities. The book discerns at least four conspicuous yet interrelated historical projects of power—colonialism, developmentalism, neoliberal globalism, and neoliberal knowledge/power/security regime—each project creating its unique mode of subjectivity and troubled environmental legacies.

Often, development is understood as the pursuit of economic growth and is taken for granted as the *raison d'être* for nation-states and their governments. The somewhat inconvenient challenge to this order presented by environmental problems has forced leaders of the international community, national governments, and business sectors to consider ways of assuring the world that development aims and economic growth can be compatible with environmental sustainability. Some scholars have also focused their attention on the interactions between nature and society. However, the central concept of power and its analysis is found lacking in existing scholarly studies in the field of development studies and environmental sociology.

The contribution of this book to the field is primarily threefold: (1) to review the existing theorizations of modernity and nature-society interactions for their accuracy and relevance in the face of contemporary environmental challenges and vulnerabilities, (2) to offer the 'double-risk society' thesis to emphasize the vulnerabilities of Third World communities under conditions of modernity, and (3) to provide case studies of the Global South to support the need for the 'double-risk society' thesis to understand how power relations between the developed and developing world affect our knowledge and experience of environmental challenges. The implication for readers is that a better understanding of the intricate relationship between power, development, and the environment may increase their awareness of Third World vulnerabilities to the environmental challenges of the twenty-first century. In this way, the book is part of the modernity project, specifically as part of what Ulrich Beck and Anthony Giddens, among others, have termed 'reflexive modernization', in which individuals come to understand the conditions of their existence and are empowered to make choices that have an impact on society and the environment. Having examined the various theories that seek to explain the relationship between power, development, and the environment, the 'double-risk society thesis' is suggested as an improvement upon Beck's 'risk-society thesis' and as a complement to the other existing theorizations in capturing the unique lived experience of Third World and other vulnerable communities. This concluding chapter adumbrates environmental and social vulnerabilities under neoliberalism with particular emphasis on the vulnerabilities of the Third World and other marginalized subaltern communities. Drawing on earlier discussions, this chapter then discerns how development has historically created different projects of power. Finally, the future of environmentalism is projected as being one that will bring a 'sustainable Earth', where ecological and social logics triumph over neoliberal economistic logic.

DISCONNECTING NATURE AND SOCIETY

The theories discussed in Chapter 4 explain the relationship between nature and society. While the theories may differ in the solutions suggested for our current environmental problems, the agreement seems to be that nature and society can and should coexist. These theories also agree by and large that consumption and production practices characteristic of modern industrialized societies may have led to an increasing disconnection between nature and society. Our consumption practices at individual and societal levels are the basis of development projects targeted at using consumption to drive the engines of economic growth. Concurrently, consumption practices have a direct relationship with our environment. The more we consume as an individual or a society in goods and services, the more depletion of natural resources is required for the production of these goods and services. Depletion of resources is also often accompanied by the polluting effects of by-products from production waste and contributes to the overall environmental degradation that humanity currently experiences. In modern industrial societies, attitudes towards nature are either ambivalent or instrumental; in the former, nature is seen as separate from society, while in the latter, nature is seen as a useful resource to be exploited for society's progress and development.

While some of these theories argue for a radical change in the political and socio-economic structures worldwide, others argue that 'sustainable development' can be achieved within existing political and social structures with the help of technological advancement—for instance, what is commonly termed as 'green technology' today. The possibility of 'sustainable development' being implementable and successful is one that remains an attractive alternative pathway for developing Third World countries to consider, according to their own circumstances.

'Sustainable development' was popularized and heralded by *Our Common Future*, a 1987 report by the World Commission on Environment and Development, and later by the 1992 Earth Summit, officially titled 'United Nations Conference on Environment and Development'. As discussed later in this chapter, although environmental protection and social equity were two fundamental objectives of 'sustainable development', along with economic growth, the world has instead witnessed even more environmental damages and social inequity and inequality. Since power remains an inherent element in, but with overarching impact on, development discourse, 'sustainable development' has been largely used as an 'ideological guise' to occlude the central dynamics of neoliberal capitalism: accumulation through exploiting human and natural resources and legitimization by creating different domains of thoughts and discourses. With this legitimacy crisis, 'sustainable development' has therefore been shifted toward and largely replaced by a new 'green discourse'. This kind of discursive shift is not entirely new in development discourse; what is new is the widening crack between nature and society.

The disconnection between nature and society seems to be widening as society progresses through what is commonly coined as 'modernity'. Industrialization has increased the need to extract more and more resources from the environment, cementing an instrumental attitude toward nature in the process. For better or for worse, the recent natural disasters to hit Japan, the U.S., and China, among others, have perhaps forced us to urgently rethink the relationship between nature and society. More importantly, it has led to international dialogues among scholars, policy-makers, politicians, non-governmental organizations (NGOs), and civil societies about the ways to meet the challenges ahead. It has certainly increased our understanding of the intricate yet interdependent relationship between nature and society and to realize that our long-term interests lie in the well-being of the environment we depend upon for our support and livelihoods. Despite this awareness, responses to these crises through, for example, repairing the crack between nature and society are largely symbolic and not genuine. Under neoliberal globalism and security regime, economic logic continues to win over social and ecological logics. Unless there is a viable resistance and change, this will perhaps go on until we come to a threshold when the whole planet will be totally unfit for living.

LIVING IN MODERNITY: THE RISK OF ENVIRONMENTAL CHALLENGES

Twenty years on after the Rio summit in 1992, Rio+20 was held as a timely assessment of the efforts at resolving environmental issues and a discussion to decide how best to move forward. The future, it seems, is fraught with dangers. As discussed throughout the book, the global environmental challenges facing humanity are characterized by increasing and intensifying social and environmental vulnerabilities experienced across national borders. The impact is greatest in the Third World, where communities have less capabilities and resources to cope with the emerging risks.

The pursuit of development throughout history from the period of colonialism to the current era of globalization—often through industrialization programs and economic restructuring—is in part driven by scientific and technological rationality. Scholars have debated over what type or what stage of modernity we are currently living in and how we should understand the social transformations brought about in part by scientific and technological progress. Giddens observes that we are now living in 'late modernity', while Beck has coined the term 'second modernity' to describe the period after modernity. Other scholars critique Becks and Giddens for assuming that there is a visible end to the period of modernity, arguing instead for understanding the project of modernity as a continuum to the extent that no visible end can be predicted. However, most scholars still agree that the modernity of contemporary times has undergone significant transformations in line with scientific and technological progress. For Beck and Giddens, this progress is characterized by a break from the traditional past, and, more importantly, it is accompanied by a radicalization and intensification of the risk experienced by individuals and society. Both scholars note that the global environmental challenges represent high-consequence risk.

Beck's risk-society thesis recognizes that individuals and society can still see hope amid all this pessimism surrounding the high levels of risk involved in contemporary life. Beck and Giddens alike are convinced that empowerment is still possible through the idea of reflexivity; people are able to reflect upon the meanings of science, modernity, and rationality and break away from traditions that are not congruent with scientific and technological rationality. For Beck, environmentalism is a result of such 'reflexivity', where the individual and society reflect on their institutions and consumption practices while confronting the role and impact of science and technology in light of new information about the environment and its relationship with human societies.

UNDERSTANDING POWER RELATIONS

The preceding discussion in this chapter has focused on our experience and understanding of environmental and developmental challenges in the current phase of modernity. How should we go on to understand the workings of power relations within and across societies? Discovery and examination of these power relations and how they work help us better understand and be aware of the governing practices that constrain and enable our everyday life. By the same token, this examination extends our understanding of the complex social techniques established in society to control the populations. In our case, they control populations across national borders, and they control—or at least attempt to control—nature as well. Let us review the four models of understanding power.

Marxian analysis understands power as being possessed by a few elites from the ruling bourgeoisie class for the purpose of controlling and sustaining their economic dominance over the other groups. Power, accordingly, is exercised through oppressive measures, such as violence, and appears legitimized through ideologies, such as religious doctrines. The elitist model of understanding power, on the other hand, emphasizes the necessity of power to fall into the hands of a small ruling elite—not necessarily bourgeoisie class, but which follows the 'law of oligarchy' stating that the masses almost always desire strong leaders to give them direction. In this analysis, there is no need for a move toward power equity: power is exercised through various means, perhaps any means necessary, to maintain the ruling elite's position and authority. Knowledge and the control of it may be used as one such means of legitimizing the elites' position.

A pluralist understanding of power recognizes the diffusion of power across various groups. Power is associated with collective interests, and any group that is able to unify behind common interests has a voice and influence in the decision-making processes within society. Power, in this view, is decentralized. In a society, there may be a set of elites dominating at any one time, but other groups can still exert their influence and fight for their interests. Power is exercised through negotiation or mediation between various groups jostling for their interests to take precedence over others and through mobilization within the groups for solidarity.

For the purposes of this book, a Foucauldian analysis of power is most appropriate for my attempts to demonstrate the relationship between power, development, and the environment. Michel Foucault views power or power relations as underlying all facets of social life and behavior. We do what we do because there are imperceptible governing mechanisms (usually established by the state) that unconsciously shape our conduct. In contemporary society, knowledge is power, which means that the state may use its ability to disseminate information and to enact discursive practices to shape our knowledge and, by extension, our worldviews, thus subsequently shaping our conduct through the internalization of social norms. The central focus of a Foucauldian study of policy is on the broader impact of state policy, particularly the effects of power across the entire social spectrum (macro-level) down to the individual's daily life (micro-level). The Foucauldian model allows us to delve into the concept of governmentality, which is a fundamental feature of the modern state for Foucault.

FROM NEOLIBERAL GOVERNMENTALITY
TO GREEN GOVERNMENTALITY

Neoliberal governmentality may refer to a set of governing practices influenced by neoliberal ideological principles to shape the conduct of people's economic activities. The ideological principles of neoliberalism prescribe minimal government intervention into economic activities. However, more governance in the form of regulations is necessary to facilitate the smooth operation of (free) market principles. For instance, strict legislation and policies may be necessary to ensure respect for private-property rights and intellectual-property rights, while removing those regulations that may inhibit the ease of doing business, ironically through more regulations and legislative provisions. While the basic neoliberal principles may be similar across nations, the economic policies and governing practices adopted in each nation are idiosyncratic; various strands of neoliberalism are contingent upon each nation's historical, cultural, and political conditions.

The spread of neoliberalism under conditions of globalization is an inegalitarian process. Societies that adopt neoliberal ideas usually enjoy economic growth, but it also results in an unequal distribution of wealth within those societies. Neoliberal globalization integrates nation-states around the world into a global economy, but at the same time it creates a disconnection between the rich and the poor, with widening income gaps and increasing economic inequality within and between societies. Neoliberal globalization is arguably the driver behind the period of 'late modernity', a term coined by Giddens to refer to the emergence of high risks and reflexivity that comes with scientific and technological progress on the one hand and the transformation of capitalism and economic growth on the other hand. Following Giddens, the late modernity period involves neoliberal strategies aimed at sustaining economic growth. Power, development, and the environment are intertwined through these neoliberal strategies. In pursing economic growth and development aims, humans are empowered by science and technology to manipulate nature while being powerless at the same time in the face of high-consequence risk generated by scientific and technological progress. One such high-consequence risk identified by Giddens involves environmental threats as a result of developments in harnessing nuclear power for energy needs. Neoliberal strategies to sustain economic growth empower the Global North through connecting them to advances in science and technology to gain competitive advantages in the global economy and to emerge as winners in the power struggle for a greater share of the wealth distribution. Concurrently, it disempowers the Global South through disconnecting these societies from their natural resources and access to scientific and technological progress in their bid for a more proportionate share of the global-wealth distribution. As argued, the mixing of neoliberalism with environmentalism produces what may be termed 'neoliberal environmentalism', which is paradoxically impeding the efforts at bringing about more radical but necessary structural changes to our economic and political structures instead of the superficial lifestyle changes advocated by business actors who encourage 'green consumerism'.

A shift from neoliberal governmentality toward green governmentality is observed. The art of governing is complex business; environmental and developmental discourses are increasingly involved in these governing practices, producing objects of knowledge and subjectivities. Anticipating Foucault, there is an increasing literature on the use of green/environmental discourses to govern populations. The term "Environmental/Green Governmentality" or "Environmentality" is first used by Timothy Luke (1995, 1997), who views it as an attempt by transnational environmental organizations to control and to dominate environmental policy and activities around the world, but especially in developing countries. Stephanie Rutherford observes the connection that green governmentality theorists make with Foucault's work:

> Green governmentality theorists propose that Foucault's work can be centrally important in analyzing the production and circulation of discourses of nature if we extend the concept of biopower to include all life. As Darier (1999) has argued, biopolitics can be reframed as 'ecopolitics' where concern for the conditions of the national population is subsumed under more intensified attempt to manage the planet's environment. The most telling way that biopolitics has been operationalized is through the use of science to tell the truth of the environment—its characteristics, its usefulness and, eventually, its crisis. (2007:297)

Individuals internalize this knowledge of the environment as truth and are convinced of the need to adopt the prescribed changes to their lifestyles and behaviors so as to 'manage the planet's environment'. The production of environmental narratives creates the necessity for deliberate management and regulation. Such environmental narratives are intertwined with the discourses on development.

DEVELOPMENT AS A 'HISTORICAL PROJECT OF POWER'

The idea of 'development' is paradoxical in being both universally accepted and contested, and in yielding environmental and social gains together with costs. The long history of development involves a transition from the colonial period to the globalization era. Before World War II, development was associated with having colonies. Nations that possessed numerous colonies were considered to be highly developed and powerful. Controlling colonies also meant gaining access to markets, raw materials, and cheap or slave labor; all these translated into economic advantages for the colonial masters and the ability to sustain economic growth for the benefit of improving the well-being and infrastructure of the colonizers' own people. Often, it comes at the expense of exploiting the land and people from the colonies.

Europe, especially Great Britain, had a lion's share of overseas colonies and was considered the superpower holding economic and political power in the world.

After World War II, development became increasingly associated with globalization. The focus remains on pursuing economic growth. Economic globalization has facilitated open flows of capital and trade in an increasingly interconnected world. Succeeding in capital accumulation earns nation-states the status of being developed, and with this status comes political and cultural power in influencing other nation-states to adopt their practices and models. The U.S. took over the superpower status from Great Britain and continues to be the benchmark for Third World development projects and aspirations around the world. Recently, the emergence of China has challenged the superpower status of the U.S. However, the development project resembles that of U.S. development path historically and comes with a neoliberal twist, as discussed in Chapters 5 and 6. Development is power: it empowers nation-states to promote economic growth and to legitimize their political rule. Lack of development or underdevelopment disempowers nation-states; they do not have the means and access to a strong voice and representation on international institutions that make important decisions, and they lack the means to provide a better life for their own populations, many of whom are caught in vicious poverty cycles. The relationship between development and power is further complicated with the former's impact on the environment. Environmental degradation is almost always a result of development manifest through industrial programs, increase in production activities, increase in extraction of raw materials to meet production demands, and higher levels of consumption that produce more waste. During the era of colonization, development in the metropolis meant the underdevelopment of the colonies: the former was organized by disorganizing the latter. After World War II, when the 'development project' was introduced based on the Western model, the outcome was problematic. It created huge environmental and social costs, and the development was highly selective. There was an inherent power relation in the project of development, empowering few while disempowering the masses.

In short, development discourses portray economic growth via industrialization programs as the only way forward for nation-states and favor a trajectory following the European and American experiences of development as the standards by which to assess all other nations. In this way, a power relation that positions the Global North as the experts on development and the Global South as backward countries aspiring to achieve development status is reinforced. Drawing on our understanding of the complex nexus between development, power, and the environment, we can discern at least four historical projects of power: colonial project, development project, neoliberal globalization project, and neoliberal security project. Table 14.1 illustrates these projects.

Table 14.1 Development as a Historical Project of Power

	Colonial Project (18th century–1940s)	Development Project (1940s–1970s)	Neoliberal Globalization Project (1970s–2000s)	Neoliberal Security Project (2001 onward)
Development	Development was understood as having colonies Developing one society (Europe) by underdeveloping other (non-European colonies) Development as a 'project of rule'	Modernization as a viable route to development National development with international aids Development shaped by Cold War rivalry; U.S. and Bretton Woods institutions as a powerful reality Green revolution and international food-aid regime	Development as 'participation in the world market' rather than state-managed national development Inculcation of neoliberal principles drawn largely from Washington Consensus Realization of global development via new inequalities	Security discourse as inevitable apparatus for neoliberal expansion and market creation Fear and terror become efficient market strategy Coercion becomes necessary and 'legitimate' where neoliberalism is questioned or resisted
Power	White-man burden vs. colonial subjectivities (through physical force and social engineering)	Creation of three worlds: First, Second, and Third World Development became a powerful apparatus in legitimizing violence and displacements State-power in forming and transforming identities of subalterns	Rise of global managers in managing and shaping the economies of the Global South Subjection of all states to neoliberal economic disciplines Developmental and environmental governmentality to discipline people and state	Rise of neoconservatives as a radical offshoot of neoliberalism A new knowledge/power/security regime projecting 'Muslims' as 'patients' Snatching the remnant of sovereign power from countries, projecting them as potential threats
Environment	Unequal ecological exchange (e.g., export monoculture) Alienating the best lands and forests for commercial exploitation	[Irreversible] ecological damage on the global commons (by, for example, green revolution) Planet of slums and unequal access to resources generating, for example, food insecurity	Planet in peril due to, for instance, climate change Neoliberal environmentality as a mitigating strategy Climate denials or with symbolic response, making economy winning over ecological and social logics	Security becomes an 'ideological devise' to hide environmental impacts of neoliberalism Superficial response to climate insecurity, but hard response to terror insecurity Unprecedented ecological catastrophes due to military-industrial-security complex

The ways of speaking about environment and development needs to produce knowledge suggesting that sustainable development is the only viable option forward. "Certain narratives gain privilege in the environmentalist critique, while others are marginalized" (Bourke and Meppem 2000, cited in Rutherford 2007:301). *The Brundtland Report* (WCED 1987) has popularized the term 'sustainable development'. The definition of the term offered in the report has been commonly cited in all subsequent national and international documents pertaining to sustainable development that take into account environmental sustainability. It is arguable that such production serves to advance and to sustain neoliberal governmentality, ensuring rules of governance that perpetuate neoliberal principles and serve the interests of the privileged while regulating the disadvantaged and vulnerable.

The sustainable-development model continues to embrace economic growth and, by extension, consumption and production of goods and services. Some observers have pointed out the dangers of a consumerist view of development: the exhaustion of natural resources given current rates of extraction. While proponents of the sustainable-development model argue that the model takes into account environmental principles and ensures that current rates of extraction will be monitored and regulated for the benefit of future generations' use, critics are yet to be convinced by the results. The latter group believes that efforts to regulate extraction rates are just not adequate in conserving the depleting resources; indeed, many from this group believe that the root of the issue is market-biased consumerism itself and that the only way to ensure that we do not drive ourselves into destruction is to uproot and to radically transform the current economic system based on unbridled consumption and production. Members of the Global South have seen an opportunity in the environmental concerns to bring up their own development agenda, culminating in the emergence of sustainable development as a model that takes into consideration both environmental concerns and the development needs of current and future generations. Members of the Global North, on the other hand, perhaps have seen an opportunity to perpetuate their dominance in global power relations through environmental governance and, as I discuss later, with neoliberal agendas. One of the key consequences of these discourses is that it subjects all nation-states to environmental regulation; developing nations may be subjected to global environmental governance for which they did not sign up, had no say in the rule making, were not consulted; and for which their rights to use and to access their natural environments are withheld.

The combined discourse preserves the imperative for economic growth and consumption of natural resources, although considerations are now being taken for future generations' right to inherit adequate resources for their own development purposes. In the final analysis, the combined discourses produce certain 'truths' about the need for continual development and economic growth. Consuming natural resources in itself is not presented as the root of the problem: the issue is with the proper management and regulation of resource utilization. It appears that global environmental governance in its current form has strong roots in neoliberal principles and preserves the neoliberal agenda of embracing economic growth based on consumerism.

As we have seen, the effectiveness of the developed world in exercising power through these discourses is alarming, as it subjugates the developing world and exacerbates the vulnerability of disempowered communities—individuals, groups, tribes (indigenous or otherwise)—who do not have the ability and resources to make their voices heard and to be fairly represented in the decision-making process. However, as Foucault's analysis of power has shown, where there is power, there is resistance. These vulnerable communities could empower themselves through self-organizing into social movements. While efforts thus far have not been successful, these communities should not give up hope of breaking the chains of neoliberalism.

RECOGNIZING THIRD WORLD VULNERABILITY

The book offers the notion of a 'double-risk society' to distinguish the experience of risk between First World and Third World societies and to more adequately describe the type and extent of risk facing Third World societies. The case study presented in Chapter 10 about the Tipaimukh Dam in India, for instance, demonstrates the vulnerabilities of Third World countries. The Tipaimukh Dam project in India reflects the power of development discourses in shaping the decisions of governments in developing countries. Elected governments may even ignore the discontentment from NGOs and local communities affected badly by such decisions as the Dam project. The Indian government employs the discourse of 'sustainable development' and 'energy security' to justify its decision despite protests from its own people. Pleas to the international community to intervene on Bangladesh's behalf have also been ineffectual. This case study reflects the power of development objectives in dominating all other concerns, including threats to the environment.

Similarly, the discussion of 'labeling practices' in Chapter 11 emphasizes the lived experience of Third World vulnerability in the Global South. As discussed, state authorities often categorize minorities and indigenous and other weaker communities as 'tribals' so as to exploit these communities' labor, land, and resources and to deprive the communities of these same rights. The power relations between dominant and subordinate groups are thus manifest when the former impose 'labels' upon the latter to justify development activities that create unequal distribution of wealth and benefits. The power relations between the dominant Global North and the somewhat powerless Global South also mean that the former often adopts policies that exploit weaker communities in the latter under the guise of development discourse. Accordingly, these weaker communities are 'labeled' as 'tribals' so as to justify the Global North's moral obligations to help develop and modernize the economies of the Global South. In addition, the label of 'tribal' assumes that local communities' 'traditional' practices are harmful and damaging for their environments, justifying intervention from the 'superior' developed countries so as to 'save' the areas. In short, discourses of development and environmentalism are employed to invent and to transform identity labels for local communities to fit the narrative of a benevolent elite group in society—often the state authorities—that must intervene, manage, and regulate the environment and the economy on behalf of these weaker communities for the benefit of humanity and the well-being of these local people from the Global South.

THE FUTURE OF ENVIRONMENTALISM: (RE)EMPOWERING COMMUNITIES AND INDIVIDUALS

In facing the challenges ahead, the international community needs to move away from producing ineffective agreements and instead focus on implementing and enforcing them. For instance, the commitments to reducing carbon emissions need to be more effectively monitored and enforced.

The future of environmentalism could be found in 'Third World environmentalism', an emphasis on the need and value of having the Third World and the Global South lead the way in pushing for more effective global environmental governance. In Chapter 3, I discuss the benefits of adopting a Community-Based Natural Resource Management (CBNRM) approach to improve the effectiveness and fairness of development projects. This approach would encourage participation from indigenous and local communities, giving them the opportunity to voice their concerns and to protect their interests in decisions made on the national and international levels. In other words, it would empower vulnerable communities. Meaningful collaboration between communities, donor agencies, and the state(s) would have to take into consideration the needs and opinions of these weaker or powerless groups.

In a paper on global environmental governance, Adil Najam (2005) argues that international environmental agreements are characterized by *contestation* before the 1970s, *participation* during the 1980s and early 1990s, and finally *engagement* from the 1990s onward. Najam observes that efforts to engage developing countries in the global environmental project have been promising. While there may be some truth to Najam's understanding of developing countries' involvement in progressive stages, this book argues that all three elements are necessary to ensure meaningful global environmental governance. Engagement should not be understood as a superior way of involving developing countries. Contestation, participation, and engagement should not be seen as mutually exclusive, nor should engagement be seen as the final stage of achievement for global environmental governance. Rather, contestation and participation should be understood as necessary and ever present throughout the history of environmentalism, specifically 'Third World environmentalism', or environmentalism of the poor.

The Global South, with the G77 as a distinct institution that represents its collective interests and voice in the international community, contests the idea of global environmental governance as an attempt by the North to use environmental concerns to limit and to impede the development plans of the poorer countries and as an excuse to maintain the North's control over the South. Such contestation is necessary as a reminder for the richer and more powerful countries to ensure that the developing countries are included in the decision-making process of setting the direction for global environmental governance. As Najam points out, contestation from the South is important as an act of solidarity to reclaim the power to decide the direction of global environmental governance. It is also necessary to ensure that the South's development rights are protected. Such contestation remains important for environmentalism of the future. All environmental and social-justice movements should mobilize their resources to create a 'global and ontological alliance' to resist as well as to engage with the neo-liberal regime. The aim will be to subvert the existing power dynamics: to generate a truly 'sustainable Earth' where ecological and social logics will win over the neoliberal economic logic.

Notes

NOTES TO CHAPTER 1

1. It has become commonplace to note that the 'Third World' and 'Second World' have ended as coherent entities. Secondly, one can think that using 'Third World' as a concept exposes its subordinate power relation with the so-called First World. The notion of 'Third World' is therefore a contested category. The concept has been used throughout the book not as an essentialized category denoting the often uncontested power relation with its First World counterpart but more as a conceptual convenience that often contests this very power relation.

NOTES TO CHAPTER 2

1. As with energy in the physical world, power pervades all dynamic social phenomena; yet it cannot be directly observed or measured (Olsen 1970). Secondly, the English language does not contain a verb 'to power,' and therefore when we discuss power in dynamic terms, we must either attach a verb to it (such as 'exercise social power') or use such verbs as 'influence' or 'control' (Olsen and Marger 1993). Thirdly, Dennish H. Wrong (1996) finds five major problems in defining social power: first, there is the issue of intentionality of power and, secondly, of its effectiveness. The latency of power, or its dispositional nature, is a third problem. The unilateral or asymmetrical nature of power relations implied by the claim that some persons have an effect on others without a parallel claim that the reverse may also be the case is fourth problem. A final question is of the nature and effects produced by power: must they be overt and behavioral, or do purely subjective, internal effects count also?

2. Bertrand Russell, for example, defines power as "the capacity of some persons to produce intended and foreseen effects on others" (cited in Olsen and Marger 1993). According to Max Weber (1993:37), "power (macht) is the probability that one actor within a social relationship will be in a position to carry out his/her own will despite resistance, regardless of the basis on which this probability rests," while quite similarly Robert Dahl (1986:37) sees "power as the control of behavior." Weber's and Dahl's approaches both focus on the idea of "power over," which has been rejected by Hannah Arendt (1986) for being too narrow. She speaks rather of political institutions as "manifestations and materialization of power." Like Arendt, Talcott Parsons (1986) also rejects the Weberian view of power as 'highly selective'. Power, for Parsons, is a system resource, a 'generalized facility or resource in the society', which enables the achievement of collective goals through the agreement of members of society

to legitimize leadership positions whose incumbents further the goals of the system, if necessary by the use of 'negative sanctions' (see also Lukes 1986). Therefore, Parsons's version of power is both 'coercion' and 'consensus', which depends on the 'institutionalization of authority'.

3. According to the analysis of Marvin E. Olsen (1993), Weber combines the first and the second bases under the headings of 'rational-legal authority', because he thinks that they are usually combined in modern societies; but subsequent research has demonstrated that much of time, they are quite separate.

4. It is important to mention here that Karl Marx's ideas have been expanded, modified, altered, and to some extent fabricated by different Marxist and non-Marxist theorists in countless ways, paving the way for several competing schools of Marxist theory. The fundamental tenets of Marxist thought expounded here are generally accepted by most Marxists.

5. The term "Environmental/Green Governmentality" or "Environmentality" is first used by Timothy Luke (1995, 1997), who views it as an attempt by transnational environmental organizations to control and dominate environmental policy and activities around the world, but especially in developing countries. See also the collection of essays in Darier 1999. Arun Agrawal's (2003) use of the term is indebted to Luke for the coinage but is different both in intent and meaning. He gives more attention to examining the shifts in subjectivities that accompany new forms of regulation rather than seeing regulation as an attempt mainly to control or dominate.

NOTES TO CHAPTER 3

1. For example, Wolfgang Sachs (1992:5) writes, "The idea of development was once a towering monument inspiring international enthusiasm. Today, the structure is falling apart and in danger of total collapse."

2. The events of 16 September 1992 is known as the Black Wednesday. On this day, being unable to keep the pound sterling above its agreed lower limit, the British Conservative government was forced to withdraw its currency from the European Exchange Rate Mechanism. The cost of the Black Wednesday was more than £3.4 billion, and George Soros alone made over a £1 billion (Tempest 2005).

3. Gramsci is an Italian political activist and theorist who wrote much of his most influential work while incarcerated in a fascist prison. Gramsci has left an enduring legacy. His notion of hegemony is quite similar to Althusser's participatory model, where even the oppressed classes happily accede to their oppression. However, Althusser's differs insofar as he thinks social change is rendered unlikely. Gramsci's theory, on the other hand, allows a much greater role for resistance to dominating influences and power from within the hegemonized groups and recognizes the opportunity for social change within a capitalist system.

NOTES TO CHAPTER 5

1. A Corn Law was first introduced in Britain in 1804, when the landowners, who dominated Parliament, sought to protect their profits by imposing a duty on imported corn. This led to an expansion of British wheat farming and to high bread prices. This legislation was hated by the people living in Britain's fast-growing towns who had to pay these higher bread prices. The industrial classes saw the Corn Laws as an example of how Parliament passed legislation that favored large landowners (See, Spartacus 2013).

2. In a paper on neoliberal pension securitization, Susanne Soederberg describes pension securitization as a phenomenon where "workers have become increasingly dependent on the economic performance of corporations for the value of their retirement savings as pension funds across the OECD area have ramped up investment in corporate stocks and bonds" (2011:224).

NOTES TO CHAPTER 9

1. Climate refugees may refer to "people who have to leave their habitats, immediately or in the near future, because of sudden or gradual alterations in their natural environment related to at least one of three impacts of climate change: sea-level rise, extreme weather events, and drought and water scarcity" (Global Governance Project 2012; also see Biermann and Boas 2008).
2. Germanwatch is a development and environmental NGO dedicated to promoting "North-South equity and the preservation of livelihoods" through addressing issues including climate change, trade and food security, and corporate accountability, among others. For more information, please visit its webpage (http://germanwatch.org/en/home).
3. JUSCANZ is a sub-set of the regional group in the United Nations that usually comprises fourteen or fifteen UN member states: Japan, the U.S., Canada, Australia, New Zealand, Switzerland, Norway, Iceland, Andorra, Korea, Liechtenstein, Mexico, San Marino, Turkey, and sometimes Israel.
4. The Bali Road Map was adopted following the 2007 Bali Climate Change Conference, and it "consists of a number of forward-looking decisions that represent the various tracks that are essential to reaching a secure climate future. The Bali Road Map includes the Bali Action Plan, which charts the course for a new negotiating process designed to tackle climate change, with the aim of completing this by 2009, along with a number of other decisions and resolutions" (UNFCCC 2012).

NOTES TO CHAPTER 10

1. The most prominent petition is online and can be accessed through the following Web address: http://www.change.org/petitions/united-nations-tipaimukh-dam-must-be-stopped.
2. The Bangladesh Rifles have been renamed the Border Guard Bangladesh (BGB) after the February 2009 mutiny by the BDR regular soldiers against their senior officials. For more information, see http://bgb.gov.bd/index.php/bgb/history_en.
3. The author was one of the participants at this seminar.

NOTES TO CHAPTER 12

1. The identity of 'Muslims' is very fluid and hybrid, although it is often used as a monolithic entity by different discourses. The concept of Muslims as a monolithic mass is something that the chapter seeks to problematize.
2. 'Development' as a mode of improving human conditions in different parts of the world by countries/experts/organizations is certainly different from 'development discourse' that contains imperial and racist connotations.
3. U.S., Office of the Press Secretary, *Remarks by the President upon Arrival*, the South Lawn, Washington, D.C., September 16, 2001.

4. U.S., Office of the Press Secretary, *President's Remarks at the National Day of Prayers and Remembrance*, the National Cathedral, Washington, D.C., September 14, 2001.

5. U.S., Office of the Press Secretary, *Remarks by the President to the NYPD Command and Control Center Personnel*, NYPD Command and Control Center, New York, February 6, 2002.

6. U.S., Office of the Press Secretary, *President's State of the Union Address*, U.S. Capitol, Washington, D.C., January 19, 2002.

7. U.S., Office of the Press Secretary, *President's State of the Union Address*, U.S. Capitol, Washington, D.C., January 29, 1991.

8. U.S., Office of the Press Secretary, *Statement of President Bush in His Televised Address to the Nation*, September 11, 2001.

9. U.S., Office of the Press Secretary, *Remarks by the President to the CEO Summit*, Pundong Shangri-La Hotel, Shanghai, People's Republic of China, October 20, 2001.

10. Remarks by Newt Gingrich, quoted by Mary Riddell, 'Just What Is This "Civilization"?', *The Observer*, October 28, 2001.

11. Remarks by Secretary of State Colin L. Powell on *The News Hour with Jim Lehrer*, PBS, September 13, 2001.

12. U.S., Office of the Press Secretary, *Remarks by the President in Announcement of Financial Aspects of Terrorism*, Financial Crime Enforcement Network, Vienna, VA, November 7, 2001.

13. Columnist Ann Coulter, *National Review Online*, September 13, 2001.

14. Gallup gathered evidence from extensive surveys conducted between 2001 and 2007. Samples taken around the world represent 90 percent of the world's 1.3 billion Muslims in more than thirty-five countries with predominantly Muslim and substantial Muslim populations. Gallup interviewed at least one thousand people in each country.

15. Gallup's data demonstrate that most Muslims do not equate terrorism with Islam. Large majorities in Muslim-majority nations, such as Indonesia, say terrorist attacks are never justified—74 percent there; 86 percent in Pakistan, 81 percent in Bangladesh, 80 percent in Iran. Nine out of ten Muslims are politically moderate.

16. John Esposito and Dalia Mogahed (2007) explain that since terrorism has unfortunately come to define Islam for many people outside the Muslim world, the definition of what makes a religious and/or political radical is important. In reality, radicals are the minority and not representative of the Muslim mainstream. It should also be noted that radicals come from different backgrounds, and many are not religious by any stretch—the 9/11 hijackers were heavy drinkers and consumers of pornography. On the other hand, not all radicals subscribe to terrorist ideologies. They may desire a greater presence of religion in public life.

17. Mamdani refers to a television image from 1985, of Reagan meeting a group of turbaned men, all Afghani, all leaders of the *Mujaheddin*. After the meeting, Reagan brought them out onto the White House lawn and introduced them to the media with these words: "These gentlemen are the moral equivalents of America's founding fathers."

NOTES TO CHAPTER 13

1. The notion of double-risk society does not mean that the risks encountered by the Third World societies are *exactly* double, but rather huge and multiple in magnitude compared with their First World counterparts.

References

AbuRabi, I. M., ed. 2003. *Islam at the Crossroads.* Albany: State University of New York Press.

Agrawal, Arun. 2003. "Environmentality: Technologies of Government and the Making of Subjects." Working chapters presented as part of York Centre for Asian Research (YCAR)'s Asian Environments Series lectures, September 29, Toronto.

Al-Mahmood, Syed Zain. 2009. "Muddying the Waters." *Star Weekend Magazine*, July 10, 2009. http://www.thedailystar.net/magazine/2009/07/02/cover.htm (accessed June 24, 2010).

Almond, Gabriel A., and Sidney Verba. 1963. *The Civic Culture: Political Attitudes and Democracy in Five Nations.* Princeton: Princeton University Press.

Amader Bangladesh. 2009. "International Court: Force Indian Government to Stop Tipaimukh Dam." http://www.change.org/petitions/international-court-force-indian-government-to-stop-tipaimukh-dam (accessed February 28, 2013).

Archibugi, Daniele. 2001. "Terrorism and Cosmopolitanism." Social Science Research Council. http://essays.ssrc.org/sept11/essays/archibugi.htm (accessed October 11, 2009).

Arendt, Hannah. 1986. "Communicative Power." In *Power*, edited by Steven Lukes, 59–74. New York: New York University Press.

Arjomand, Said Amir. n.d. "Can Rational Analysis Break a Taboo? A Middle Eastern Perspective." Social Science Research Council. http://essays.ssrc.org/sept11/essays/arjomand.htm (accessed October 11, 2009).

Armstrong, Karen. 2000. *Islam: A Short Story.* New York: Random House.

———. 2006. "We Cannot Afford to Maintain These Ancient Prejudices against Islam." *The Guardian*, September 18. http://www.guardian.co.uk/commentisfree/2006/sep/18/religion.catholicism (accessed October 24, 2009).

Ash, Roberta. 1972. *Social Movements in America.* Chicago: Markham Publishing.

Askari, Rashid. 2012. "Tipaimukh Dam and Indian Hydropolitics." Forum: A Monthly Publication of *The Daily Star* 6 (1). http://www.thedailystar.net/forum/2012/January/tipaimukh.htm (accessed June 26, 2012).

Azad India Foundation. 2009. *Poverty in India.* http://www.azadindia.org/social-issues/poverty-in-india.html (accessed April 20, 2009).

Baker, Christopher J. 2009. "Frogs and Farmers: The Green Revolution in India and Its Murky Past." In *Understanding Green Revolutions*, edited by Tim Bayliss-Smith and Sudhir Wanmali, 37–52. London: Cambridge University Press.

Baker, Peter. 2009. "Poor Nations Reject a Target on Emission Cut." *New York Times*, July 8. http://www.nytimes.com/2009/07/09/world/europe/09prexy.html?pagewanted=all (accessed July 10, 2009).

Bakker, Karen. 1999. "The Politics of Hydropower: Developing the Mekong." *Political Geography* 18:209–232.

Bannerji, Himani. 1991. *Inventing Subjects: Studies in Hegemony, Patriarchy and Colonialism.* New Delhi: Tulika Books.

———. 1996. "On the Dark Side of the Nation: Politics of Multiculturalism and the State of Canada." *Journal of Canadian Studies* 31 (3): 103–128.

Barbosa, Luiz C. 2009. "Theories in Environmental Sociology." In *Twenty Lessons in Environmental Sociology,* edited by Kenneth A. Gould and Tammy L. Lewis, 25–44. New York: Oxford University Press.

Barrett, C. B., and D. G. Maxwell. 2005. *Food Aid after Fifty Years: Recasting Its Role.* London: Routledge.

Barry, John. 1999. *Environment and Social Theory.* London: Routledge.

Baudrillard, Jean. (1970). *The Consumer Society: Myths and Structures* (Translated by Chris Turner, and an Introduction by George Ritzer). London: SAGE Publications.

BBC. 2009a. "Why Did Copenhagen Fail to Deliver a Climate Deal?" *BBC News,* December 10. http://news.bbc.co.uk/2/hi/8426835.stm (accessed June 5, 2012).

———. 2009b. "Where Countries Stand on Copenhagen." *BBC News,* December 3. http://news.bbc.co.uk/2/hi/8345343.stm (accessed June 1, 2012).

———.2010. "UNClimateChangeTalksinCancúnAgreeaDeal." *BBCNews,* December 11. http://www.bbc.co.uk/news/science-environment-11975470 (accessed June 1, 2012).

Beck, Ulrich. 1992. *Risk Society: Towards a New Modernity.* London: SAGE Publications.

———. 1999. *World Risk Society.* Cambridge, UK: Polity Press.

———. 2006. "Living in the World Risk Society." *Economy and Society* 35 (3): 329–345.

———. [2007] 2009. *World at Risk.* Cambridge, UK: Polity Press.

Beck, Ulrich, Wolfgang Bonss, and Christoph Lau. 2003. "The Theory of Reflexive Modernization: Problematic, Hypotheses and Research Programme." *Theory, Culture and Society* 20 (2): 1–33.

Bell, Michael M. 2009. *An Invitation to Environmental Sociology,* 3rd ed. Thousand Oaks, CA: Pine Forge Press.

Benedict XVI, Pope. 2006. "Faith, Reason, and the University—Memories and Reflections." Rosenberg Lecture. University of Rosenberg, Germany. September 12.

Bhabha, Homi. 1990. "The Other Question: Difference, Discrimination, and the Discourse of Colonialism." In *Out There: Marginalization and Contemporary Cultures,* edited by Russell FergusonMartha Gever, Trinh T. Minh-ha, and Cornel West, and illustrated by Gonzales-Torres, 71–89. New York: New Museum of Contemporary Art.

Bhalla, N. 2009. "India Malnourishment Rates Worse Than Africa." Reuters AlertNet Foundation. http://www.alertnet.org/thenews/newsdesk/DEL334973.htm (accessed April 10, 2009).

Biermann, Frank, and Ingrid Boas. 2008. "Protecting Climate Refugees: The Case for a Global Protocol." *Environment* 50 (6). http://www.environmentmagazine.org/Archives/Back%20Issues/November-December%202008/Biermann-Boas-full.html (accessed June 10, 2012).

Blalock, Hubert M., Jr. 1989. *Power and Conflict: Toward a General Theory.* Newbury Park, CA: Sage Publications.

Blumer, Harbert G. 1969. "Collective Behaviour." In *Principles of Sociology,* edited by Alfred McClung Lee, 65–121. New York: Barnes and Noble Books.

Bom, Philip C. 2008. "Obama as a War President." *American Thinker,* October 23. http://www.americanthinker.com/2008/10/obama_as_a_war_president.html (accessed March 17, 2010).

Bond, Patrick. 2011. "From Copenhagen to Cancún to Durban: Moving Deckchairs on the Climate Titanic." *Capitalism Nature Socialism* 22 (2): 3–26.

Booth, Ken, ed. 1998. "Cold Wars of the Mind." In *Statecraft and Security: The Cold War and Beyond*, 29–55. Cambridge, UK: Cambridge University Press.

Bose, Sugata. 1997. "Instruments and Idioms of Colonial and National Development: India's Historical Experience in Comparative Perspectives." In *International Development and Social Science: Essays on the History and Politics of Knowledge*, edited by Frederick Cooper and Randall Packard, 45–63. Berkeley: University of California Press.

Bottomore, T. B., and Maximillen Rubel. 1956. *Karl Marx: Selected Writings in Sociology and Social Philosophy*. London: C. A. Watts.

Boudia, Soraya, and Nathalie Jas. 2007. "Introduction: Risk and 'Risk Society' in Historical Perspective." *History and Technology* 23 (4): 317–331.

Bourdieu, Pierre. 1998. "The Essence of Neoliberalism." *Le Monde Diplomatique*. http://mondediplo.com/1998/12/08bourdieu (accessed March 20, 2012).

Boychuk, Rick. 1992. "The Blue Revolution." *New Internationalist* 234 (August). http://www.newint.org/issue234/blue.htm (accessed June 15, 2007).

Boyd, C. E., and J. R. Clay. 1998. "Shrimp Aquaculture and the Environment." *Scientific American* 278 (6): 59–65.

Bracken, Patrick, Joan E. Giller, and Derek Summerfield. 1997. "Rethinking Mental Health Work with Survivors of Wartime Violence and Refugees." *Journal of Refugee Studies* 10 (4): 431–442.

Brookfield, Harold, Lesley Potter, and Yvonne Byron. 1995. *In Place of the Forest: Environmental and Socio-economic Transformation in Borneo and the Eastern Malay Peninsula*. Tokyo, Japan: United Nations University Press.

Brosius, J. Peter. 1999. "Green Dots, Pink Hearts: Displacing Politics from the Malaysian Rain Forest." *American Anthropologist* 101 (1): 36–57.

Brosius, J. Peter., Anna Lowenhaupt Tsing, and Charles Zerner. 1998. "Representing Communities: Histories and Politics of Community-Based Natural Resource Management." *Society and Natural Resources* 11 (2): 157–168.

Brown, Elaine C. 1994. "Grounds at Stake in Ancestral Domains." In *Patters of Power and Politics in the Philippines*, edited by James Eder and Robert Youngblood, 43–76. Phoenix, Arizona: Arizona State University Press.

Brown, Mark. 2000. "Calculations of Risk in Contemporary Penal Practice." Pp. 93–108 in *Dangerous Offenders: Punishment and Social Order*, edited by M. Brown and J. Pratt. London: Routledge.

Bullard, Robert D. 2001. "Anatomy of Environmental Racism and the Environmental Justice Movement." In *The Environment and Society Reader*, edited by R. Scott. Frey, 97–105. Boston: Allyn and Bacon.

Bunker, Stephen. 1988. *Underdeveloping the Amazon: Extraction, Unequal Exchange, and the Failure of Modern State*. Chicago: University of Chicago Press.

Burns, E. Bradford. 1980. *The Poverty of the Progress: Latin America in the Nineteenth Century*. Berkeley, California: University of California Press.

Buttel, F. H. 2000. "Classical Theory and Contemporary Environmental Sociology: Some Reflections on the Antecedents and Prospects for Reflexive Modernization Theories in the Study of Environment and Society." In *Environment and Global Modernity*, edited by G. Spaargaren, A.P.J. Mol, and F. H. Buttel, 17–40. London: SAGE Publications.

———. 2002. "Has Environmental Sociology Arrived?" *Organization and Environment* 15 (1): 42–54.

———. 2003. "Environmental Sociology and the Exploration of Environmental Reform." *Organization and Environment* 16 (3): 306–344.

———. 2004. "The Treadmill of Production: An Appreciation, Assessment, and Agenda for Research." *Organization and Environment* 17 (3): 323–336.

CAIR. 2006. *American Public Opinion about Islam and Muslims 2006.* http://www.cair.com/Portals/0/pdf/american_public_opinion_on_muslims_islam_2006.pdf (accessed October 24, 2009).

Caldwell, Malcom. 1977. *The Wealth of Some Nations.* London: Zed Press.

Cameroon, William Bruce. 1966. *Modern Social Movements: A Sociological Outline.* New York: Random House.

Campbell, David. 1998. *Writing Security: United States Foreign Policy and the Politics of Identity.* Minneapolis: University of Minnesota Press/Manchester University Press.

Campbell, Elizabeth H. 2009. "Corporate Power: The Role of the Global Media in Shaping What We Know about the Environment." In *Twenty Lessons in Environmental Sociology,* edited by Kenneth A. Gould and Tammy L. Lewis, 68–84. New York: Oxford University Press.

Campbell, J. L., and O. K. Pedersen, eds. 2001. *The Rise of Neoliberalism and Institutional Analysis.* Princeton: Princeton University Press.

Castree, Noel. 2009. "Crisis, Continuity and Change: Neoliberalism, the Left and the Future of Capitalism." *Antipode* 41 (S1): 185–213.

Catton, W. R., Jr., and R. E. Dunlap. 1978. "Environmental Sociology: A New Paradigm." *American Sociologist* 13 (1): 41–49.

Chung, Do Kim. 1998. "Assessment of Household and Village Level Impacts of IPM: Evaluation of IPM Programs—Concepts and Methodologies." *Pesticide Policy Project Publication Series,* Institute for Economics in Horticulture. Hanover: University of Hanover.

Clapp, Jennifer. 2011. "Environment and Global Political Economy." In *Global Environmental Politics: Concepts, Theories and Case Studies,* edited by Gabriela Kütting, 42–55. New York: Routledge.

Clark, Brett, and John B. Foster. 2009. "Ecological Imperialism and the Global Metabolic Rift: Unequal Exchange and the Guano/Nitrates Trade." *International Journal of Comparative Sociology* 50 (3–4): 311–334.

Clark, Robert P. 1998. "Bulk Flow Systems and Globalization." In *Space and Transport in the World-System,* edited by Paul S. Ciccantell and Stephen G. Bunker, 196–209. Westport, CT: Greenwood Press.

Clausen, Rebecca. 2009. "Healing the Rift: Metabolic Restoration in Cuban Agriculture." In *Environmental Sociology: From Analysis to Action,* edited by Leslie King and Deborah McCarthy, 425–437. Lanham: Rowman and Littlefield.

Colaneri, Robert. 2006. "The Not So Green Revolution." http://www2.hn.psu.edu/faculty/jmanis/eng15/sp2006/greenrevolution_sp2006.htm. (accessed June 13, 2012).

Cole, Juan. 2003. "Review of Bernard Lewis' *What Went Wrong*: Western Impact and Middle Eastern Response," *Global Dialogue,* January 27.

Collins, Randall, and Michael Makowsky. 1998. *The Discovery of Society.* New York: McGraw-Hill.

Cooper, Frederick. 1997. "Modernizing Bureaucrats, Backward Africans, and the Development Concept." In *International Development and the Social Sciences: Essays on the History and Politics of Knowledge,* edited by Frederick Cooper and Randall Packard, 64–92. Berkeley: University of California Press.

Cooper, Frederick, and Randall Packard, eds. 1997. "Introduction." Pp. 1–43 in *International Development and Social Science: Essays on the History and Politics of Knowledge.* Berkeley: University of California Press.

Cooper, R. G. 1979. "The Tribal Minorities of Northern Thailand: Problems and Prospects." In *Southeast Asian Affairs,* edited by Leo Suryadinata, 323–332. Singapore: Institute for Southeast Asian Studies.

Cornell News. 2004. "Fear Factor: 44 Percent of Americans Queried in Cornell National Poll Favor Curtailing Some Liberties for Muslim Americans." http://

www.news.cornell.edu/releases/Dec04/Muslim.Poll.bpf.html (accessed October 24, 2009).

Coulter, Ann. 2002a. "Murder for Fun and Prophet." *TownHall: Conservative News and Information* 3, September 6. http://www.townhall.com (accessed December 16, 2002).

———. 2002b. "Media Muslim Makeovers!" *TownHall: Conservative News and Information* 3, October 31. http://www.townhall.com (accessed December 16, 2002).

Cowen, M. P., and R. W. Shenton. 1996. *Doctrines of Development*. London: Routledge.

Cozier, Muriel. 2011. "Restoring Confidence at the Cancún Climate Change Conference." *Greenhouse Gases: Science and Technology* 1 (1): 8–10.

Crick, Bernard. 2002. *Democracy: A Very Short Introduction*. New York: Oxford University Press.

Dahl, Robert. 1956. *A Preface to Democratic Theory*. Chicago: University of Chicago Press.

———. 1986. "Power as the Control of Behavior." In *Power*, edited by Steven Lukes, 37–58. New York: New York University Press.

Dahrendorf, Ralf. 1959. *Class and Class Conflict in Industrial Society*. Stanford, CA: Stanford University Press.

———. 1989. *Modern Social Conflict: An Essay on the Politics of Liberty*. California: University of California Press.

Darier, Éric. 1996a. "The Politics and Power Effects of Garbage Recycling in Halifax, Canada." *Local Environment* 1 (1): 63–86.

———. 1996b. "Environmental Governmentality: The Case of Canada's Green Plan." *Environmental Politics* 5 (4): 585–606.

———, ed. 1999. "Foucault and the Environment: An Introduction." Pp. 1–34 in *Discourses of the Environment: An Introduction*. Oxford: Blackwell.

Daquila, T.C. 2005. *The Economies of Southeast Asia: Indonesia, Malaysia, Philippines, Singapore and Thailand*. New York: Nova Science Publishers.

Demotix. 2009. "Protest against Tipaimukh Project." Demotix, October 18. http://www.demotix.com/news/162154/protest-against-tipaimukh-project (accessed July 25, 2010).

Denny, David. 2005. *Risk and Society*. London: SAGE Publications.

Department of Social Affairs. 1994. *Isolated Community Development: Data and Information*. Jakarta: Directorate of Isolated Community Development, Directorate General of Social Welfare Department, Department of Social Affairs.

DeSombre, Elizabeth R. 2002. *The Global Environment and World Politics*. New York: Continuum.

Dewar, J. A. 2007. *Perennial Polyculture Farming*. Santa Monica, CA: RAND Pardee Center.

Dickens, Peter. 1998. "Life Politics, the Environment and the Limits of Sociology." In *Theorising Modernity: reflexivity, environment and identity in Giddens' Social Theory*, edited by Martin O'Brien, Sue Penna, and Colin Hay, 98–120. New York: Addison Wesley Longman.

Dietz, Thomas, R. Scott Frey, and Eugene Rosa. 2001. "Risk Assessment and Management." In *The Environment and Society Reader*, edited by R. Scott Frey, 272–299. Boston: Allyn and Bacon.

Dimitrov, R. S. 2010. "Inside Copenhagen: The State of Climate Governance." *Global Environmental Politics* 10 (2): 18–25.

Doty, R. L. 1996. *Imperial Encounters*. Minneapolis: University of Minnesota Press.

Dunlap, R. E., F. H. Buttel, P. Dickens, and A. Gijswijt, eds. 2002. *Sociological Theory and the Environment: Classical Foundations, Contemporary Insights*. Lanham, MD: Rowman and Littlefield.

The Economist. 2009. "Wanted: Fresh Air Poor Countries Wrangle with Rich Ones about Who Can Burn What and When." July 9. http://www.economist.com/node/14009113 (accessed June 4, 2012).

———. 2011a. "Climate Change Summit: A Deal in Durban." December 17. http://www.economist.com/node/21541806 (accessed December 28, 2011).

———. 2011b. "Canada and Climate Change: Kyoto and Out." December 17. http://www.economist.com/node/21541849 (accessed December 28, 2011).

———. 2011c. "A Deal in Durban: Something Came Out of it, Which Is Probably Better Than Nothing." December 17. http://www.economist.com/node/21541806 (accessed June 5, 2012).

Erikson, Kai T. 1994. *A New Species of Trouble: Explorations in Disaster, Trauma, and Community*. New York: Norton.

Escobar, Arturo. 1992. "Reflections on 'Development': Grassroots Approaches and Alternative Politics in the Third World." *Futures* 24 (5): 411–436.

———. 1995. *Encountering Development: The Making and Unmaking of the Third World*. Princeton, NJ: Princeton University Press.

Esposito, John, and Dalia Mogahed. 2007. *Who Speaks for Islam? What a Billion Muslims Really Think?* New York: Gallup Press.

Etzoni, Amita. 1964. *Modern Organizations*. Englewood Cliffs, N.J.: Prentice-Hall.

———.1993. *The Spirit of Community: Rights, Responsibilities and the Communitarian Agenda*. New York: Crown Publishers, Inc.

Evers, Peter J. 1995. "Preliminary Policy and Legal Questions about Recognizing Traditional Land in Indonesia." *Ekonesia: A Journal of Indonesia Human Ecology* 3:1–24.

Fallaci, Oriana. 2002. *Rage and Pride*. New York: Rizzoli International Publications.

Ferguson, James. 1990. *The Anti-Politics Machine: "Development," Depoliticization, and Bureaucratic Power in Lesotho*. Minnesota: University of Minnesota Press.

Finger, Matthias, and James Kilcoyne. 1997. "Why Transnational Corporations Are Organizing to 'Save the Global Environment'." *The Ecologist* 27 (4): 138–142.

Fitzgerald, Scott T., and Beth A. Rubin. 2010. "Risk Society, Media, and Power: The Case of Nanotechnology." *Sociological Spectrum: Mid-South Sociological Association* 30 (4): 367–402.

Flynn, James. 2003. "Nuclear Stigma." In *The Social Amplification of Risk*, edited by Nick Pidgeon, Roger E. Kasperson, and Paul Slovic, 326–352. Cambridge: Cambridge University Press.

Fontana, Benedetto. 1993. *Hegemony and Power: On the Relation between Gramsci and Machiavelli*. Minneapolis: University of Minnesota Press.

Ford, Lucy. 2011. "Transnational Actors in Global Environmental Politics." In *Global Environmental Politics: Concepts, Theories and Case Studies*, edited by Gabriela Kütting, 27–41. New York: Routledge.

Foster, J. B. 1999. "Marx's Theory of Metabolic Rift: Classical Foundations for Environmental Sociology." *American Journal of Sociology* 105 (2): 366–405.

Foucault, Michel. 1979. "On Governmentality." *Ideology and Consciousness* 6:5–21.

———. 1982. "The Subject and Power, Afterword." In *Michel Foucault: Beyond Structuralism and Hermeneutics*, edited by H. Dreyfus and P. Rabinow, 208–226. London: Harvester Wheatsheaf.

———. 1984. "Space, Knowledge, and Power." In *The Foucault Reader*, edited by Paul Rabinow, 239–256. New York: Pantheon Books.

———. 1986. *The Use of Pleasure*. New York: Pantheon Books.

————. 1991. "Governmentality." In *The Foucault Effect: Studies in Governmentality*, edited by Graham Burchell, Colin Gordon, and Peter Miller, 87–104. London: Harvester Wheatsheaf.

————. 2000. *Power*, edited by James D. Faubion and translated by Robert Hurley. New York: New Press.

Frey, R. Scott, ed. 2001a. "Environmental Problems." In *The Environment and Society Reader*, 4–25. Boston: Allyn and Bacon.

————, ed. 2001b. "The Hazardous Waste System." In *The Environment and Society Reader*, 106–120. Boston: Allyn and Bacon.

————, ed. 2001c. "Preface." In *The Environment and Society Reader*, v–xii. Boston: Allyn and Bacon.

Friedmann, Harriet. 1982. "The Political Economy of Food: The Rise and Fall of the Postwar International Food Order." *American Journal of Sociology* 88:248–286.

————. 1990. "The Origin of Third World Food Dependence." In *The Food Question: Profits Versus People*, edited by H. Bernstein, Ben Crow, Maureen Mackintosh, and Charlotte Martin, 13–31. London: Earthscan Publications.

Gallup. 2008. *Muslim West Facts Project: What the People Really Think*. http://www.muslimwestfacts.com/MWFHOMEPAGE/home.aspx (accessed October 24, 2009).

Ganguly, Saby. 2006. *From the Bengal Famine to the Green Revolution*. http://www.indiaonestop.com/Greenrevolution.htm (accessed June 13, 2012).

Gamble, Andrew. 2001. "Neoliberalism." *Capital and Class* 75:127–135.

Garst, Rachel, and Tom Barry. 1991. *Feeding the Crisis: US Food Aid and Farm Policy in Central America*. Lincoln: University of Nebraska Press.

Gaud, William. 1968. *The Green Revolution: Accomplishments and Apprehensions*. Agency for International Development, Department of State: Shorehan Hotel, Washington, D.C., March 8. http://www.agbioworld.org/biotech-info/topics/borlaug/borlaug-green.html (accessed June 13, 2012).

Gereffi, Gary, and Miguel Korzeniewicz. 1994. *Commodity Chains and Global Capitalism*. Westport, CT: Greenwood Press.

Giddens, Anthony. [1981] 1995. *A Contemporary Critique of Historical Materialism*, Vol. 1. Stanford, CA: Stanford University Press.

————. 1984. *The Constitutions of Society: Outline of a Theory of Structuralization*. Cambridge: Polity Press.

————. 1990. *The Consequences of Modernity*. Cambridge: Polity Press.

————. 1991. *Modernity and Self-Identity: Self and Society in the Late Modern Age*. Cambridge: Polity Press.

————. 1994. *Beyond Left and Right: The Future of Radical Politics*. Cambridge: Polity Press.

Gitlin, Todd. 2003. *The Whole World Is Watching: Mass Media in the Making and Unmaking of the New Left*. Berkeley: University of California Press.

Global Governance Project. 2012. "Forum on Climate Refugees." http://www.glogov.org/?pageid=80 (accessed June 10, 2012).

Goldblatt, David. 1996. *Social Theory and the Environment*. Cambridge: Polity Press.

Goldman, Michael. 2005. *Imperial Nature: The World Bank and Struggles for Social Justice in the Age of Globalization*. New Haven: Yale University Press.

Goodman, David, and Michael Redclift. 1991. *Refashioning Nature: Food, Ecology and Culture*. New York: Routledge.

Gordon, Colin. 1991. "Governmental Rationality: An Introduction." In *The Foucault Effect: Studies in Governmentality*, edited by Graham Burchell, Colin Gordon, and Peter Miller, 1–51. Chicago: University of Chicago Press.

Gould, Kenneth A., and Tammy L. Lewis, eds. 2009. "An Introduction to Environmental Sociology." In *Twenty Lessons in Environmental Sociology*, 1–8. New York: Oxford University Press.

Griffin, Keith B. 1989. *Alternative Strategies of Economic Development*. London: MacMillan/OECD Development Centre.

Grinspun, Ricardo. 2003. "Exploring the Links among Global Trade, Industrial Agriculture, and Rural Underdevelopment." In *Rural Progress Rural Decay: Neoliberal Adjustment Policies and Local Initiatives*, edited by Lisa L. North and John D. Cameron, 46–68. West Hartford, Connecticut: Kumarian Press.

The Guardian. 2011. "Global Climate Change Treaty in Sight after Durban Breakthrough." December 11. http://www.guardian.co.uk/environment/2011/dec/11/global-climate-change-treaty-durban (accessed June 5, 2012).

Guha, R. 2000. *Environmentalism: A Global History*. New York, USA: Longman.

Guha, Ramachandra, and Joan Martinez-Alier. 1997. *Varieties of Environmentalism: Essays North and South*. London: Earthscan Publications.

Gulati, A., N. Minot, C. Delgado, and S. Bora. 2005. *Growth in High-Value Agriculture in Asia and the Emergence of Vertical Links with Farmers*. Washington, DC: The World Bank.

Gupta, Akhil. 1997. "Agrarian Populism in the Development of Modern Nation (India)." In *International Development and the Social Sciences: Essays on the History and Politics of Knowledge*, edited by Frederick Cooper and Randall Packard, 320–344. Berkeley: University of California Press.

Gupta, Avijit. 1998. *Ecology and Development in the Third World*, 2nd ed. London, UK: Routledge.

Hall, Stuart. 1991. "Old and New Identities, Old and New Ethnicities." In *Culture, Globalization and the World System: Contemporary Conditions for the Representation of Identity*, edited by Anthony D. King, 41–68. Basingstoke: McMillan.

———. 1996. "Introduction: Who Needs 'Identity'?" In *Questions of Cultural Identity*, edited by Stuart Hall and Paul du Gay, 1–17. London: Sage Publishers.

Hameed, A. Khan. 1997. "The Orangi Pilot Project: Uplifting Periurban Settlement near Karachi." In *Reasons for Hope: Instructive Experiences in Rural Development*, edited by Anirudh Krishna, Norman Uphoff, and Milton J. Esman, 25–40. West Hartford: Kumarian Press.

Hannigan, John. 2006. *Environmental Sociology*, 2nd ed. New York: Routledge.

Harmeling, Sven. 2012. "Global Climate Risk Index 2012: Who Suffers Most from Extreme Weather Events? Weather-Related Loss Events in 2010 and 1991 to 2010." Germanwatch. http://germanwatch.org/de/download/2193.pdf (accessed June 1, 2012).

Harris, Paul G. 2011. "Climate Change." In *Global Environmental Politics: Concepts, Theories and Case Studies*, edited by Gabriela Kütting, 107–118. New York: Routledge.

Harvey, David. 2005. *A Brief History of Neoliberalism*. New York: Oxford University Press.

Hawken, Paul, Amory Lovins, and L. Hunter Lovins. 1999. *Natural Capitalism: Creating the Next Industrial Revolution*. Boston, New York, London: Little, Brown and Company.

Hawley, Amos H. 1963. "Community Power and Urban Renewal Success." *American Journal of Sociology* 68:422–431.

Hayami, Y. and M. Kikuchi. 2000. *A Rice Village Saga: Three Decades of Green Revolution in the Philippines*. London: MacMillan Press.

Heilbroner, Robert L. 1980. *Marxism: For and Against*. New York: W. W. Norton.

Hirschman, A. O. 1970. *Exit, Voice and Loyalty.* Cambridge, MA: Harvard University Press.

Hoogvelt, Ankie. 2001. *Globalization and the Postcolonial World: New Political Economy of Development.* Baltimore: Johns Hopkins University Press.

Huber, J. 1982. *Die verlorene Unschuld der Ökologie: Neue Technologien und Superindustrielle Entwicklung (The Lost Innocence of Ecology: New Technologies and Superindustrial Development).* Frankurt am Main: Fischer.

———. 1985. *Die Regenbogengesekkschaft: Ökologie and Sozialpolitik (The Rainbow Society: Ecology and Social Policy).* Frankurt am Main: Fischer.

Humphrey, Craig R., Tammy L. Lewis, and Frederick H. Buttel. 2002. *Environment, Energy, and Society: A New Synthesis.* Belmont: Wadsworth Thomson Learning.

Hunt, Diana. 1989. *Economic Theories of Development: An Analysis of Competing Paradigms.* New York: Harvester Wheatsheaf.

Hunter, Floyd. 1953. *Community Power Structure: A Study of Decision Makers.* Chapel Hill: University of North Carolina Press.

Huntington, S. P. 1996. *The Clash of Civilizations and the Making of the World Order.* New York: Simon and Schuster.

IPCC (Intergovernmental Panel on Climate Change). 2007. *Climate Change 2007: Synthesis Report.* Cambridge: Cambridge University Press.

Isenman, Paul, and H. W. Singer. 1977. "Food Aid: Disincentive Effects and Their Policy Implications." *Economic Development and Cultural Change* 25 (2): 205–238.

Islam, Md Nazrul. 2009. "Information Please: Impact of Tipaimukh Dam on Bangladesh." http://impact-tipaimukh-dam.blogspot.com/2009/08/information-please.html (accessed July 27, 2011).

Islam, Md Saidul. 2005. "Muslims in the Capitalist Discourse: September 11 and Its Aftermath," *Journal of Muslim Minority Affairs* 25 (1): 3–12.

———. 2008. "From Pond to Plate: Towards a Twin-driven Commodity Chain in Bangladesh Shrimp Aquaculture." *Food Policy* 33 (3): 209–223.

———. 2009. "From 'Development Project' to Globalization: Understanding Third World Politics, Class Relations and Development Choices." In *Globalization: Understanding, Management and Effects*, edited by H. V. Baines and J. R. Ursah, 107–124. New York: Nova Publishers.

———. 2013. *Confronting the Blue Revolution: Industrial Aquaculture and Sustainability in the Global South.* Toronto: University of Toronto Press.

Jahangir, Nadim. 2009. "Tipaimukh Dam Controversy." *Forum* 3 (7). http://www.thedailystar.net/forum/2009/july/tipaimukh.htm (accessed July 25, 2010).

Jensen, Mette, and Anders Blok. 2008. "Pesticides in the Risk Society: The View from Everyday Life." *Current Sociology* 56 (5): 757–778.

Johnson, Cassidy. 2011. "Kernels of Change: Civil Society Challenges to State-Led Strategies for Recovery and Risk Reduction in Turkey." *Environment and Urbanization* 23 (2): 415–430.

Jonsson, Hjorleifur. 1996. "Rhetorics and Relations: Tai States, Forests and Upland Groups." In *State Power and Culture in Thailand*, edited by E. Paul Durrenberger, 166–200. New Haven, CT: Yale Southeast Asia Studies.

Kahn, Joel S. 1993. *Constituting the Minaukabau: Peasants, Culture and Modernity in Colonial Indonesia.* Providence: Berg.

Kahn, Joel S. 1999. "Culturalizing the Indonesian Uplands." In *Transforming the Indonesian Uplands: Marginality, Power and Production*, edited by Tania Murry Li, 81–106. Amsterdam: Harwood Academic Publishers.

Kain, E. D. 2009. "Obama as the War President." *American Times*, December 10. http://trueslant.com/erikkain/2009/12/10/obama-the-war-president/ (accessed March 17, 2010).

Kamei, Namdingpou. 2006. "Controversial Hydro Electric (Multi-purpose) Project." *Sangai Express* (India), December 15.

Kaplan, Robert. 1993. *Balkan Ghosts: A Journey through History*. New York: St. Martin's Press.

Kazmi, Mamoona Ali. 2009. "Tipaimuk Dam: A Hazard for Bangladesh." *South Asian Research and Analysis Studies*, August 28. http://saras.org.pk/printpreview.php?topicid=1337 (accessed July 25, 2010).

Keck, Margaret E., and Kathryn Sikkink. 1998. *Activists beyond Borders: Advocacy Networks in International Politics*. Ithaca, NY: Cornell University Press.

Keynes, John M. [1936] 2008. *The General Theory of Employment, Interest and Money*. New York: Classic House Books.

Khan, Muqtedar, and John Esposito. 2008. "Islam in the West: the Threat of Internal Extremism." *Al-Bayyinah* 8 (3): 26–30.

Khor, Martin. 2001. *Rethinking Globalization: Critical Issues and Policy Choices*. London: Zed Books.

Kornhauser, William. 1959. *The Politics of Mass Society*. New York: Free Press.

Kotz, David. M. 2009. "The Financial and Economic Crisis of 2008: A Systemic Crisis of Neoliberal Capitalism." *Review of Radical Political Economics* 41 (3): 305–317.

Kuznets, Simon. 1955. "Economic Growth and Income Inequality." *American Economic Review* 45 (March): 1–28.

Lacey, Colin, and David Longman. 1993. "The Press and Public Access to the Environment and Development Debate." *Sociological Review* 41 (2): 207–243.

Latour, Bruno. 2003. "Is re-modernization occurring—and if so, how to prove it? A commentary on Ulrich Beck." *Theory, Culture and Society* 20:35–48.

Laungaramsri, Pinkaew. 1998. *The Ambiguity of Watershed: The Politics of People and Conservation in Northern Thailand. A Case Study of the Chom Thong Conflict*. Seattle: University of Washington.

Lefeber, Louis 2003. "Problems of Contemporary Development: Neoliberalism and Its Consequences." In *Rural Progress Rural Decay: Neoliberal Adjustment Policies and Local Initiatives*, edited by Lisa L. North and John D. Cameron, 25–45. Connecticut: Kumarian Press, Inc.

Leupp, G. 2002. "Challenging Ignorance on Islam: A Ten-Point Primer for Americans." *Counterpunch*, July 24. http://www.counterpunch.org/leupp0724.html (accessed December 12, 2006).

Lewis, Bernard. 1993. *Islam and the West*. Oxford: Oxford University Press.

———. 2002a. "What Went Wrong," *The Atlantic*. January 2002 Issue.

———. 2002b. *What Went Wrong: Western Impact and Middle Eastern Response*. New York: Oxford University Press.

Lewis, Tammy L. 2009. "Environmental Movements in the Global South." In *Twenty Lessons in Environmental Sociology*, edited by Kenneth A. Gould and Tammy L. Lewis, 244–254. New York: Oxford University Press.

Leys, Colin. 1996. *The Rise and Fall of Development Theory*. Bloomington: Indiana University Press.

Li, Tania M. 1999a. "Marginality, Power and Production: Analyzing Upland Transformations." Pp. 1–46 in *Transforming the Indonesian Uplands: Marginality, Power and Production*, edited by Tania Murry Li. Amsterdam: Harwood Academic Publishers.

———. 1999b. "Compromising Power: Development, Culture and Rule in Indonesia." *Cultural Anthropology* 14 (3): 1–28.

———. 2000a. "Recognizing, Fixing, and Fudging: The Politics of Culture and Nature in Indonesia." Presentation at York University, January 26.

———. 2000b. "Articulating Indigenous Identity in Indonesia: Resource Politics and the Tribal Slot." *Comparative Studies in Society and History* 42 (1): 149–179.

————. 2002. "Engaging Simplifications: Community-Based Resource Management, Market Processes and State Agendas in Upland Southeast Asia." *World Development* 30 (2): 265–283.

Liebig, Justus von. 1859. *Letters on Modern Agriculture*. London: Walton and Maberly.

Lohmann, Larry. 1993. "Land, Power and Forest Colonization in Thailand." In *The Struggle for Land and Fate of the Forests*, edited by M. Colchester and L. Lohmann, 198–227. London: Zed Books.

————. 1999. "Forest Cleansing: Racial Oppression in Scientific Nature Conservation." *The Corner House*. Briefing No. 13: Forest Cleansing.

Loon, Joost Van. 2000. "Virtual Risks in an Age of Cybernetic Reproduction." Pp. 165–182 in *The Risk Society and Beyond: Critical Issues for Social Theory*, edited by Barbara Adam, Ulrich Beck and Joost Van Loon. London: Sage Publications.

Los Angeles Times. 2009. "What Lessons Have We Learned Since 9/11, and When Should He Send American Troops into Harm's Way?" January 16. http://articles. latimes.com/2009/jan/16/opinion/ed-leadership16 (accessed March 17, 2010).

Luke, Timothy. 1995. "On Environmentality: Geo-Power and Eco-Knowledge in the Discourses of Contemporary Environmentalism." *Cultural Critique* 31 (2): 57–81.

————. 1997. *Ecocritique: Contesting the Politics of Nature, Economy, and Culture*. Minneapolis: University of Minnesota Press.

————. 1999. "Environmentality as Green Governmentality." In *Discourses of the Environment*, edited by Éric Darier, 121–151. Oxford: Blackwell.

Lukes, Steven, ed. 1986. *Power*. New York: New York University Press.

————. 2005. *Power: A Radical View*. New York: Palgrave Macmillan.

Lynch, Owen, Kirk Talbot, Kirk Talbott, and Marshall Berdan. 1995. *Balancing Acts: Community-Based Forest Management and National Law in Asia and the Pacific*. Washington, DC: World Resource Institute.

Mamdani, Mahmood. 2004. *Good Muslim, Bad Muslim: America, Cold War, and the Roots of Terror*. New York: Three Leaves Press.

Mann, Charles. 1997. "Reseeding the Green Revolution." *Science* 277 (5329): 1038–1043.

Margolis, Eric. 2008. "Obama, the Democratic 'War President'," in *Lewrockwell*, June 22. http://www.lewrockwell.com/margolis/margolis117.html (accessed March 17, 2010).

Martell, Luke. 1994. *Ecology and Society: An Introduction*. Cambridge, MA: Polity Press.

Marx, Karl. [1844] 1972. "Economic and Philosophic Manuscripts of 1844: Selections." In *The Marx-Engels Reader*, edited by Robert C. Tucker, 52–103. New York: W. W. Norton.

————. 1998. *The Communist Manifesto*. New York: Verso.

————. 1964. Selected Writings in Sociology and Social Philosophy. (translated by T.B. Bottomore). London: McGraw-Hill.

Marx, Karl, Frederick Engels, and Valdimir Lenin. 1975. *Dialectical and Historical Materialism*. Moscow: Progress Publishers.

McAdam, D., John D. McCarthy, and Myer N. Zald. 1988. "Social Movements." In *Handbook of Sociology*, edited by Neil J. Smelser, 695–737. Newbury Park, California: Sage Publications.

McDermott, Melanie Hughes. 2000. "Boundaries and Pathways: Indigenous Identities, Ancestral Domain, and Forest Use in Palawan, Philippines." Presented at the 8th Biennial Conference of the International Association for the Study of Common Property (IASCP), May 31 to June 4, Bloomington, Indiana.

McMichael, Philip. 1992. "Tensions between National and International Control of the World Food Order: Contours of a New Food Regime." *Sociological Perspectives* 35 (2): 343–365.

———. 2008. *Development and Social Change: A Global Perspective*. Thousand Oaks, CA: Pine Forge Press.

Melucci, Alberto. 1980. "The New Social Movements: A Theoretical Approach." *Social Science Information* 19 (2): 119–126.

Merinews. 2010. "People Oppose the Construction of Tipaimukh Dam." April 12. http://www.merinews.com/article/people-oppose-construction-of-tipaimukh-Dam/15803796.shtml (accessed June 26, 2010).

Michels, Robert. 1968. *Political Parties*. New York: Free Press.

Mills, C. Wright. [1956] 2000. *The Power Elite*. New York: Oxford University Press.

———. 1962. *The Marxist*. New York: Dell Publishing.

Mirza, Monirul Qader. 2009. "Fallacies of India's Tipaimukh Dam." *Holiday International*, September 4. http://www.weeklyholiday.net/2009/040909/anniv09/21.html (accessed June 17, 2010).

Mohanty, Chandra. 1991. "Cartographies of Struggle: Third World Women and the Politics of Feminism." In *Third World Women and the Politics of Feminism*, edited by Chandra Mohanty, Ann Russo, and Lourdes Torres, 1–47. Bloomington: Indiana University Press.

Mol, A.P.J., and Gert Spaargaren. 2003. "Towards a Sociology of Environmental Flows: A New Agenda for 21st Century Environmental Sociology." Paper presented at the International Conference on "Governing Environmental Flows." Wageningen, The Netherlands, June 13–14.

Morrison, Denton E. 1978. "Some Notes toward Theory on Relative Deprivation, Social Movements and Social Change." In *Collective Behaviour and Social Movements*, edited by Louis E. Genevie, 202–209. Itasca, IL: Peacock.

Mosca, Gaetano. 1939. *The Ruling Class*. New York: McGraw-Hill.

Mousseau, Frederic. 2005. *Food Aid or Food Sovereignty? Ending World Hunger in Our Time*. Oakland, CA: Oakland Institute.

Mudge, Stephanie Lee. 2008. "The State of the Art: What Is Neoliberalism?" *Socio-Economic Review* 6:703–731.

Murray, G. F. 1997. "A Haitian Peasants Tree Chronicle: Adaptive Evolution and Institutional Intrusion." In *Reasons for Hope: Instructive Experiences in Rural Development*, edited by Anirudh Krishna, Norman Uphoff, and Milton J. Esman, 241–254. West Hartford: Kumarian Press.

Muscati, Sina Ali. 2003. "Reconstructing 'Evil': A Critical Assessment of Post-September 11 Political Discourse." *Journal of Muslim Minority Affairs* 23 (2): 249–269.

Najam, Adil. 2005. "Developing Countries and Global Environmental Governance: From Contestation to Participation to Engagement." *International Environmental Agreements* 5:303–321.

Nandy, Ashis (1983). *The Intimate Enemy: Loss and Recovery of Self under Colonialism*. Delhi: Oxford University Press.

Nazrul, Asif. 2010. "There Is No Way to Believe That Tipaimukh Project Will Not Hurt Bangladesh." *Daily Naya Diganto* (Dhaka), February 4.

Nesar, Moinuddin. 2009. "India Secretly Hands over Tipai Project to State-Owned Entity." *Holiday International*, August 7. http://www.weeklyholiday.net/2009/070809/front.html (accessed July 25, 2010).

Newell, Peter. 2000. *Climate for Change: Non-State Actors and the Global Politics of the Greenhouse*. Cambridge: Cambridge University Press.

Newman, Bryan. 2006. "Indian Farmer Suicides: A Lesson for Africa's Farmers." *Food First Backgrounder* 12 (4): 2.

The New Nation. 2009a. "Tipaimukh Protest March to Ottawa." August 14. http://nation.ittefaq.com/issues/2009/08/14/news0639.htm (accessed July 25, 2010).

———. 2009b. "Tipai Dam: IAB Submits Memo to UN." August 18. http://nation. ittefaq.com/issues/2009/08/18/news0965.htm (accessed July 25, 2010).

———. 2009c. "Bangladesh Needs Natural Flood: Three Rivers to Dry If Tipai Dam Constructed." August 21. http://nation.ittefaq.com/issues/2009/08/21/ news0207.htm (accessed July 25, 2010).

———. 2009d. "People Urged to Join Tipaimukh Dam." August 30. http://www. ittefaq.com/issues/2009/08/30/all0337.htm (accessed June 24, 2010).

NFB (News from Bangladesh). 2009. "Assam Joins Manipur to Decry Tipaimukh Dam Project." July 29. http://newsfrombangladesh.net/view. php?hidRecord=277048 (accessed July 25, 2010).

North, Col. Oliver. 2009. "Barack Obama: War President?" Fox News, December 1. http://www.foxnews.com/story/0,2933,580042,00.html (accessed March 17, 2010).

O'Connor, James. 1998. *Natural Causes.* New York: Guilford.

———. 2001. "Uneven and Combined Development and Ecological Crisis: A Theoretical Introduction." In *The Environment and Society Reader*, edited by R. Scott Frey, 151–159. Boston: Allyn and Bacon.

O'Malley, Pat. 2000. "Risk Societies and the Government of Crime." In *Dangerous Offenders: Punishment and Social Order*, edited by M. Brown and J. Pratt, 17–34. London: Routledge.

Oberthür, Sebastian, and Hermann E. Ott. 1999. *The Kyoto Protocol: International Climate Policy for the 21st Century.* Berlin: Springer.

Olsen, Marvin E., ed. 1970. *Power in Societies.* New York: MacMillan Publishing.

———. 1993. "Forms and Levels of Power Exertion." In *Power in Modern Societies*, edited by Marvin Olsen and Martin Marger, 29–36. Boulder, CO: Westview Press.

Olsen, Marvin E., and Martin N. Marger, eds. 1993. *Power in Modern Societies.* Boulder, CO: Westview Press.

Öniş, Ziya. 2000. "Neoliberal Globalization and the Democracy Paradox: The Turkish General Elections of 1999." *Journal of International Affairs* 54 (1): 283–306.

Öniş, Ziya, and Ahmet Faruk Aysan. 2000. "Neoliberal Globalisation, the Nation-State and Financial Crises in the Semi-Periphery: A Comparative Analysis." *Third World Quarterly* 21 (1): 119–139.

Packard, Randall. 1997. "Visions of Post-War Health and Development and Their Impact on Public Health Intervention in the Developing World." In *International Development and the Social Sciences: Essays on the History and Politics of Knowledge*, edited by Frederick Cooper and Randall Packard, 93–118. Berkeley: University of California Press.

Paddock, W. C. 1970. "How Green Is the Green Revolution?" *BioScience* 20 (16): 897–902.

Pakulski, Jan. 1993. "Mass Social Movements and Social Class." *International Sociology* 8 (2): 131–158.

Panitch, Leo, ed. 1977. *The Canadian State: Political Economy and Political Power.* Toronto: University of Toronto Press.

Pareto, Vilfredo. 1935. *The Mind and Society*, translated by A. Bongiorno and edited by A. Livingston. New York: Harcourt, Brace.

Parsons, Talcott. 1986. "Power and Social Systems." In *Power*, edited by Steven Lukes, 94-143. New York: New York University Press.

Pearce, Fred, and Catherine Brahic. 2010. "Cancún Analysis: Dawn Breaks on the Low-Carbon World." *New Scientist* 208 (2791): 8–9. http://www.newscientist.com/article/dn19861-cancun-analysis-dawn-breaks-on-lowcarbon-world. html?full=true (accessed June 5, 2012).

Peck, Jamie, Nik Theodore, and Neil Brenner. 2009. "Postneoliberalism and Its Malcontents." *Antipode* 41 (S1): 94–116.

Pett, Richard, and Elaine Hartwick. 1999. *Theories of Development*. New York: Guilford Press.

Pine, John C. 2009. *Natural Hazards Analysis: Reducing the Impact of Disasters*. New York: Auerbach Publications, Taylor and Francis Group.

Polanyi, Karl. 2001. *The Great Transformations: The Political and Economic Origins of Our Time*. Boston: Beacon.

Pray, C. E. 1981. "The Green Revolution as a Case Study in Transfer of Technology." *Annals of the American Academy of Political and Social Science* 458:68–80.

Presthus, Robert. 1964. *Men at the Top: A Study in Community Power*. New York: Oxford University Press.

Public Citizen. 2005. *Fishy Currency: How International Finance Institutions Fund Shrimp Farms*. Pennsylvania: Public Citizen.

Rahman, Mirza Zulfikur. 2009. "India, Bangladesh and Tipaimukh Dam." *IPCS (Institute of Peace and Conflict Studies) Bulletin*, No. 2945, August 17. http://www.ipcs.org/article_details.php?articleNo=2945 (accessed June 24, 2010).

Rasborg, Klaus. 2012. "(World) Risk Society or New Rationalities of Risk? A Critical Discussion of Ulrich Beck's Theory of Reflexive Modernity." *Thesis Eleven* 108 (1): 3–25.

Rashid, M. 2009. "Tipaimukh Protest March to Ottawa: Bangladeshis Urged India to be benevolent to the neighbor Bangladesh." *News From Bangladesh*. August 13, 2009. http://www.bangladesh-web.com/view.php?hidRecord=279416 (accessed February 25, 2013).

Reuters UK. 2009. "George Galloway Joins Bangladesh Dam Protest." November 29. http://uk.reuters.com/article/idUKTRE5AT1BF20091130 (accessed June 24, 2010).

Riaz, Ali. 2011. "Bangladesh." In *Climate Change and National Security: A Country Level Analysis*, edited by Daniel Moran, 103-114. Washington D.C.: Georgetown University Press.

Rist, Gilbert. 2002. *The History of Development: From Western Origin to Global Faith*. New York: Zed Books.

Roberts, J. T. 2001. "Global Inequality and Climate Change." *Society and Natural Resources* 14 (6): 501–509.

———. 2009. "Climate Change: Why Old Approaches Aren't Working." In *Twenty Lessons in Environmental Sociology*, edited by Kenneth A. Gould and Tammy L. Lewis, 191–208. New York: Oxford University Press.

———. 2011. "Multipolarity and the New World (Dis)order: US Hegemonic Decline and the Fragmentation of the Global Climate Regime." *Global Environmental Change* 21 (3): 776–784.

Roberts, J. Timmons, and Bradley C. Parks. 2007. *A Climate Inequality: Global Inequality, North-South Politics, and Climate Policy*. Cambridge, MS: MIT Press.

Rose, Jerry D. 1982. *Outbreaks*. New York: Free Press.

Rose, Nikolas. 1999. *Powers of Freedom: Reframing Political Thought*. London: Cambridge University Press.

Rosenblat, R. 1984. "Who Cares? [Review of Shawcross (1984)]." *New York Review of Books*, August 16.

Rosset, Peter. 2000. "Lessons from the Green Revolution." *Food First*, March/April. http://www.foodfirst.org/media/opeds/2000/4-greenrev.html (accessed July 23, 2006).

Rostow, Walt W. 1960. *The Stages of Economic Growth: A Non-Communist Manifesto*. Cambridge: Cambridge University Press.

Rozelle, Scott, Gregory Veeck, and Jikun Huang. 1997. "The Impact of Environmental Degradation on Grain Production in China." *Economic Geography* 73:44–66.

Ruiter, Tine. 1999. "Agrarian Transformations in the Upland of Langkat: Survival of Independent Caro Batak Smallholders." In *Transforming the Indonesian Uplands: Marginality, Power and Production*, edited by Tania Li, 281–312. Amsterdam: Harwood Academic Publishers.

Rutherford, Stephanie. 2007. "Green Governmentality: Insights and Opportunities in the Study of Nature's Rule." *Progress in Human Geography* 31 (3): 291–307.

Sachs, Wolfgang. 1992. "Development: A Guide to the Ruins." *New Internationalists* 232:2–8.

Sader, Emir. 2009. "Postneoliberalism in Latin America." *Development Dialogue* 51:171–179.

Safi, L. M. 2001. "Global Justice, Not Global Revenge." *Balanced Development*, October 9. Virginia: Center for Balanced Development. http://www.balanced-development.org/trends/global_justice.htm (accessed October 21, 2001).

Said, Edward. 1979. *Orientalism*. New York: Vintage Books.

———. 2003. "The Academy of Lagado." *LRB (London Review of Books)* 25 (8). http://www.lrb.co.uk/v25/n08/print/said01_.html (accessed April 20).

Salleh, Ariel. 2010. "From Metabolic Rift to 'Metabolic Value': Reflections on Environmental Sociology and the Alternative Globalization Movement." *Organization and Environment* 23 (2): 205–219.

———. 2011. "Cancún and After: A Sociology of Climate Change." *Political Economy of the World-System News* 11 (1): 4–5.

Schaffer, B. B. 1975. "The Problem of Access to Public Services." *Development and Change* 6 (2): 3–11.

———. 1977. *Official Providers—Access to Equity and Participations*. Paris: UNESCO.

———. 1985. "Policy Makers Have Their Needs Too: Irish Itinerants and the Culture of Poverty." *Development and Change* 16 (3): 375–408.

Schmidt, Volker H. 2006. "Multiple Modernities or Varieties of Modernity?" *Current Sociology* 54 (1): 77–97.

Schnaiberg, Alan. 1980. *The Environment: From Surplus to Scarcity*. New York: Oxford University Press.

Schnaiberg, Allan, and Kenneth Gould. 2009. "Treadmill predisposition and technological change." In *Environmental Sociology: From Analysis to Action*, edited by Leslie King and Deborah McCarthy, 51–62. Maryland: The Rowan & Littlefield Publishers, Inc.

Schneider, Mindi, and Philip McMichael. 2010. "Deepening, and Repairing, the Metabolic Rift." *Journal of Peasant Studies* 37 (3): 461–484.

Schroeder, Richard. 1995. "Contradictions along the Commodity Road to Environmental Stabilization: Foresting Gambian Gardens." *Antipode* 25 (4): 325–342.

Schubert, J. N. 1981. "The Impact of Food Aid on World Malnutrition." *International Organization* 35 (2): 329–354.

Schumpeter, Joseph. 1962. *Capitalism, Socialism and Democracy*. New York: Harper and Row.

Scott, James C. 1998. *Seeing Like a State: How Certain Schemes to Improve Human Condition Have Failed*. New Haven: Yale University Press.

———. 2009. *The Art of Not Being Governed: An Anarchist History of Upland Southeast Asia*. New Haven: Yale University Press.

Scott, John and Gordon Marshall. 2005. *Oxford Dictionary of Sociology*. Oxford: Oxford University Press.

Shaw, D. J. 2001. *The UN World Food Programme and the Development of Food Aid*. New York: Palgrave.

Shaw, J., and E. Clay, eds. 1993. *World Food Aid*. Portsmouth: Heinemann.

Shiva, Vandana. 1995. "The Damaging Social and Environmental Effects of Aquaculture." *Third World Resurgence* 59:22–24.

———. 2000. *Stolen Harvest: The Hijacking of the Global Food Supply*. London: Zed Books.

Sider, Gerald. 1987. "When Parrots Learn to Talk, and Why They Can't: domination, deception and self-deception in Indian-White relations." *Comparative Studies in Society and History* 29(1):3–23.

Sklair, Leslie. 1995. *Sociology of the Global System*. Baltimore: Johns Hopkins University Press.

Slevin, P. 2002. "Bush White House Reconsidering Reagan's 'Evil Man': Gaddafi's Gesture May Change Policies." *Washington Post*, March 11.

Smalley, W. 1994. *Linguistic Diversity and National Unity: Language Ecology in Thailand*. Chicago: University of Chicago.

Smart, Barry. 2003. *Economy, Culture and Society*. Buckingham and Philadelphia: Open University Press.

Smelser, Neil J. 1962. *Theory of Collective Behavior*. New York: Free Press.

Smith, Dorothy E. 1990. *The Conceptual Practices of Power: A Feminist Sociology of Knowledge*. Toronto: University of Toronto Press.

Smith, Jackie. 2004. "Transnational Processes and Movements." In *The Blackwell Companion to Social Movements*, edited by David A. Snow, Sarah A. Soule, and Hanspeter Kriesi, 311–336. Oxford, UK: Blackwell Publishing.

Soederberg, Susanne. 2011. "Cannibalistic Capitalism: The Paradoxes of Neoliberal Pension Securitization." *Socialist Register* 47:224–241.

Soja, Edward, and Barbara Hooper. 1993. "The Space That Difference Makes: Some Notes on the Geographical Margins of the New Cultural Politics." In *Place and the Politics of Identity*, edited by Michael Keith and Steve Pile, 183–205. London: Routledge.

Spartacus. 2013. "1846 Corn Laws." http://www.spartacus.schoolnet.co.uk/Lcorn46.htm (accessed February 26, 2013).

Speth, James Gustave. 2008. *The Bridge at the Edge of the World: Capitalism, the Environment, and Crossing from Crisis to Sustainability*. New Haven: Yale University Press.

Stanfield, J. Ronald, and Michael C. Carroll. 2009. "The Social Economics of Neoliberal Globalization." *Forum for Social Economics* 38 (1): 1–18.

Steger, Manfred B., and Ravi K. Roy. 2010. *Neoliberalism: A Very Short Introduction*. New York: Oxford University Press.

Stiglitz, Joseph. 2000. "The Insider: What I Learnt at the World Economic Crisis." *New Republic Online*, April 17. http://www.tnr.com/article/politics/the-insider (accessed July 22, 2012).

Stonich, Susan, and Conner Bailey. 2000. "Resisting the Blue Revolution: Contending Coalitions Surrounding Industrial Shrimp Farming." *Human Organization* 59:23–36.

Strange, Susan. 1996. *The Retreat of the State: The Diffusion of Power in the World Economy*. New York: Cambridge University Press.

Sun, Xiaohua. 2009. "Pollution Problems Serious: Survey" *China Daily*, January 19.

Sutton, P. W. 2004. *Nature, Environment and Society*. Basingstoke: Palgrave Macmillan.

Tapp, Nicholas. 1989. *Sovereignty and Rebellion: The White Hmong of Northern Thailand*. Oxford: Oxford University Press.

Tarafdar, Mustafizur Rahman. 2009. "Tipaimukh Dam: An Alarming Venture." *The Daily Star*, April 25. http://www.thedailystar.net/newDesign/news-details. php?nid=85451 (accessed June 24, 2010).

Tarrow, Sidney. 1994. *Power in Movement: Social Movements, Collective Action and Politics*. London: University of Cambridge.

Taylor-Gooby, Peter, and Cebulla, Andreas. 2010. "The Risk Society Hypotheses: An Empirical Test Using Longitudinal Survey Data." *Journal of Risk Research* 13 (6): 731–752.

Tempest, Matthew. 2005. "Treasury papers reveal cost of Black Wednesday." *The Guardian*. 09 February, 2005. http://www.guardian.co.uk/politics/2005/ feb/09/freedomofinformation.uk1 (accessed February 25, 2013).

Tocqueville, Alex de. [1835] 1961. *Democracy in America, Vol. 2*, translated by Henry Reeves. New York: Schocken Books.

Trivett, Vincent. 2011. "25 US Mega Corporations: Where They Rank If They Were Countries." *Business Insider*. http://www.businessinsider.com/25-corporations-bigger-tan-countries-2011–6?op=1 (accessed October 1, 2012).

Trouillot, M.-R. 1991. "Anthropology and the Savage Slot: The Poetics and the Politics of Otherness." In *Recapturing Anthropology: Working in the Present* (Advanced Seminar), edited by Richard G. Fox, 18–44. Santa Fe, NM: School of American Research.

TSR (Trilateral Statistical Report). 2006. http://www.trilateral.net/statistics/ tsr/2006.html (accessed February 26, 2013).

UNCGG (United Nations Commission on Global Governance). 1995. *Our Global Neighbourhood*. Oxford: Oxford University Press.

UNCTAD (United Nations Conference on Trade and Development). 2008. *World Investment Report 2008: Transnational Corporations and Export Competitiveness*. New York: United Nations.

UNDP Human Development Report. 1993.

UNEP (United Nations Environment Programme). 2002. *Global Environmental Outlook 3: Past, Present and Future Perspectives*. London: Earthscan Publications.

———. 2010. "UN Climate Change Chief Urges Nations to Find Common Ground at Climate Talks." http://www.unep.org/Documents.Multilingual/Default.asp? DocumentID=649&ArticleID=6765&l=en (accessed June 5, 2012).

———. 2011. *UNEP Year Book 2011: Emerging Issues in Our Global Environment*. Nairobi, Kenya: UNEP Publications.

———. 2012. *21 Issues for the 21st Century: Result of the UNEP Foresight Process on Emerging Environmental Issues*. Edited by J. Alcamo and S. A. Leonard. United Nations Environment Programme (UNEP), Nairobi, Kenya.

UNFCCC (United Nations Framework Convention on Climate Change). 2012. "Bali Road Map." UNFCCC Home: Bali Road Map. http://unfccc.int/key_documents/bali_road_map/items/6447.php (accessed June 11, 2012).

Uvin, P. 1992. "Regime, Surplus, and Self-interest: The International Politics of Food Aid." *International Studies Quarterly* 36 (3): 293–312.

Vandergeest, Peter. 2003. "Racialization and Citizenship in Thai Forest Politics." *Society and Natural Resources* 16(1):19–37.

Vandergeest, Peter, and Nancy Peluso. 1995. "Territorialization and State Power in Thailand." *Theory Society* 24 (3): 385–426.

Vaughan, A. 2010. "Cancún Climate Agreements at a Glance." *The Guardian*, December 12. www.guardian.co.uk/enviornment/2010/dec/13/cancun-climate-agreement (accessed January 26, 2012).

Veblen, Thorstein. [1899] 1967. *The Theory of the Leisure Class*. New York: Funk and Wagnalls.

Veeck, Gregory, and Wang Shaohua. 2000. "Challenges to Family Farming in China." *Geographical Review* 90:57–82.

Victor, David G. 2001. *The Collapse of the Kyoto Protocol and the Struggle to Slow Global Warming.* Princeton: Princeton University Press.

Von Werlhof, Claudia. 2008. "The Consequences of Globalization and Neoliberal Policies. What Are the Alternatives?" http://www.globalresearch.ca/index.php?context=vaandaid=7973 (accessed March 20, 2012).

Wacquant, Loic. 1985. "Heuristic Models in Marxian Theory." *Social Forces* 64 (1): 17–46.

Wallerstein, Immanuel M. 2011. *The Modern World-System: Capitalist Agriculture and the Origins of the European World-Economy in the Sixteenth Century.* California: University of California Press.

———. 1995. "The Rise and Future Demise of the Capitalist World Economy." In *Sociological Worlds: Comparative and Historical Readings on Society,* edited by Stephen K. Sanderson, 50–63. New York: Oxford University Press.

———. 2004. *World Systems Analysis: An Introduction.* Durham, NC: Duke University Press.

———. 2008. "The Demise of Neoliberal Globalization." *MRZine,* February. http://mrzine.monthlyreview.org/2008/wallerstein010208.html (accessed March 20, 2012).

Walsh, Bryan. 2011. "U.N. Global-Warming Talks: Good for Diplomats, Indifferent for the Climate." *TIME,* December 11. http://ecocentric.blogs.time.com/2011/12/11/u-n-global-warming-talks-good-for-diplomats-indifferent-for-the-climate/ (accessed June 5, 2012).

Watt, Michael. 2003. "Development and Governmentality." *Singapore Journal of Tropical Geography* 24 (1): 6–34.

Weber, Max. 1947. *The Theory of Social and Economic Organization.* Translated by A. M. Hendreson and Talcott Parsons. Glencoe, IL: Free Press.

———. 1978. *Economy and Society: An Outline of Interpretive Sociology.* Berkeley: University of California Press.

———. 1993. "Power, Domination and Legitimacy." In *Power in Modern Societies,* edited by Marvin Olson and Martin Marger, 18–28. Boulder, CO: Westview Press.

Weisbrot, Mark, et al. 2001. "Growth May Be Good for the Poor—But Are IMF and World Bank Policies Good for Growth? A Close Look at the World Bank's Most Recent Defense of Its Policies." Centre for Economic and Policy Research. *Briefing Paper.*

Williamson, James. 2004. "A Short History of the Washington Consensus." Presented at Forum Barcelona, Barcelona, Spain, September 24–25. http://www.iie.com/publications/papers/williamson0904-2.pdf (accessed February 10, 2012).

Wood, Aston. 2011. "Agriculture at a Crossroads." *The Gleaner,* February 13. http://jamaicagleaner.com/gleaner/20110213/focus/focus5.html (accessed June 14, 2012).

Wood, Geoffrey. 1985. *Labelling in Development Policy.* London: Sage.

———. 1997. "States without Citizen: The Problem of Franchise State." In *NGOs, States and Donors: Too Close for Comfort?,* edited by David Hulme and Michael Edwards, 79–92. New York: St. Martin's Press.

World Commission on Environment and Development (WCED). 1987. *Report of the World Commission on Environment and Development: Our Common Future.* http://conspect.nl/pdf/Our_Common_Future-Brundtland_Report_1987.pdf (accessed July 30, 2012).

World Food Program. 2011. "7 Facts about Climate Change and Hunger." Revised December 4. http://www.wfp.org/stories/7-facts-about-climate-change-and-hunger (accessed June 1, 2012).

Wrong, Dennis H. 1996. *Power: Its Forms, Bases, and Uses*. New Jersey: Transaction Publishers.

Wu, Changhua, Crescencia Maurer, Yi Wang, Shouzheng Xue, and Lee Davis. 1999. "Water Pollution and Human Health in China." *Environmental Health Perspectives* 107:251–260.

Young, Zoe. 2002. *A New Green Order? The World Bank and the Politics of the Global Environment Facility*. London: Pluto Press.

ZeeNews. 2010. "Rally against Construction of Tipaimukh Dam." *ZeeNews*, March 10. http://www.zeenews.com/news610051.html (accessed July 25, 2010).

Zeitlin, Irving M. 1967. *Marxism: A Re-Interpretation*. Princeton: Princeton University Press.

Zerner, Charles. 1990. "Community Rights and, Customary Law and the Law of Timber Concessions in Indonesia's Forests: Legal Options and Alternative in Designing the Commons." *Report* UTF/INS/066, Forestry Studies.

Index